The U.S. Bill of Rights and the Canadian Charter of Rights and Freedoms

Edited by William R. McKercher

Ontario Economic Council
Special Research Report

© 1983
Ontario Economic Council
81 Wellesley Street East
Toronto, Ontario
M4Y 1H6

Printed in Canada

Canadian Cataloguing in Publication Data

Main entry under title:

The U.S. Bill of Rights and the Canadian Charter of Rights and Freedoms

(Special research report / Ontario Economic Council,
ISSN 0225-591X)
Includes United States Bill of Rights and Canadian
Charter of Rights and Freedoms.
Bibliography: p.
Includes index.
ISBN 0-7743-8164-7
1. United States. Constitution. 1st-10th amendments.
2. Canada. Canadian Charter of Rights and Freedoms.
I. McKercher, William Russell, 1944–   II. Ontario
Economic Council. III. United States [Constitution.
1st-10th amendments] IV. Canada [Canadian Charter
of Rights and Freedoms] V. Series: Special research
report (Ontario Economic Council)

K3240.4.B5   342'.085   83-093020-5

These papers reflect the views of the authors and not necessarily those of the
Ontario Economic Council. The Council establishes policy questions to be
investigated and commissions research projects, but it does not influence the
conclusions or recommendations of authors. The decision to sponsor publication
of these papers was based on their competence and relevance to public policy.

THE U.S. BILL OF RIGHTS AND THE
CANADIAN CHARTER OF RIGHTS AND FREEDOMS

Contents

Introduction 3
WILLIAM R. MCKERCHER

PART ONE: COMPARING BILLS OF RIGHTS

The United States Bill of Rights: Implications for Canada 7
WILLIAM R. MCKERCHER

The United States Bill of Rights and the Canadian Charter:
A Socio-Political Analysis 27
ALAN F. WESTIN

PART TWO: THE AMERICAN EXPERIENCE WITH RIGHTS

The Rights of Americans: An Historical View 53
PAUL L. MURPHY

Rights in the United States Constitution since 1940 72
WILLIAM M. BEANEY

The Legislative Protection of Rights 94
WALTER BERNS

The Judicial Protection of Rights 107
PAUL BENDER

Enforcing a Bill of Rights 122
ARYEH NEIER

PART THREE: THE CANADIAN PERSPECTIVE ON RIGHTS

Rights and Constitutional Change in Canada:
A Roundtable Discussion 139

The Canadian Charter of Rights and Freedoms: An Ontario View 151
HON R. ROY MCMURTRY

Entrenchment Revisited: The Effect of the Canadian
Charter of Rights and Freedoms 158
DOUGLAS A. SCHMEISER

Collective versus Individual Rights: The Canadian Tradition
and the Charter of Rights and Freedoms 174
M. JAMES PENTON

Judicial Statesmanship and the Canadian
Charter of Rights and Freedoms 184
RAINER KNOPFF AND F.L. MORTON

PART FOUR: THE CANADIAN
CHARTER OF RIGHTS AND FREEDOMS

Some Perspectives on the Canadian Charter of Rights and Freedoms 203
WALTER S. TARNOPOLSKY

The Canadian Charter of Rights and Freedoms
with Special Emphasis on Quebec-Canada Relations 218
DONALD SMILEY

The Implications of the Canadian Charter of Rights and Freedoms 226
BARRY STRAYER

Panel: Questions and Answers 235

APPENDICES

A Authors and Contributors 245

B The Canadian Charter of Rights and Freedoms 247

C The United States Bill of Rights 256

D Select Bibliography 259

THE U.S. BILL OF RIGHTS AND THE
CANADIAN CHARTER OF RIGHTS AND FREEDOMS

Introduction

The literature pertaining to bills of rights has expanded steadily over the past two decades not only to accommodate a rising interest in the subject, but also to keep pace with the rapid growth in statutory and constitutional protections throughout the world. It has been increasingly recognized that bills of rights serve an important declaratory function, as well as forming a foundation upon which to build law. Although, ultimately, their significance is in their application, they do provide a valuable source of principles to be articulated and laws to be applied.

The United States Bill of Rights, which is among the oldest in the world, warrants particular study in this regard, for over the years, it has been applied in such a way as to expand the protection offered to citizens of that country. Indeed, the decisions of the Supreme Court in the 1950s, 60s and 70s, a high point of judicial activism, have led to a strengthening of the provisions of the Bill of Rights beyond the hopes of the most optimistic of rights advocates of half a century ago. In the view of some observers, the United States has undergone a 'rights revolution,' which has fundamentally altered many aspects of the American legal and political culture. The past two decades, fraught with the tensions of civil rights protests, race riots, Vietnam, and feminist and religious militancy, have produced a whole new body of constitutional law based upon the Bill of Rights, with repercussions that have touched every group and interest in American society. The result has been to make Americans even more conscious of their rights and vigilant of their protection. Though the American bar, judges, academics and politicians often disagree over the application of the Bill of Rights, there are few among them who do not uphold its principles as the hallmark of American democracy in action.

It was with these ideas in mind, and with the impending proclamation of the Canadian Constitution Act, 1982, that we decided to hold a conference on 'The U.S. Bill of Rights: Implications for Canada,' at The University of Western Ontario in March 1982. Accordingly, a group of eminent American and Canadian scholars and government officials was brought together to explore, in a series of seminars and public lectures, specific topics and issues pertinent to a political system which was about to adopt for the first time a constitutionally entrenched bill of rights. The Americans brought to the task an array of skill and experience developed in the analysis of the United States Bill of Rights. It was from this vantage point that they were able to speculate upon the applicability of their experience to what might eventually also be the experience of Canadians. Canadian scholars, in turn, tended to draw upon their wealth of experience in the study of a political and legal system in which the protection of rights had been a matter of convention rather than statute. The cross-fertilization of ideas was rewarding and fruitful, as can be seen from the Commentaries, the Roundtable, and the Panel Discussions included in this volume.

As conference coordinator and editor of this volume, I am honoured to have had the opportunity to work with such a distinguished group of scholars and grateful for their co-operation in preparing their oral presentations for publication. Even those who had not anticipated publication admirably rose to the occasion, thereby making the job of editor considerably easier than is often the case. Many others contributed to this project from beginning to end. The conference was sponsored and funded by the Faculty of Social Science at The University of Western Ontario, where the then Dean, B.B. Kymlicka, was instrumental in making it possible. Special thanks are due to the members of the programme committee for the conference: chairman David H. Flaherty, Bruce Bowden, Robert A. Hohner, Ian A. Hunter, A.M.J. Hyatt and Martin W. Westmacott. My colleagues S.V. LaSelva and S.J.R. Noel helped me to prepare this manuscript and Tom Courchene and David Conklin of the Ontario Economic Council had enough faith in it to support its publication. Sharon E. Lannon, Carol McDonald, Ann Nagy, Barry Bartmann, Marilyn Belch, Geoffrey Painter, Faye Murphy and R. Murray McKercher all rendered valuable assistance. I thank them all for their support.

William R. McKercher
Department of Political Science
The University of Western Ontario

PART ONE: COMPARING BILLS OF RIGHTS

The United States Bill of Rights: Implications for Canada

William R. McKercher*

The United States Bill of Rights came into being as a result of a promise made by the Federalists to the states during the struggle for the ratification of the Constitution in 1787–88. Many citizens in the states, among them Thomas Jefferson of Virginia, were concerned that the absence of a bill of rights left the door open to federal domination, if not tyranny.[1] Alexander Hamilton[2] and James Madison,[3] on the other hand, saw no need for such guarantees since the enumerated powers of the federal government did not include the power to abridge freedom of religion, speech, the press or any other of the liberties which were commonly specified in state bills of rights. Indeed, the unamended Constitution guaranteed some basic rights, including jury trial, *habeas corpus*, and protections against bills of attainer and *ex post facto* laws. In short, they argued that exclusive powers not specifically delegated to the federal government could not be exercised.

---

* William R. McKercher is an Assistant Professor of Political Science at the University of Western Ontario.
1 'A bill of rights is what the people are entitled to against every government on earth ...' Thomas Jefferson to James Madison, 20 December 1787. Thomas Jefferson, *The Papers of Thomas Jefferson*, ed Julian P. Boyd, vol 12: 7 August 1787 to 31 March 1788 (Princeton, NJ: Princeton University Press, 1955), p 440
2 The views of Hamilton, as a believer in national supremacy, are expressed in *The Federalist* no 22, his position on bills of rights in *The Federalist* no 84.
3 Madison reluctantly accepted the argument that a bill of rights was necessary, but he wanted it to apply to the states as well in the areas of the rights of conscience, freedom of speech and the press, and trial by jury. He, having committed himself to a bill of rights, viewed the judiciary as the guardians of these rights. See 'Speech Placing the Proposed Bill of Rights Amendments Before the House of Representatives,' *Annals of Congress*, I (1789–91), p 457.

To Hamilton, the constitution of a state *was* its bill of rights, so why '... declare that things shall not be done which there is no power to do?'[4] Ironically, for Canadians, who see the adoption of a bill of rights as a sign of creeping Americanism, Hamilton, a staunch republican, took it as a sign of creeping monarchism:

... bills of rights are in their origin, stipulations between kings and their subjects, abridgments of prerogative in favor of privilege, reservations of rights not surrendered to the prince.

(bill of rights) ... have no application to constitutions professedly founded upon the power of the people ... in strictness the people surrender nothing, and as they retain everything, they have no need of particular reservations.[5]

Those representing state authorities, particularly in New York, New England, South Carolina and Virginia, were somewhat wary of these arguments. They had had first-hand experience with the rights supposedly guaranteed to every British subject and had found them wanting. Tucker, of South Carolina, wanted powers not *expressly* delegated to Congress, reserved to the states so as to limit the powers of the federal government.[6] The word 'expressly' was not included in what became the Tenth Amendment. But the fears of the Anti-Federalists as to the creation of new federal powers, by implication, were well founded. In 1819, Chief Justice John Marshall legitimized the doctrine of *implied* powers, thereby establishing that the 'necessary and proper' clause could be used as the constitutional basis for the execution of delegated powers.[7] Thus, the stage was set. Powers 'reserved to the states respectively or to the people' were circumscribed by the doctrine of national supremacy.

THE PROTECTION OF RIGHTS

That the Bill of Rights was designed to protect individuals from the power of the federal government *only* was a view pronounced in a direct fashion by

---

4 *The Federalist* no 84 (New York: Bantam Classic, 1982), p 437 (All citations are to this edition)
5 *Ibid*, pp 436–37
6 Madison, in opposing this addition, knew full well the limitations it could impose on the federal government. See *The Federalist* no 44, pp 229–30.
7 *McCulloch* v *Maryland*, 4 Wheat (17 US) 316 (1819). The decision marked the beginning of Chief Justice Marshall's doctrine of national supremacy and the expansion of the federal domain despite state claims that the Tenth Amendment prohibited such encroachments.

Marshall when he asserted, in 1833, that it did not afford protection to individuals against actions which were within the jurisdiction of the states.[8] In spite of such restrictions, however, the inclusion of the Bill of Rights in the Constitution seems to have accomplished something that was psychologically of great importance: it gave credence to the Jeffersonian view that individuals had 'inalienable rights' that could not be taken away by *any* government, a view which, from the outset of the republic, seems to have been commonly held by the people, if not by their leaders. To some extent, the popular view was supported by the Constitution, but not exactly in ringing terms. Although the first eight amendments gave individuals protection from the federal government, the last two amendments reserved certain unspecified powers and rights *to the people*, as well as to the states. The people had *rights*, as Americans, which were *apparently* recognized by the Ninth Amendment: 'The enumeration in the Constitution, of certain rights, shall not be construed to deny or disparage others retained by the people.' They also had *powers*, again unspecified according to the Tenth Amendment. 'The powers not delegated to the United States by the Constitution, nor prohibited by it to the States, are reserved to the States respectively, or to the people.' These rights and powers of the people were indeterminate and not easily understood. Some scholars have contended that the people have rights and powers only by virtue of the fact that they are citizens of the various states and had acted in such a capacity in the creation of the federation.[9] Others have argued that these amendments are '... but a truism that all is retained which has not been surrendered.'[10] Still others appear to attach great importance to them. In support of one such right, for example, Mr Justice Douglas said: 'We deal with a right of privacy older than the Bill of Rights – older than our political parties, older than our school system.'[11] In the same case, Mr Justice Goldberg's concurring opinion provided a highly unorthodox but original interpretation:

---

8 'We are of the opinion that the provision in the Fifth Amendment to the Constitution, declaring that private property shall not be taken for public use without just compensation is intended solely as a limitation on the powers of the United States, and is not applicable to the legislation of the states,' *Barron* v *Baltimore*, 7 Pet. (32 US) 243 (1833)
9 '... the Constitution was in fact the creation of states and of people within each of the states.' See W.J. Brennan, Jr 'The Bill of Rights and the States' in *The Great Rights*, ed Edward Cahn (New York: Macmillan, 1963), p 70. This view conforms to Marshall's in *Barron* v *Baltimore* 7 Pet. (32 US) 243 (1833).
10 See the opinion of Justice Stone, speaking for a unanimous Court in *United States* v *Darby*, 312 US 100, 123–4 (1940).
11 *Griswold* v *Connecticut*, 381 US 479, 486 (1965)

... the Ninth Amendment, in indicating that not all such liberties are specifically mentioned in the first eight amendments, is surely relevant in showing the existence of other fundamental personal rights, now protected from state, as well as federal, infringement.

... The Ninth Amendment simply lends strong support to the view that the 'liberty' protected by the Fifth and Fourteenth Amendments from infringement by the Federal Government or the States is not restricted to rights specifically mentioned in the first eight amendments ...[12]

In short, Goldberg argued that the people possessed rights which could not be violated by any government. It seems that this is the pith and substance of the belief in the inalienability of individual rights to be found in the American political culture, and a strong force in allaying the fears that people have about the indomitable powers of government at any level.

In 1865, John A. Macdonald, who in two years would be the first prime minister of Canada, proudly proclaimed his faith in a document which was to become the British North America Act. Addressing the Legislative Assembly of the United Canadas, Macdonald pointed out that the division of legislative powers in the new constitution

... confers on the General Legislature the general mass of sovereign legislation, the power to legislate on 'all matters of a general character, not specially and exclusively reserved for the local governments and legislatures.' This is precisely the provision which is wanting in the Constitution of the United States. It is here that we find the weakness of the American system – the point where the American Constitution breaks down. (Hear, hear.)[13]

He was only one of many, during the Confederation Debates, who recognized the import and significance of the American experience. George Brown was fearful of the expansionist tendencies inherent in an armed nation for 'The Americans are now a warlike people.'[14] George-Étienne Cartier was most

12 *Ibid* p 493. Mr Justice Goldberg did not, however, consider the Ninth Amendment to be an *independent* source of rights. See Thomas I. Emerson, 'Nine Justices in Search of a Doctrine' *Michigan Law Review* Vol 64 (December 1965) pp 227-8.
13 P.B. Waite ed, *The Confederation Debates in The Province of Canada/1865* (Toronto: McClelland and Stewart, 1963), pp 47–8
14 Brown referred to the American experience time and time again as he spoke in support of united provinces. *Ibid*, p 73

blunt in his assertion that '... either we must obtain British American Confederation or be absorbed in an American Confederation (Hear, hear, and dissent).'[15] The very existence of the United States had a profound effect upon the constitution-makers of Canada and American institutions and experiences were very much on their minds. Yet, as British North Americans, they could not accept the doctrine of revolution, republican government, the sovereignty of the people, the separation of powers, or the concept of a bill of rights. There was no mention whatsoever of such a bill in the Confederation Debates. An 'entrenched' bill of rights was simply not a part of a governmental tradition which had at its heart the supremacy of parliament and the symbolic unity of the Crown. The Fathers of Confederation, however, had the enviable advantage of using the American experiments in federalism as so many beacons in the night forewarning them of dangers already discovered. Above all, they tried to ensure that all the residual powers were granted to the federal government '... to make laws for the Peace, Order and Good Government of Canada.' As it turned out, the highest Court of Appeal for Canada until 1949, the Judicial Committee of the Privy Council, did not wholly concur. Their early decisions set the stage for what is now considered to be one of the most decentralized federal systems in the world.[16]

A more sudden, but perhaps equally profound reversal of the intentions of the Fathers of Confederation is the adoption in 1982 of the Canadian Charter of Rights and Freedoms. Whereas before the adoption of the Charter Canadian legislatures were supreme, having power without limit within their jurisdictions, they now have debatable supremacy within altered jurisdictions. Moreover, although no powers or rights have been explicitly 'reserved' to the people, supporters of the Charter nevertheless appear to give Canadians hope that the possibility may exist.

If it comes to be the case that Canadians look to the Charter to the same extent that Americans look to their Bill of Rights, it could be most important in encouraging the growth of a popular belief that certain rights are inalienable – that there are areas where no government may legislate. Prime Minister Trudeau has stated that the Charter 'gives' rights to Canadians and limits the power of the governments so that Canadians now possess a *national*

---

15 *Ibid*, p 50
16 See *Attorney-General for Ontario* v *Attorney-General for Canada*, [1896] AC 348; *Attorney-General for Canada* v *Attorney-General for Alberta*, [1916] 1 AC 589; *Toronto Electric Commissioners* v *Snider*, [1925] AC 396; *Atlantic Smoke Shops Ltd.* v *Conlon*, [1943] AC 550; and Peter H. Russell, *Leading Constitutional Decisions* 3rd ed (Ottawa: Carleton University Press, 1982).

standard of rights protection.[17] Most of the legal battles surrounding the United States Bill of Rights have been to make it a truly national document – such that states may not violate its provisions. The doctrine of incorporation, which finally made this possible, will not be a point of debate in Canada.[18] But the 'notwithstanding' clause almost certainly will. This clause, contained within section 33 of the Charter, allows provincial legislatures and the Parliament of Canada to override, for an initial period of five years (which can be renewed thereafter), the provisions protecting Fundamental Freedoms, Legal Rights, and Equality Rights.

The defenders of the 'notwithstanding' clause have interestingly argued that it will be used only sparingly, because no legislature would want to have to justify its use to the electorate. Whether that will be so remains to be seen. The adoption of the 'notwithstanding' clause, however, is also reminiscent of an argument put forth by the American Federalists, namely that rights can be protected within separate jurisdictions in a federal state. This is an argument based very much on faith – that certain events will not occur. But it is also very consistent with the view that Canadian society should be one of 'unity with diversity,' which this clause would allow by permitting provincial variations in the protection of rights. The constituent units in the constitutional bargain have clearly won a major concession to their own aspirations and regional interests, but there may also develop a *national* standard from which they will be unable to deviate too much without paying too great a political price. The American Bill of Rights limited the power of the federal government; it now limits the powers of the state governments as well. In the Canadian Charter, the 'notwithstanding' clause gives flexibility to the provincial legislatures and the federal Parliament: but the Charter also makes the protection of rights a national, as opposed to a mainly provincial, concern.

FEDERALISM

The federal structure of Canada led to the curious phenomenon whereby individual rights were protected, not only by common law, but also by the

---

17 See Canada, 'Prime Minister's Remarks at Close of Discussion on the Charter of Rights, 10 September 1980' (Document 800-14/078), *Federal-Provincial Conference of First Ministers on the Constitution*, Ottawa: 8–13 September 1980, p 1.
18 The doctrine of incorporation in the United States holds that the Fourteenth Amendment should be so construed so as to apply the provisions of the federal Bill of Rights to the states. In Canada, the Charter is national in scope and applies to the federal and provincial governments except when Parliament or the legislatures choose to invoke section 33.

Supreme Court (especially in the 1950s) in their decisions which arose out of constitutional disputes over legislative jurisdiction. Civil liberties were protected on many occasions as an *incidental* outcome of these decisions.[19] While, to the individuals and groups involved, to civil libertarians and rights advocates, the results of these cases were far more important than the legal rationale used to justify the divisions of power in Canadian federalism. In constitutional law, it was the federal principle which was at issue rather than any fundamental principle of freedom or justice. Still, it remained true that civil liberties protections in Canada were, on the whole, enhanced by the federal system because there were instances whereby zealous provincial governments were limited through the use of a mechanism which was unavailable to citizens of a unitary state. Creative and compassionate lawyers, such as F.R. Scott,[20] were able to turn the divisions of powers to the advantage of harassed minorities, thus making jurisdictional disputes an adjunct to statutory and common law protections in the area of rights.

Both federal and provincial legislatures in Canada have created a myriad of statutory protections to enhance rights, but it should be added that this has been a fairly recent practice which has coincided with the international human rights movement of the post World War II era. Prior to the Charter, the most ambitious attempt was the Diefenbaker Bill of Rights, but to this must be added provincial human rights codes and numerous other statutes. On the face of it, Canada's record on rights protection is clearly amongst the best in the world, suggesting that the British model of justice has served us well. As truth would have it, however, Canadians do not *know* their rights. The protections afforded to the individual varied not only with geographical location, from province to province, but also depended to some extent upon such 'suspect' categories as sex, race and religion.[21] It has been the avowed intention of supporters of the Charter to rid Canada of this confusing and often unjust patchwork of rights protection by nationalizing fundamental rights and freedoms.

The Canadian Charter of Rights and Freedoms, it has been argued, will give Canadians just such a national standard by which federal and provincial

---

19 For an in-depth discussion, see Walter S. Tarnopolsky, *The Canadian Bill of Rights*, 2d rev ed (Toronto: McClelland and Stewart Ltd, 1975), ch II.
20 Professor Scott argued for a Canadian bill of rights in 'Dominion Jurisdiction over Human Rights and Fundamental Freedoms,' *Canadian Bar Review* 22 (1944): p 598. He fought and won two important cases in Quebec in the 1950s. *Switzman* v *Elbling*, [1957] SCR 285 and *Roncarelli* v *Duplessis*, [1959] SCR 121
21 The following decisions had a *bearing* on each category: Race: *Regina* v *Drybones*, [1970] SCR 282. Sex: *Attorney-General for Canada* v *Lavell*, [1974] SCR 1349. Religion: *Walter et al.* v *Attorney General of Alberta*, [1969] SCR 383.

legislation and actions alike can be judged. For many politicians, rights protection is subsumed under the grander vision of 'national unity' in the federal sphere or of 'unity with diversity,' a view popular with provincial authorities. The compromise, which led to the inclusion of section 33, *appears* to have been a victory for the provincial viewpoint. On the other hand, the inclusion of language and education rights, which are not subject to the 'notwithstanding' clause, gives force to the federal Liberal view that Canada should be a multicultural but bilingual nation.

In the American experience, however, the path to recognition of a national standard of rights protection has been long and hard. As early as 1868, Congress attempted to extend the application of the Bill of Rights to the States as a means to unify a divided country and strengthen the authority of the federal government. Contrary to the intentions of some of the authors of the Fourteenth Amendment, who saw it as the constitutional vehicle for nationalizing rights,[22] the Supreme Court did not accept such a view. The 'incorporation thesis,' first proposed in a Supreme Court case in 1884,[23] acknowledged in dissent in a case in 1908,[24] was not legitimized by the Court in a majority opinion until 1925.[25] In 1931, the 'incorporation doctrine' was applied when the justices declared, for the first time, that a state law was unconstitutional on the grounds that it conflicted with the Bill of Rights.[26] Through a process known as 'selective incorporation,' virtually all of the Bill of Rights has now been 'nationalized.'[27]

In the United States, the politics of rights was very much a product of the federal structure of the nation, even though today we tend to view the states as

22 The author of the 'privileges and immunities,' 'due process' and 'equal protection' clauses, Rep John A. Bingham of Ohio, believed that the Fourteenth Amendment would 'incorporate' the Bill of Rights. '(T)he privileges and immunities of citizens of the United States ... are chiefly defined in the first eight amendments to the Constitution ... these eight articles ... were never limitations upon the power of the States, until made so by the Fourteenth Amendment.' Irving Brant, *The Bill of Rights: Its Origin and Meaning* (Indianapolis: Bobbs-Merrill Company, 1965) as quoted in *The Supreme Court and Individual Rights* (Washington, DC: Congressional Quarterly Inc, 1980), p 3.
23 *Hurtado* v *California*, 110 US 516 (1884)
24 *Twining* v *New Jersey*, 211 US 78 (1908)
25 *Gitlow* v *New York*, 268 US 652 (1925)
26 *Near* v *Minnesota*, 283 US 697 (1931)
27 See *Palko* v *Connecticut*, 302 US 319 (1937) with special attention to Justice Cardozo's opinion. See also Felix Frankfurter, 'Memorandum on "Incorporation" of the Bill of Rights into the Due Process Clause of the Fourteenth Amendment,' *Harvard Law Review* 78 (1965): 746. Amendments not incorporated are: the right to bear arms (A.II); protection against the quartering of soldiers (A.III); the guarantee of a grand jury hearing (A.V); and the right to a jury trial in civil cases (A.VII).

rather weak and obedient partners, who rarely mount any serious challenges to the power of Washington. Historically, the whole process of incorporation attests to the fact that the states wanted to preserve their jurisdictional competence in the area of rights. For the most part, with the acquiescence of the Court, they were able to do so until well into the twentieth century. Eventually, however, their resistance was broken. No sooner had the battle over government regulation been won in the 1940s,[28] giving the federal government immense new regulatory power, than the scene shifted to the 'nationalizing' issue of civil rights. That fight, carried on by special interests working for aggrieved minorities, was engaged in with the purpose of creating a national, unifying identifiable standard of rights protection, which would be guaranteed to every citizen, regardless of geographical location, race, colour, or religion.

Sexual equality, however, not being a part of the Bill of Rights except with regard to voting, could not be guaranteed without another amendment to the Constitution. The recent fight for ratification of the Equal Rights Amendment in many ways exemplifies the politicization of rights in a federal society.[29] Much of the opposition to ERA in Congress and the state legislatures was premised on the belief that state rights are more fundamental than equality rights (at least if the latter were to fall into the realm of federal jurisdiction, as they would have, had the amendment been ratified). Supporters of ERA, on the other hand, argue for the nationalization of rights, even if it means forcing them upon 'parochial' state legislatures. This centrist view holds that the federal government is the only national institution which has sufficient resources to implement and enforce equal rights. The Stop ERA movement is composed mostly of conservative elements, who concur with the promise in the Republican party platform (since 1980) to deal with women's rights through changes in the law rather than through constitutional amendment. Those who support the 'New Federalism' of Ronald Reagan clearly resent the extension of federal power into those domains 'reserved' to the states. The politics of rights in the United States has always been contingent upon the ever-shifting perceptions about the powers and responsibilities of both levels of government. Thus, 'It is manifest that no view of the Bill of Rights or interpretation of any of its provisions which fails to take into account [federalism] can be considered constitutionally sound.'[30]

28 *United States* v *Darby*, 312 US 100 (1941) supplies an invaluable constitutional 'history' of congressional attempts to create a 'police power' through regulatory practices.
29 The defeated amendment reads: 'Equality of rights under the law shall not be denied or abridged by the United States or by any State on account of sex.'
30 John M. Harlan, 'The Bill of Rights and the Constitution,' *American Bar Association Journal* 50 (1964): p 920

This statement may be equally applied to Canada, whose political history is very much one of federal-provincial relations, intergovernmental bargaining, mutual accommodation, and the preservation of the 'unity with diversity' which arose from the bargain of Confederation. Inevitably, Canadian federalism will be altered by the Charter, perhaps in ways that cannot now be foreseen, for Canadians have at a stroke acquired a national set of standards for rights protection applicable to both jurisdictions – even though it includes a disclaimer that its operation will not increase the legislative powers of any body.[31] It is no coincidence, however, that the power of the American federal government, in terms of the range of its enforcement powers, increased dramatically as the Supreme Court continued down the road of incorporation. The United States Department of Justice and other federal agencies use their legal powers of enforcement to virtually force the states into complying with the rulings of the United States Supreme Court. This has unquestionably given Washington, with its vast financial resources, a 'big stick' with which to establish national standards and priorities, for example, in such areas as education, criminal law, and penal reform. Viewed in this fashion, one must conclude that the formal powers of legislatures are not *necessarily* relevant to the issue of rights protection. It is the American federal executive and its bureaucratic machinery, acting upon the ruling of the highest court of the land, which has gained a greatly expanded capacity to deal with its more numerous partners at the state level of the federal system. In Canada, similarly, the legislative distribution of power may remain formally unaltered, but the true power relationships between governments cannot help but be changed, perhaps drastically, if Canadians look to the Government of Canada for the enforcement required in the guaranteeing of their rights. When the loyalty of the population shifts from one jurisdiction to another, so too does the balance of power in a federal system.

It is likely, as well, that the Canadian concern with rights will grow. Canadians have been told, on many occasions, that entrenchment will *transfer* power to the people.[32] The official position of the Government of Canada was to promote this rather American view in order to rally popular support behind their particular vision of rights protection. 'Entrenchment is there-

31 Canada, Constitution Act, 1982, *Canadian Charter of Rights and Freedoms*, s 31
32 For example, the Honourable Jean Chrétien declared, 'Entrenchment of these rights will not increase my power or your power, in fact it will reduce both my power and your power. What entrenchment will do is transfer power to the people.' Canada, Statement by the Honourable Jean Chrétien, 'Continuing Committee of Ministers on the Constitution – Charter of Rights and Freedoms' (Document 830-81/025), *Meeting of the Continuing Committee of Ministers on the Constitution*, Montreal: 8–11 July 1980, p 2

fore not a redistribution of powers between governments, rather it is a redistribution from governments *to the people* ... "the fact is that the losers in the 'power game' under an (entrenched) Bill of Rights are the totality of governments and the winners are the people."'[33] Such statements appear to echo the sentiments expressed in the Ninth Amendment to the United States Constitution. They give the *impression* that some rights are indeed 'reserved' to the people, and that there has been a transfer of power by guaranteeing a set of rights against governments. These rights are defined by governments, but within limits, if their actions are deemed by the courts to be 'reasonable ... in a free and democratic society.' A reading of the Charter does not give cause to readily accept that Canadians are now in possession of inalienable rights, since sections 1 and 33 make it very clear that there is a standard and a process for limiting rights. In American constitutional law, it must be remembered, *governments are limited*, not only by the Bill of Rights, but by other constitutional provisions. The Bill of Rights is, thus, only *one* limiting factor. In Canada, where limitations on governmental power depended only upon jurisdictional authority, governments *were not* limited. This means that the Charter of Rights and Freedoms as part of the written constitution is a more prominent document for it stands as the major constitutional barrier between limited and unlimited power. If one accepts that Canadians have *guaranteed* (if not absolute or inalienable) rights, such rights have to be determined through creative Supreme Court decisions. If rights not mentioned specifically in the Charter were *found* by the Court, one might plausibly argue that the 'emanations'[34] flowing from the language of the Charter could give rights *to the people*, thus making the Canadian federal system not only a bargain between governments, but between governments and the people of Canada. For the first time, governments would be limited. The responsibility for defining these limitations now rests with the courts, which could make the judiciary – who can use the Charter rather than considerations of federalism as a reference – the ultimate guardians of the rights of the people.

33 Canada, 'Background Notes: Entrenching a Charter of Rights' (Document 830-81/026), *Meeting of the Continuing Committee of Ministers on the Constitution*, Montreal: 8–11 July 1980, p 3
34 In justifying and helping to create the right to privacy, Justice Douglas, who delivered the opinion of the Court said: '... [T]he First Amendment has a penumbra where privacy is protected from governmental intrusion ...' for precedents suggest that '... specific guarantees in the Bill of Rights have penumbras, formed by emanations from those guarantees that help give them life and substance ...' *Griswold* v *Connecticut*, 381 US 479, 484 (1965).

THE JUDICIARY

Largely because of the Bill of Rights, the American Supreme Court, especially over the last thirty years, has played an increasingly significant role in the political process and indeed in the everyday lives of Americans. It is important, therefore, in view of the American experience, to ask if the new role established for the Canadian Supreme Court will give it similar prominence. And, in turn, will the Canadian legal system as a whole, and Canadian legal attitudes, as many fear, become Americanized even further? If by 'Americanized' we mean influenced by the American experience, I think the answer is clear. The Charter puts the whole of the judiciary and the legal profession into a position which is very much closer to that of their American counterparts and, most importantly, forces the Supreme Court into the centre of Canadian political life, which hitherto has been dominated almost exclusively by the executive branch of governments.

The Charter was written by those who are as familiar, if not more so, with the Harvard Law School as they are with the Inns of Court. One can attest to the influence of the American experience in the very language of the Charter and the rights it seeks to enshrine. Hindsight has already allowed Canadians to avoid some of the pitfalls experienced during the development of the body of law surrounding the United States Bill of Rights. Thus, the Charter does *not* contain a 'due process of law' clause, or the 'protection of property' (or 'the right to bear arms') clause. Again, with an eye to the American experience, it *does* include 'rights and freedoms ... equally to male and female persons,'[35] an 'affirmative action' clause, a prohibition against 'cruel and unusual treatment or punishment,' a standard for judging the limits of rights,[36] language and educational rights, mobility rights, and numerous other minority protec-

---

35 Section 28, which gives this guarantee, cannot be overridden by the 'notwithstanding' clause, but 'equality before and under the law' and 'equal protection and benefit of law' on the basis of sex (section 15(1)) can be limited by legislatures. There seems to be a wariness in using 'sex' as a classification. Sections 28 and 15(1) are a source of potential conflict. Opponents of ERA in the United States objected to the word as well. See Phyllis Schlafly, 'ERA and Homosexual "Marriages,"' *The Phyllis Schlafly Report* 8:2 (September, 1974), s 2. This could be seen in many ways to be a bogus issue for a major concern of the movement was one of federal domination. See Phyllis Schlafly, 'The Effect of ERAs in State Constitutions,' *The Phyllis Schlafly Report* 13:1 (August, 1979), s 2.

36 'The Canadian Charter of Rights and Freedoms guarantees the rights and freedoms set out in it, subject only to such reasonable limits prescribed by law as can be demonstrably justified in a free and democratic society.' Canada, Constitution Act, 1982, *Canadian Charter of Rights and Freedoms*, s 1

tions against discrimination.[37] Clearly, the United States Bill of Rights has been immensely influential in the composition of the Charter, and even the ubiquitous man on the street will now be correct for once in assuming that his rights, as in the television shows, must be read to him upon request – an assumption already in the minds of many who had previously demanded their 'constitutional rights' from an unmoved Canadian policeman.

The drafters of the Charter, having benefited from American constitutional law, now leave it to the judges to rule upon and interpret the language of the document as the repercussions of its enactment work their way through the legal system. It is highly likely that judges will look to the American experience with an ever sharper eye and keener interest than they have in the past.[38] American constitutional law is a mother lode of information and inspiration – or, to take a more jaundiced view, a minefield of thoughts and opinions yet to be detonated among an unsuspecting Canadian public. This is not to say that the British legal tradition will vanish. But in the area of the formal protection of rights, this tradition is very thin.[39] To save time and money, if for no other reason, judges will find American case law an invaluable guide when making rights judgments, writing their opinions, and justifying their arguments within the Canadian context. Everyone in Canada is susceptible to and makes use of the American influence, from federal politicians and provincial governments to the ordinary citizen.[40] There is no reason to believe that it will not be just as strong in the halls of justice during a period when the whole legal profession must accommodate itself to a dramatic change in the law of the constitution.

37 *Ibid*, Aboriginal rights, s 25; denominational, separate or dissentient schools, s 29
38 For examples of Canadian justices referring to the American legal experience, see Mr Justice Tysoe's opinion in *Regina* v *Gonzales*, [1962] 32 DLR (2d) 290; Mr Justice Ritchie in *Robertson and Rosetanni* v *The Queen*, [1963] SCR 651; Mr Justice Laskin in *Regina* v *Appleby*, [1972] SCR 303; and *Curr* v *The Queen*, [1972] SCR 889.
39 See Albert S. Abel, 'The Bill of Rights in the United States: What Has it Accomplished?' *The Canadian Bar Review* 37 (1959): pp 153–61.
40 To cite but one example, Manitoba Premier Sterling Lyon stated 'We have not had the experience of our neighbours to the south, where judges create rights – on occasion in direct defiance of the peoples' elected and accountable representatives ...' Manitoba, 'Entrenchment of Rights Fundamentally Wrong: Lyon,' Press Release, 10 September 1980 (Document 800-14/076), *Federal-Provincial Conference of First Ministers on the Constitution*, Ottawa: 8–13 September 1980, p 1.
Mr Lyon, a Progressive Conservative, was defeated at the polls on 17 November 1981. His successors, a government of the New Democratic Party, reversed his position. See Richard Cleroux 'Manitoba Becomes First Province to Endorse Rights Charter Outright,' *Globe and Mail* 25 January 1982, pp 1–2.

One cannot assume that the Canadian Supreme Court will automatically take on a more activist role, although most civil libertarians presumably would welcome such a development. In this regard, it would be beneficial to look at judges as individuals, with varying jurisprudential backgrounds, for a clue in ascertaining whether their decisions, as a Court, would be acceptable to those in Canada holding a variety of ideological viewpoints. For example, an activist conservative Court may not be as welcome to a liberal as one which is judicially restrained. What is important, then, will be the positions taken by *individual* judges *vis-à-vis* the language of the Charter – will they interpret it broadly, or will they become 'strict constructionists' who find little room for latitude? The constructionist approach would be a safe and, some might say, very Canadian way of dealing with the Charter. Each interpretation of the law would thus serve to hone and refine the definition of words and concepts in the Charter. What is or is not judged to be a 'reasonable' limitation in a free and democratic society in particular will determine the course of the Charter in its formative years. Whatever approach and definitions they eventually adopt, the justices will have to confront one question very quickly: what will they do in cases that involve conflicting rights? Are some rights to be 'preferred' over others, or are they all to be given equal weight? If some rights are to be preferred over others, then the judiciary can, to some degree, choose between alternatives, given that some ranking of preference can be made. If they are to be given equal weight, then any conflict is almost beyond resolution. Lawyers representing the Government of Quebec have argued before the Superior Court of Quebec that there are occasions when community interest must supersede individual interests.[41] Strictly speaking, they are arguing that individual rights can only be claimed if they do not take away the rights of the community. But what are community rights and when, if ever, should they prevail over individual rights?

The American Supreme Court, having created its own standards for judging rights, has, over the years, evolved the practice of *balancing* rights and creating preferential status for particular rights. Those rights designated as 'the great rights' or the fundamental freedoms are 'preferred.' The First Amendment states that 'Congress shall make no law ...' abridging such rights – yet Congress has done so, much to the chagrin of absolutist justices like Hugo Black. Congress has done so on the grounds that it was given the authority in article I:8 to make laws 'necessary and proper for carrying into execution' the

---

41 *Quebec Association of Protestant School Boards* c *P.G. du Québec* 8 septembre 1982, Cours Supérieure, Montréal, Jugement no 82-888

powers enumerated to the federal government. The Court has balanced that power, granted for the protection of the community or national interest, against individual rights as protected in the Bill of Rights. Such balancing often allows Congress to do anything the courts believe to be 'reasonable.' This implies that Congress is able to overcome the prohibitions in the Bill of Rights on the grounds that it is the protector of the national interest against any 'pernicious' claim to individual rights, at least under *certain circumstances*. One of the most glaring instances of this view was Justice Holmes' opinion on the guarantees of free speech in the *Schenck* case,[42] in which he argued that, while the Bill of Rights was meant to limit Congress, it was not meant to do so if a 'radical' attempted to persuade those under arms to be insubordinate and others to obstruct the draft. The Bill of Rights did not protect Schenck, for since he did not engage in protected 'speech,' his right to it had not been limited.

The Canadian Supreme Court, in looking at the Charter, could take an equally constructionist view of section 1, and interpret it in such a way as to protect the 'national interest' from many forms of behaviour or organized activities deemed detrimental to life in the Canadian polity. The Charter, thus, contains a *built-in* standard by which the Court may balance the rights of the people with the legitimate powers of the legislatures. Section 1 will be particularly useful in times of national emergency, for it helps eliminate the *necessity* for the judiciary to create their own standards of judgment for justifying a limited claim of constitutional rights. This has been the case with the United States Supreme Court when it was forced to rely upon such judicially created standards as the 'clear and present danger' and 'bad tendency' tests.[43]

Since the 1930s, some justices on the United States Supreme Court have considered the First Amendment freedoms to be 'preferred,' '... where the usual presumption supporting legislation is balanced by the preferred place given in our scheme to the great, the indispensable democratic freedoms secured by the First Amendment.'[44] This meant that laws conflicting with

---

42 'The most stringent protection of free speech would not protect a man in falsely shouting fire in a theatre, and causing a panic.' *Schenck* v *United States*, 249 US 47 (1919)
43 Holmes' 'clear and present danger' test developed in *Schenck* v *United States*, 249 US 47 (1919) was used as a standard from *Thornhill* v *Alabama* 310 US 88 (1940) until *Dennis* v *United States*, 341 US 494 (1951). The 'bad tendency' test can be traced back to *Frohwerk* v *United States*, 249 US 204 (1919) but is normally associated with *Gitlow* v *New York*, 268 US 652 (1925). See Edward S. Corwin, 'Bowing Out "Clear and Present Danger,"' *Notre Dame Lawyer* 27 (1952): pp 325.
44 See the opinion of Justice Rutledge in *Thomas* v *Collins*, 323 US 516 (1945) as quoted in Alpheus Thomas Mason and William M. Beaney, *American Constitutional Law: Introductory Essays and Selected Cases*, 6th ed (Englewood Cliffs, NJ: Prentice-Hall, 1978), p 545.

these freedoms would be given 'stricter scrutiny' and that some rights in the Bill of Rights and the Constitution, as a class, would be given more weight and consideration than others.

In the balancing of rights, some Justices, such as Rutledge, Black and Douglas, took the 'preferred freedoms' approach while others, most prominently Justice Frankfurter, took the view that the Court ought to 'examine all legislative and official action against the standard of "reasonableness," with the presumption of validity applying in freedom cases as in all others.'[45] In the Canadian Charter, the courts are clearly instructed by section 1 to balance rights by some standard of 'reasonableness' as well. Nonetheless, this does not prevent them from recognizing *classes* of rights whereby one class could be interpreted as preferable, and, hence, 'preferred' to others. To follow this logic, we must look at section 33.

Section 33, the 'notwithstanding' clause, allows legislatures to override section 2 and sections 7 to 15. I would suggest that those rights guaranteed by the Charter that *cannot* be overridden by section 33 could be considered to be 'preferred' over those which can be overridden by simple legislative majority. Although section 1 allows that all rights may be limited if such limitations are judicially deemed to be 'reasonable,' I would argue that the ones not subject to the 'notwithstanding' clause could cause the courts to apply a standard of stricter scrutiny to governmental actions which could possibly conflict with them. Legislatures are limited, therefore, by the doctrine of 'reasonableness' as interpreted by the courts on the one hand, while on the other they are given the power to limit Fundamental Freedoms, Legal Rights and Equality Rights. There are clearly two classes of rights. One class could thus be designated as 'preferred rights.'

One cannot be certain that the framers of the Charter wanted to create two classes of rights since the Constitutional Accord was very much a *political* bargain. It seems clear that Prime Minister Trudeau and his negotiators were determined to protect Language and Education Rights at all costs, whereas the premiers of the predominantly English-speaking provinces were concerned about the repercussions the Fundamental and Equality Rights provisions might have on provincial areas of jurisdiction. Nonetheless, it could be argued that the end result could, in the long run, help the justices to resolve some dilemmas by allowing for a hierarchy of preference in the protection of rights in Canada. If the Court were forced to choose between Language Rights

---

45 *Ibid.* For an extended discussion see Henry J. Abraham, *Freedom and the Court: Civil Rights and Liberties in the United States*, 4th ed (New York: Oxford University Press, 1982), pp 15–27.

and Equality Rights, or between Legal Rights and Educational Rights, which would predominate? If a court were forced to choose between individual rights based upon the Legal Rights of the individual and individual rights based upon Education Rights, which right would prevail? If the justices wanted to create a hierarchy of preference, then such a judicial standard as 'preferred rights' would seem to be a 'reasonable' method of choosing between the rights contained within the Charter or balancing rights with the legislation and official acts they will be forced to examine in the future, as the latter pertain to the limitation of rights. This would help establish a doctrine of reasonable limitation which goes beyond the standard of 'reasonableness' as practised by the United States Supreme Court.[46] The Canadian courts will be given new opportunities to rule upon the most controversial of rights issues, discrimination between 'male and female persons,' native rights, and Language and Educational Rights, among others on the basis of 'reasonable' limitation. But many of the most political of issues – the Fundamental Freedoms, and Legal and Equality Rights will remain the ultimate responsibility of changing majorities – the provincial and federal legislatures. It is now the case that within the schema of Canadian constitutional law, the rights of linguistic minorities and others are of a differing status than those guaranteed those groups such as women and native peoples whose rights are subject to legislative overrides and future constitutional amendments. The view that bilingualism and educational freedom should supersede many other claims to rights is a testament to the understanding of the drafters of the Charter who were cognizant of what the Canadian cultural heritage might demand. The Charter protects, in a firmer fashion, those rights which the drafters felt should take on a special status, rather than those rights and freedoms which are considered, as part of the political bargain, to be less important to the development of Canadian culture. To this extent, the Charter is a revolutionary document which promotes, rather than guarantees, a vision of the future, to no less degree than the American supporters of their Bill of Rights sought to establish a society unique in its time – an expression of a few who sought to enforce their vision on the many.

THE POLITICS OF RIGHTS

Over the years, political scientists have theorized that Canadian federalism has functioned relatively smoothly due to the operation of a process they

46 For an authoritative discussion of what 'reasonable' implies in American constitutional law, see James Bradley Thayer, 'The Origin and Scope of the American Doctrine of Constitutional Law' in *Judicial Review and the Supreme Court: Selected Essays*, ed Leonard W. Levy (New York: Harper & Row, 1967), pp 43–63.

refer to as elite accommodation.[47] Simply stated, federal-provincial relations are often characterized by compromise reached between the executives of the two levels of government. The ensuing bargains, made without formal constitutional amendment, take into account consultations made with the leaders of various interests in the population, who articulate the demands of those regional and functional interests. In such an environment, where accommodation and compromise tend to prevail, regional and provincial loyalties often take precedence. The Constitutional Accord was perhaps a rather forced example of this process in action. Accommodation was reached through executive bargaining at the elite level, not through popular participation.[48] Although Prime Minister Trudeau proposed holding a referendum on the constitutional package, the provincial premiers balked at such a suggestion.[49] The means to the final Accord were, therefore, perfectly in keeping with the traditional methods of constitution-making in Canada. The role of the legislatures, with minor exceptions, was one of acquiescence. However, in the process of determining *which* rights were to be contained in the Charter, interest groups were vocal and, to some degree, effective in having their interests addressed.[50] The spectacle of politicians bargaining over rights reinforces the view that we are entering into a new era where the elite accommodation model will be rejected in favour of more active citizen participation on rights issues, possibly precipitated by the adoption of the Charter.

Connected to and arising out of the nationalization of rights is the politicization of rights. Since World War II, rights and politics have been closely intertwined in the United States. As the National Association for the Advancement of Colored People, the American Civil Liberties Union, the National

47 See Robert Presthus, *Elite Accommodation in Canadian Politics* (Toronto: Macmillan of Canada, 1973), and S.J.R. Noel, 'Political Parties and Elite Accommodation: Interpretations of Canadian Federalism' in *Canadian Federalism: Myth or Reality*, 2d ed, ed J. Peter Meekison, (Toronto: Methuen, 1971).
48 There were 100 groups and individuals, who appeared and gave evidence before the Special Joint Committee of the Senate and the House of Commons on the Constitution. Another 1439 provided written submissions, on or before 2 February 1981. See Government of Canada, *The Charter of Rights and Freedoms: A Guide for Canadians* (Ottawa: Supply and Services, 1982) pp 41–76.
49 See John Gray 'Referendum Gamble by PM Powerful Lever against Gang of Eight,' *Globe and Mail*, 5 November 1981, p 10.
50 See Robert Sheppard, 'Lobby Groups Taste Blood, and Ottawa Quaking,' *Globe and Mail* 26 November 1981, p 8. Edwin Webking, 'Why Canada Needs the Charter of Rights,' *Canadian Association of University Teachers Bulletin* 28 (December, 1981), pp 15–16. Edward McWhinney, *Canada and the Constitution 1979–1982: Patriation and the Charter of Rights* (Toronto: University of Toronto Press, 1982), pp 105–8

Organization of Women and the AFL-CIO have done in the United States, so too in all probability will their counterparts in Canada. Pressure group activity could become more obvious and sustained as legal funds are established to fight the causes of the special interests in the courts. By doing so, they could bypass the traditional processes of compromise and accommodation, bypass provincial authorities and institutions, and engage in political activities to protect rights in the national forum. This would suggest that the conventional recipients of the lobbyists' attention, the federal and provincial executives, could find their leverage less valued, their decisions less final, and their power subsequently diminished. Barring a change of the structure of the parliamentary system, the impact of special interests cannot become as great as it has become in the United States. But the special interests will, nevertheless, find that a new avenue has been opened to them.

One can anticipate that those whose interests are allied with some activist group will be the ultimate beneficiaries in the struggle to define their rights in relation to the new limitations set upon governmental authorities. Two particular groups, women and native peoples, now have the opportunity to expand their influence within the political process. Rights issues will enter into the mainstream of Canadian political debate.

Will demands for national protections erode the traditional structures of provincial loyalty, namely those areas of government action which distinguish one region or one province from the other? If provincial governments, through the use of the 'notwithstanding' clause, deprive citizens of what special interests consider to be a fundamental or national right, then a shift of loyalty is bound to occur, with all its repercussions. The federal government, as is the case in the United States, will come to be seen as the ultimate guardian of minority interests. This could lead to a greater reluctance to find provincial solutions, not only to rights issues, but perhaps to other areas of concern, such as health and education. The result could make the federal government dominant and the federal system more centralized. To avoid this possible scenario, provincial governments must ensure that they are not viewed as impediments to the expansion of rights and freedoms. To help preserve their provincial autonomy, they must lead, rather than follow the national standards of rights protection, for nothing prevents them from guaranteeing *more* rights and freedoms than are guaranteed under the Charter, for example, in such areas as privacy legislation or freedom of information. As the Governors of American states have learned, one cannot fight a determined Attorney-General who is acting to enforce the moral authority of Supreme Court decisions on recalcitrant states. Similarly, one would suspect, the Minister of Justice will be in a strong position to act in Canada. Should this occur often, however, federal dominance in the politics of rights could be a major nationalizing factor in the years ahead – or a major source of tension in federal-provincial relations.

The Canadian Charter of Rights and Freedoms promises to alter, fundamentally and irrevocably, the way Canadians perceive their rights, thus transforming the rules and understandings of political life. On the whole, the American experience gives cause for optimism that the entrenchment and nationalization of rights can, in the long run, be made to serve both justice and national unity. To ensure that it does so in Canada is ultimately a challenge, not only of law, but of politics.

The United States Bill of Rights and the Canadian Charter: A Socio-Political Analysis

Alan F. Westin*

This is a very exciting time for Canadians. They have a new constitution entrenching some new statements about rights and freedoms and liberties for Canadian citizens. This calls forth some fascinating speculation about what effect the Charter of Rights and Freedoms will have on federal-provincial relations, on the future role of courts, in particular the Supreme Court of Canada, and on a wide range of specific issues of civil liberties and civil rights which are now going to be coming up for re-examination in the light of the new Charter. There will be renewed attention paid to matters such as censorship, freedom of information, police practices, women's rights, and so forth.

It is also an exciting but rather different time in the United States with regard to rights and freedoms. Americans are facing efforts to curb the jurisdiction of the United States Supreme Court, and of the judiciary in general. Specifically, Americans are confronting efforts to overturn major Supreme Court decisions on abortion, school prayer, and on busing to achieve racial balances in the schools. Indeed, Americans face efforts to overturn some central 'due process' definitions and their enforcement in the courts; for example, through the use of exclusion of illegally obtained evidence in state and federal trials.[1] For Canadians, the time of excitement is rather positive. For Americans, at the moment, it is highly defensive.

This points out the fact that no statement of liberty tends to be static. There are moments in some societies in which there may be public question-

---

* Alan F. Westin is a Professor of Public Law and Government at Columbia University.
1 The 'exclusionary rule' was first referred to by the Supreme Court, in dealing with federal prosecutions, in *Weeks* v *United States*, 232 US 383 (1914). This led to inconsistent and conflicting practices in the courts at the state and federal level, which were eventually clarified in *Mapp* v *Ohio*, 367 US 643 (1961).

ing about whether the pendulum of rights protection has swung too far, and whether retrenchment – rather than of expanding incorporation that Canadians are building into the Constitution Act, 1982 – is the right policy for the moment.

I would like to speculate upon what the short-term future may be, in terms of bringing the Charter into operation in Canadian society. To avoid even the slightest suspense about my main thesis, let me suggest it at the outset. I think that the treatment of rights and freedoms in any democratic society is best understood as a part of its politics. In that case, using politics in the broad and non-pejorative sense of the word, it is a 'special politics,' just as the politics of federal/state relations or the politics of defence or the politics of welfare are subsets of the larger study of politics. Clearly, civil liberties politics has its own distinctive rules, its conventions, its procedures and its ideology. But it is best understood in terms of analysing aspects of the political struggle in societies.

With that as my fundamental premise, I want first to suggest what kind of factors political scientists would see as those that shape the civil liberties politics of democratic societies. Second, I want to apply this to the United States, initially in a kind of general discussion, and then particularly by tracing some of the historical developments of rights and liberties in the United States. This can be done by looking at the role that the Supreme Court has played in civil liberties politics in American history, under a written constitution with a Bill of Rights. Third, I would like to ask some questions in the same vein about Canadian history and Canadian experience in the protection of rights and freedoms. By way of comparison, I shall use one topic in which I have a special interest: the topic of privacy. As such, we will be able to discern the way in which the two societies have dealt with traditional privacy issues and how they have dealt with some of the recent, new issues of privacy involving information, record keeping, and high technology. Lastly, I will try to suggest what some of the implications for the near future in Canada may be in the move towards a hybrid system, part way between the British and American systems in terms of rights, liberties, and the role of courts.

Liberal societies write a bill of rights to express the ideals that they aspire to. Which ideals they select is obviously very important. It is interesting that the new constitution in Canada does not use the word 'privacy.'[2] Updating

---

2 The United States Constitution does not explicitly mention privacy as such but judicial interpretation has in effect led to the judicial creation of a right of privacy beyond the protection against 'unreasonable searches and seizures' in the Fourth Amendment. See *Griswold* v *Connecticut*, 381 US 479 (1965); and *Roe* v *Wade*, 410 US 113 (1973); and *Doe* v *Bolton*, 410 US 179 (1973).

the concepts of the individual's relationship to the state (and the collection and use of personal information) did not seem to the framers of the Charter to be worth mentioning explicitly. It is also interesting that the Charter did not include social and economic rights, as many democratic socialist constitutions have done. In Japan, for example, the Basic Law talks about the right to form labour unions and the right to bargain collectively. There is no mention about work and leisure and health and other socialist definitions in the Charter of Rights.

Although each liberal society starts with a statement of ideals that it aspires to, rights and freedoms it actually installs and enforces will depend on the social and political realities of that society. The task for historians and for political analysts is to look at the process by which each liberal society tries to apply its ideal goals to the realities of governance in a complex society, to changing social and economic conditions. This is so especially where parts of a statement of ideal goals will conflict either between or among rights. There are familiar conflicts between equality and liberty, between fair trial and free press, and other quite well-known intramural conflicts in the world of civil liberties and civil rights. Civil liberties claims can also conflict with other social interests of public order, interests of community, interests of stability, and other equally important fundamentals to the management and continuance of the society.

My view of civil liberties politics in the United States is a rather Hegelian one. That is, governmental office holders in the United States approach the 'giving of liberties,' or 'the observance of liberties,' almost instinctively by denying claims of liberty, justice, and equality whenever these are inconvenient to the administration of public affairs. Almost inevitably, they reject any *new* statement of rights and liberties, in which some previously discriminated against group – by race, colour, sex, ideology, or life style – demands to enjoy the same rights as those that make up the mainstream of the citizenry. This is generally predictable, even though every now and then a particular public official may have some special personal or intellectual proclivity that leads him or her to be more civil libertarian in a given instance. But the instinctive posture of a public official in the American political system is to find most expansive liberty claims *inconvenient* and, therefore, to try to find ways to limit the claims of liberty, equality, and due process in the interests of more placid administration.

This then brings into play the opposite Hegelian forces, political movements by groups denied liberty, equality, and justice, and support for them by various groups that speak on their behalf. This leads either to defensive advocacy of already well-defined rights in the United States Bill of Rights (free press, free exercise of religion, the privilege against self-incrimination, etc. ...) or to the voicing of new demands, as for racial equality, sexual equality, or other claims that emerged later in American history than the writing of the original eighteenth century Bill of Rights.

In the best of all situations, this point and counterpoint produces a policy in which advocacy of civil liberties leads to better social or governmental policy than would have been the case were it not for the active advocacy of civil liberties claims upon power. This notion has been expressed eloquently by people like Reinhold Niebuhr, Frederick Douglass, Martin Luther King Jr, and others, when they have said that those in power give nothing without challenge, and that the history of the expansion of rights and liberties is always a matter of demanding change from those who only reluctantly give minorities access to opportunities, benefits, and rights in the society.

This is the reason why I think, for example, that the American Civil Liberties Union, who many regard as the 'scold' of American society, performs a highly useful function. It is not necessarily the case that the ACLU *never* comes up with a policy which, if instituted, would work in the real world (in a government agency, a corporation, or a university), but I would submit that it would be a rare case, in terms of the kinds of positions which the ACLU generally puts forward. This is because the ACLU's basic role is to assert the full *opposite* value position in order to move government policy closer to a fair balance between the claims of liberty and the claims of order. It is essentially a dialectical process.

This describes a great deal of the way in which, in historical terms, I see the evolution of new rights of equality, justice, and freedom in American history. Restrictive actions have been confronted in political struggle, have been looked at in terms of the basic ideals of the society as expressed in its constitution and Bill of Rights, and then subjected to the test of civil liberties politics. Whether the decision comes from a court or legislature or administrative agency, the key issue will be: 'Is the new demand legitimate, after various conflicts and testing, and therefore to be incorporated in the mainstream of the society's perception of how to apply ideals into real world situations?'

Having given the general conception of civil liberties politics in the United States, I would suggest that there are at least six factors that are primary in shaping the civil liberties politics of any democratic society. One could frame these factors differently and produce a list of four or eight or ten factors, but what is important is to see the kinds of elements that are involved.

It is logical to start with the 'Act of Founding' in the United States – the circumstances under which the thirteen colonies emerged as a nation. Professor Louis Hartz and his colleagues have stressed here, rightly, the unique experience of the United States in escaping feudalism, monarchy and aristocracy as vested institutions.[3] That, plus a century of open frontier, produced an extraordinarily broad liberal consensus, as Hartz has called it. Both aristocracy, on the one hand, and radical and socialist-type ideologies, on the other hand, have not been able to generate large political movements as an alternative to a centrist, libertarian society. At the same time, the colonists' revolt from England was a sharp break from the mother system. Though many elements remained common (the language, the common law, etc.), the writing of the United States Constitution and the interpretation in the first few decades was seen as a deliberate act of state-making, drawing on ideas about the separation of powers and the fundamental rights of man, that the new Americans wanted to treat very differently than the law and practice of their motherland. These are some of the key aspects of the act of creation of the United States as a nation that clearly imprinted the Bill of Rights into its larger constitutional framework.

The second aspect to look at is the ideology or political culture of the society. Americans are inordinately distrustful of government, and are, for the most part, suspicious of all authority, religious, economic, or otherwise. Americans believe that power inevitably corrupts. If government is necessary, it is a necessary evil, and one gets nothing from government without paying the price. Those ideas, which revolutionary leaders as diverse as John Adams, Thomas Jefferson and Alexander Hamilton all voiced, are still current. This is true not only in the stance of the conservative president Ronald Reagan, but also in the positions that many liberals currently adopt. This American orientation deeply affects notions of rights and liberties, and how Americans expect such rights to be protected. This negative orientation toward government illustrates the kind of political ideology that is fundamental to understanding the American civil liberties experience.

Third, one must look at the structures of government that were created by a written constitution. America is a federal system dividing power between central and constituent governments, with much overlapping of authority, and with a complex mixture of interdependence and autonomy. This creates the need, at many critical moments, for some authoritative body to decide what power belongs to the central government, and what resides in the state governments or their local subdivisions. Similarly, the checks and balances

---

3 Louis Hartz, *The Founding of New Societies: Studies in the History of the United States, Latin America, South Africa, Canada and Australia* (New York: Harcourt, Brace and World, 1964)

system that the United States Constitution installed amongst the legislative, executive, and judicial branches creates expectations on the part of the public that some agency will provide authoritative statements about which power belongs to the executive and which to the legislative, and when the judiciary is being transgressed upon by the elected branches. Federalism and the separation of powers were structures that, in the American ideological setting, invited, if not even demanded, the exercise of an interventionist, 'political' brand of judicial review.

Fourth, one turns to the political processes that a society has. There is a weak party system in the United States. It is non-ideological, with most of the fractured power held by local and state political systems. The role of the Supreme Court is much enhanced by the weakness of the American party system. In countries that have strong parties, it would be much less likely that programs that had been enunciated by parties and put to the test of elections would as easily be revised or overturned by a high court. This Americans accept because of the weak and non-ideological character of the national party system. One of the most important cases in the United States Supreme Court in the last decade was the Nixon tapes case, in which the tapes made by President Richard Nixon were required by the United States Supreme Court to be turned over to a judge for use in a criminal trial involving obstruction of justice.[4] The Supreme Court rejected the claim of 'executive privilege' in favour of a need to have a fair trial, and to have the administration of justice proceed with the evidence necessary to adjudicate guilt or innocence. That would never happen in a parliamentary system. Nixon would have been voted out of office in late 1973 or early 1974. It would have been regarded as unseemly for the Court to pass upon the executive privilege of a president, since there would have been a political resolution of the question of Nixon policies and the credibility of Nixon's statements about his involvement in Watergate. Thus, many of the processes of politics in the United States enhance expectations of judicial review, and lead people to believe that it is appropriate for the Court to make decisions like the Nixon tapes decision.

I would also put under this heading a mixed ideological-structural aspect, namely the low programmatic responsibility that often marks American government. Americans often start out with the assumption that the federal government should come into play with programmes only when the private sector has failed or only when local and state governments prove inadequate. That explains the long history of delaying social programmes and economic

---

4 *United States* v *Nixon*, 418 US 683 (1974)

programmes that many industrial nations began to develop in the nineteenth and early twentieth centuries. This is most obvious in the areas of factory health and safety protection, social security, child labour and the protection of women in the workplace. In the American political system, the notion prevailed for many decades that somehow it was not appropriate for the national government to engage in these kinds of social activities.

A fifth factor I would cite is the sociological makeup of the population; the heterogeneous or homogeneous aspects of the given society, whether it has sharp race cleavages or religious cleavages, and the impact this has on the expectation that these issues need to be worked out with as low a 'political' content as possible in terms of applying noble and broad concepts of equality, rather than as part of the everyday 'pull and haul' of politics.

Finally, one comes to the legal culture of the society. The United States is the most litigious society known to the world. Even ancient Athens never had as much of a zest for litigation as the American political culture has produced. Alexis de Tocqueville remarked that lawyers were the 'American aristocracy' and that they were the element that made up for what in Europe would have been an aristocratic class to manage public affairs.[5] American judges consider it quite appropriate to decide test cases, and their rules about 'standing to sue' are extraordinarily broad. Compared to Britain or to Canada and many other countries, Americans invite cheap and relatively quick lawsuits for a wide variety of interest groups. Americans use the test case mechanism to receive quick decisions about real controversies in a way that shocks many of the societies that believe that this is not an appropriate role for the judiciary to play so frequently on such wide and far reaching issues.

In the United States, there is a great debate going on now about alternatives to litigation. It has arisen out of the criticism of the high litigiousness of Americans. This is not simply a reaction to liberal-activist judicial trends of the 1960s and 70s. There is much to be said for creating dispute resolution mechanisms that do not involve such lengthy and costly devices as trials have become in the United States. But one has to note that many of these critics come from the same business community that brought the test case to a high art in the latter half of the nineteenth and early twentieth centuries. In the process, they disadvantaged labour unions, blacks, and women, and evaded the business regulation that was voted by reform political movements first in the South and mid-West and then at the national level. Such

---

5 In his 'Introduction' to de Tocqueville's book, John Stuart Mill states: 'We recommend special attention to the section devoted to this topic. (Vol. ii. p 165)' See Alexis de Tocqueville, *Democracy in America*, 2 vols (New York: Schocken Books, 1961), p xliii.

was the case with the Sherman Anti-trust law of 1890, the first major anti-trust mechanism. When business critics say that consumer, environmental, civil liberties, and civil rights groups are impeding the orderly exercise of democratic government by excessive litigation, we do well to remember how business used litigation when the judicial majorities were ready to champion their claims.

There are some other things that could be mentioned, in terms of major factors that shape civil liberties politics and application of a bill of rights. However, these six factors do illustrate the kinds of conditions and factors that are critical to look at in any society, when one tries to understand why it developed the kind of bill of rights it has, and how the society has applied it.

What is the political history of the United States Bill of Rights, and what are some of the complex interactions of elected-branch conduct and judicial activity involving the Bill of Rights? The United States started off in the 1790s with a system analogous to the Athenian Republic, that is, an elite society dedicated to reason and liberty but built upon a slave economy. Persons who were part of the mainstream of the society, as political participants, were very few. The dominant elite championed the rights of free speech, free press, and freedom of religion because those were rights claimed and used in the revolutionary struggle against Britain. They produced a constitution and bill of rights which expressed a strong commitment to freedom and the limited state.

In the nineteenth century, the central struggle of civil liberties politics was the effort of groups outside the dominant elite to widen that consensus to include their interests and rights. Jews, Catholics, and later, Mormons, atheists and other groups, tried to expand the definition of religious liberty to one that would be broad enough to give those groups religious equality. Other aspects of this nineteenth century struggle include the struggle of small property holders and others in the Jacksonian era to win equality rights in voting and other forms of political participation; the fight by slaves, first to be free, and then to win some kind of equal treatment after the Civil War; the struggle of women trying to bring themselves within the new equality definition after the Civil War, being totally rebuffed by the courts; the struggles of Indians and others who were pushed back by the expansion of the United States across the continent, finding themselves largely set apart from the main society, on reservations; the struggle of organized labour throughout the nineteenth century to win the right to engage in organizing activity, to bargain over wages and working conditions, and to be able to strike, finding themselves for the most part blocked in such aspirations by the contract and property doctrines applied by American law at that time.

During the nineteenth century and until the 1930s, the United States Supreme Court was of little or no help in these struggles for equality, liberty, or justice. Before the Civil War, there was hardly any federal case law on equality or liberty. After the Civil War, up until the 1930s, the Supreme Court was notable mostly for emasculating rather than applying the new equality guarantees for newly-freed blacks; for rejecting women's groups' efforts to apply equality protections; and for upholding restrictions on labour unions and radical, political groups. There were a few isolated decisions that talked about 'free press rights' or 'fair trial rights' in these decades, but they were marginal decisions, if one looks at the primary thrust of judicial review in the politics or economics of the era. This continued until the late 1930s, and can really be applied until the 1950s in terms of the Supreme Court's largely restrictive rather than expansive role in civil liberties politics.

Sir Henry Maine once remarked that a major development in English law in the post-feudal era was that it moved from a law of status, governed by feudal relations, to a law of contract, based on negotiated positions among presumed equals, thereby enhancing the development of capitalism.[6] I would suggest that it was the law of contract, which the United States Supreme Court had as its central jurisprudence between Chief Justice John Marshall's day and the 1930s. It was a conception that protected business and conservative interests to a high degree. But in the Warren Court era, the United States Supreme Court moved into a jurisprudence of status, in which the Court expanded definitions of liberty, equality, and due process to protect the 'statuses' of people, in terms of their rights vis-à-vis higher authorities.

In that sense, let me suggest a way of thinking about what the Supreme Court did that adopts a 'nasty' result-oriented approach. It takes as its measuring rod the issue of which groups were really helped and which were hurt by the presence of the United States Supreme Court in the constitutional life of the American nation from 1790 until the present.

From the late eighteenth century until 1937, most of the people who were helped by the Supreme Court were property holders, slave owners, the new capitalist and corporate groups, and those conservative, party, and ideological interests that saw the defence of property rights and laissez-faire notions as the right course for the United States. To them, the Supreme Court was the 'sheet anchor' of the Republic, keeping the ship of state on course. Nine wise individuals, independent and not subject to political passion, would

---

6 Sir Henry J.S. Maine, *Ancient Law: Its Connection with the Early History of Society and Its Relation to Modern Ideas*, 4th ed (London: J. Murray, 1870)

strike down actions of 'mere majorities' where they intruded upon property rights and those 'minority rights' associated with propertied groups.[7] For example, David Lawrence in the 1930s wrote an interesting book called *Nine Honest Men*, which was a reply to the so-called 'nine-old-men' charge of New Dealers that a Supreme Court majority was striking down vital New Deal economic and social programs, and that this was an unconscionable thwarting of the public will.[8] To David Lawrence and his associates, the Supreme Court was a Platonic Nocturnal Council, revising in the cool of the morning those bad or ill-considered measures that were passed by overheated legislatures in the passions of the day.

Who were the critics of the Court in the same period? They were primarily leaders of the movements of social reform and social change: Jefferson, Jackson, Lincoln, Bryan, Teddy Roosevelt, Senator La Follette and Franklin Roosevelt. Each criticized the United States Supreme Court directly, not just for specific decisions but because they saw the Court as an institution that interposed an aristocratic, unresponsive set of judgments for the wisdom of majorities trying to widen the American economic and political system to the participation and rights of disenfranchised groups and groups which were discriminated against. The reform majorities had run the gauntlet of the American political system and separation of power, and had managed to achieve the power in Congress, in the presidency, and the state capitals to enact social reforms. Yet they were being denied the ability to put their programs fully into effect because of judicial vetoes. To these critics, the Supreme Court was irresponsible and anti-democratic.

Then came the shift in 1937, in what T.R. Powell called 'the switch in time that saved nine.'[9] This was the shift in the Supreme Court majority's view of the constitutionality of New Deal measures, which produced a majority that upheld major social and economic legislation against almost all challenges, and began to shift instead to a new 'jurisprudence of status.' Again, who was helped and hurt by the Supreme Court from the later 1930s until at least the 1970s? The beneficiaries of the Supreme Court's new jurisprudence were: blacks, religious minorities, political dissenters, the women's rights movement, consumer groups, and environmental groups. On labour-management

---

7 For a convenient summation of the legal history surrounding these questions, see Robert F. Cushman, *Leading Constitutional Decisions*, 14th ed (Englewood Cliffs, NJ: Prentice-Hall, 1971), pp 197–213.
8 David Lawrence, *Nine Honest Men* (New York and London: D. Appleton-Century Company, 1936)
9 See Alpheus T. Mason and William M. Beaney, *American Constitutional Law: Introductory Essays and Selected Cases*, 6th ed (Englewood Cliffs, NJ: Prentice-Hall, 1978), pp 258–60.

issues, the Court moved into a neutral position in that period, and allowed a now economically strong trade-union movement to compete with business in the economic and political arenas.

Not surprisingly, the great defenders of the Supreme Court were now the American Civil Liberties Union, the National Association for the Advancement of Colored People, the AFL-CIO, the American Jewish Congress, and the other liberal groups. Now, these groups saw the Court as not really antidemocratic after all. As with the business and conservative groups earlier, liberals now called the Court legitimate. When it struck down majority measures which were out of keeping with the higher law principles of the Constitution, it was fulfilling the highest duty that the Framers had envisaged for it, and what the written Constitution and Bill of Rights required. The same David Lawrence who wrote *Nine Honest Men* became Editor-in-Chief of the conservative magazine, *U.S. News and World Report*, and called for Earl Warren to be impeached. He and fellow conservatives cried out that a Supreme Court elected by no one, responsible to no one, was an institution running amuck.

From a 'who gets what' and 'who defends what' analysis comes the division of general Supreme Court political impact in the United States from 1790 to 1937, and then from 1937 through the 1970s. To put it another way, until 1937, the Court was largely irrelevant to civil liberties and civil rights politics in America. After 1937, reaching a high point in the 1950s, 60s, and early 70s, the Supreme Court began to be an engine of change for rights of new claimant groups. The judiciary operated in these years as a body that put its thumb on the scale, often, on behalf of civil libertarian and equality claims in the political system.

However, I do not mean to suggest that the Supreme Court was, in the first period I mentioned, operating in some *conspiratorial* way against the public will. The United States, from 1790 to 1937, was a republic with representative institutions. If the Supreme Court was not speaking on behalf of what was the dominant politics in these decades, the Court could and would have been brought to heel. Its decisions could have been overturned by constitutional amendments, and/or new appointees, reflecting angry majorities, would have changed the jurisprudence of the Court. This did not happen because most of the Court's conservative rulings reflected the dominant ideas and political systems of those eras. In the 1896 presidential election, for example, in which William Jennings Bryan attacked the Supreme Court for its income tax decision, its anti-trust decisions, and its decisions in the Eugene Debs labour contempt conviction, the country went to the polls and voted overwhelmingly, not for Bryan and social reform, but for William

McKinley and the business-oriented status quo. Therefore, one has to conclude that Supreme Court doctrines were generally in keeping with the dominant politics of the day.

The same conclusion seems justified about political realities and the post-1937 Court. Since 1937, those decisions of the Supreme Court that have expanded equality rights, expression rights, religious rights and due process rights have generally been supported by a public majority, at least until recently. Up to now, no effort to amend the Constitution, to overturn any Supreme Court civil liberty or civil rights decision in the past several decades has succeeded. There *were* efforts to overturn the legislative reapportionment decision, the school prayer decisions, the abortion decision, and loyalty/security rulings. All of those, when put to the test of 'yes' or 'no,' have not passed out of Congress. In that sense, I would submit that both the jurisprudence of contract from 1790–1937 and the jurisprudence of status, from 1950 to the mid-70s, followed the dominant politics of the United States in both eras.

In turning to Canada, I shall refer to the analytic factors and socio-political experiences that I have used for the United States. It is helpful at the outset to note swiftly some broad differences between the two societies. If one looks at the 'act of founding,' for example, I would see Canada not as the rebellious runaway, but as a sister who decides to leave home and live abroad and who still likes to see mother often. Canada did not have the break and the discontinuities with England as did the United States, and that seminal difference in the 'act of founding' of Canadian society has had important consequences.

The Canadian ideology, my second 'factor,' has Canadians much less distrustful of government and authority. Most Canadians see government as more positive, and more often acting in the interests of the citizenry, than is the case in the United States. In the United States, the assumption will be that if it could be done wrongly, the government will do it wrongly. This is not the way the public opinion polls and sociological studies characterize Canadian attitudes toward government.

In terms of governmental structures, it is clear that Canada – at least under the Charter – has reflected the British tradition, which sees parliamentary supremacy as the central feature of government. This puts in the hands of the legislature the responsibility, in law and in politics, of holding the society's balance true between liberty claims on the one hand, and competing claims of order and community on the other hand. There is in Canada a broad public sense, not shared in the United States, that legislatures and cabinets are appropriate bodies to conduct those kinds of weighing processes wisely and well. At least Canadians have felt that the judges do not have a monopoly on that process. As I read Canadian public opinion, the dominant view seems to have been that those decisions are better thrashed out in the administrative and legislative processes than in the courts. Relating this to political processes, the Canadian party system, and the parliamentary process with its vote of no confidence for changing governments, produces a different relationship between liberty issues and the political process than is the case in the United States. For example, in Canada, had there been a prime ministerwho had acted the way President Nixon did and h ad tried to cover up actions as he did, parliamentary mechanisms, not the courts, would have passed upon the basic issues.

In sociological terms, Canada shares some of the same problems of heterogeneity of population, of language differences, and of 'original native population' as the United States. In this dimension, there are many similarities between the two countries, in terms of definition and reconciliation of minority rights, that have been central to civil liberty politics, and will probably be central issues under the Charter.

There are other comparisons that could be made, and the legal culture is a good case in point. In Canada, there is neither the popular penchant for litigation nor the presence of large interest-group activity in test cases. There is obviously less readiness by judges under Canadian law to entertain venturesome test case litigation, and the Canadian Bar itself does not seem to regard test-case litigation as a road to legal fame and fortune as in the United States.

There are important differences in the legal culture that need to be noted in terms of civil liberties politics in Canada. As an example of the different ways in which the civil liberties politics of the two countries have operated in the past, one could look at the issue of privacy. In the United States, the judiciary has been reasonably competent in some aspects of protecting the right to privacy. In the last twenty or thirty years, the United States Supreme Court has expanded the notion of protection against 'unreasonable searches and seizures' to take into account wiretaps, parabolic microphones, or other micro-miniaturized listening devices. By defining what is a *reasonable* expectation of privacy that an individual can assert, the Supreme Court has done a creative job in modernizing the traditional protection of people from unreasonable penetration by government.

The Supreme Court has been good also in many personal autonomy issues, such as sexual freedom, abortion, and other issues in which the privacy question arises of what individuals will be allowed to do by themselves, or in private with adult persons who consent, and where the law ought not to intrude.

Where the United States Supreme Court has not been wise or effective, in my judgment, is in the area of record-keeping and informational privacy. There are a series of decisions, which I think are disastrous, that have dealt with privacy questions in bank records, in arrest records, and in government medical data banks. These are issues fundamental to a credential-oriented society where large organizations increasingly use personal and judgmental information to make important decisions about who gets what in the society. Individuals have received very little *constitutional* protection in this area in the last twenty years. Rather, it has been in the legislative arenas that the protection of informational privacy has proceeded, often with reasonable success. Politicians aware of (and usually sharing) popular worry about misuse of computer data banks by government and private institutions, have frequently stepped in where the Supreme Court has not found (or been willing to create) constitutional protection. Many well known statutes have been passed: the federal Fair Credit Reporting Act, and its counterparts in state legislation; the federal Privacy Act of 1974, dealing with federal data banks and creating fair informational laws; the federal Buckley Amendment dealing with the family and educational privacy issues in school and college records; the federal Financial Right to Privacy Act of 1978, dealing with privacy in bank records; and a wide range of state legislation on employee privacy, insurance privacy, medical record privacy, and criminal history records. Where informational privacy is concerned, civil liberties politics have really not been dominated by the Supreme Court and the judicial function in the past two decades, but have centred on a political struggle to write legislation that defines new rights of privacy in a high technology age.

In terms of that political struggle, the impetus for much of this came from Richard Nixon. Those people, who were talking in 1970 or 1972 about the possible abuse of power and the dangers that could come from misuse of information technology, were always met by the comment: 'Yes, that's all okay in terms of hypotheticals, but show me any government official that really would abuse power in this case.' After Watergate, that was never much of a problem for privacy advocates. Watergate was all about information – about breaking into a psychiatrist's office to steal medical records, about breaking into the Democratic Party headquarters to plant microphones and eavesdropping equipment, and about attempting to use Internal Revenue Service records to retaliate against critics. All of the 'plumbers and tappers' were actively involved in the misuse of information, and intrusion by the highest levels of government into protected group privacy and individual privacy. The Nixon exposures made possible the enactment of much privacy legislation.

If one looks at Canada, there are some interesting similarities. Canada also had the kind of early alarms about the potential invasion of privacy, with writings and media exposures in the 1960s. Canada had a similar federal privacy commission that tried to get a look at the empirical realities in the early 1970s. With the advent of the Canadian Human Rights Act of 1977, legislation set in place a federal Privacy Commissioner for federal data banks, with fair information principles applied at that level. Many provinces today are considering the same kind of fair information practices laws for dealing with provincial data collections about individuals. Similarly, there is some provincial legislation on credit bureaus, on wiretapping, and on confidentiality of health records. Such parallel legislation dealing with new record-keeping and data bank issues, and the absence of major judicial decisions in this area, suggests that both societies have wound up dealing with new informational privacy issues in rather similar ways.

Since popular distrust of institutional power is often at the heart of concern about privacy and technology, as the Nixon Watergate episode shows, it is important to note that in Canada there have been some incidents which, had they happened in the United States, would probably have led to great *causes célèbres*. Most Canadians seem to have accepted Royal Canadian Mounted Police break-ins without warrants between 1970 and 1978, and also the RCMP's secret access to income tax information, and to personal health information from the Ontario Health Insurance Plan. If I read the Canadian scene correctly, those did not shock and outrage most Canadians. They upset some Canadian civil liberties groups, some legal groups and various academics, but the public seems to have decided that there was enough justification for what the government had done in those cases. And, if a little too much *had* been done, government could be expected to receive the protests and make some calibrated adjustments to put the RCMP back into their proper practices.

But what are some of the implications of the adoption of the Constitution Act, 1982 for the next decade of Canadian political life? It is rather interesting to note just what Canadian politicians have chosen to do. Canada now has the Charter of Rights and Freedoms which covers the federal and provincial governments; that sets out fundamental freedoms, democratic rights, legal rights, and equality rights. Canadians have also added mobility rights and language rights. Interestingly enough, the Charter legitimates affirmative action in the constitutional definition of equality rights. At the same time, the United States is wrestling with these issues in the courts and in the legislatures, as to whether 'colour blind' or 'colour conscious' will be the rule that governs the American constitutional tradition.

When one looks at the balancing standard set out in section 1, something has been created which would warm the hearts of those law teachers in the

United States who teach what the Supreme Court of the United States actually does, rather than what the justices sometimes say they will do. The Charter says that all of those rights 'are subject only to those reasonable limits as prescribed by law as can be demonstrably justified in a free and democratic society.'

That is the kind of balancing standard which the United States Supreme Court has used in a great majority of civil liberties and civil rights cases. It is an invitation to look at values and weigh their importance and their immediacy. While not quite as specific as something like the 'clear and present danger test'[10] in dealing with free speech, it is the kind of reasonable statement about the potential conflict of values among liberties or between liberty and other social values which is very much the way in which the American judiciary tends to approach the hard balancing questions.

Very different, of course, is the political override clause in section 33. Here, despite the fundamental freedoms of section 2 and the legal rights of sections 7 through 14, legislatures, federal or provincial, are given the power to pass legislative acts which will operate 'notwithstanding' a provision above. This opportunity to have a parliamentary 'veto' over decisions under the Charter is a continuation of Canada's parliamentary tradition, and seems to me a basic unwillingness to leave the written bill of rights entirely in the hands of the judiciary.

Where does this lead? There are at least three indications that the Charter could make a difference in the civil liberties politics of Canada. First of all, the Charter will stimulate the elites that manage organizations and government to be much more sensitive to legitimate interests of liberty, equality, and justice issues, because of the very fact that they are stated as fundamental rights which are now binding in Canadian society. I do not think one should minimize the importance of what a society says is important to it, what it puts in a constitution, and which then becomes the standard of judgment with which one starts debates about whether something is right or wrong, good or bad, necessary or unnecessary. Symbols are powerful, and I think that the symbolism of what has been done here will have an enormous rippling effect in the society over time.

Second, I suspect that this will give the media a lot of events to write about that will have the effect of continuing the popularization of liberty and equality claims in the society. It may be that the Canadian Supreme Court will find more excitement and limelight in the future as a result of the substantive material with which it will be dealing. More political importance could be

---

10 Mr Justice Holmes enunciated this 'test' while delivering the opinion of the Court in *Schenck* v *United States* 249 US 47 (1919).

invested in the Supreme Court of Canada as a result of this than has been traditional previously.

Third, the Charter may well provide the bar and legal system in Canada with an interesting choice: to go American or to remain British, or to invite more test litigation and invite judges to see themselves as personages dealing with fundamental values and political questions in the state, using the Charter as the ground for assessing legitimacy for such action. If this is so, it is an invitation to the courts to be much more interventionist than previously. In the near term, since my assumption is that the approach one takes to these issues is powerfully shaped by the political culture and socialization, one should not hold one's breath for the present judges or the present bar becoming overnight great adherents to a very different style and a very different sense of legitimate action just because the Charter was passed and becomes operative over the next three years. It may take a decade. It may take two decades, before the people coming up in the universities and the law schools and innovative people on the bench begin to see what it is to use a written bill of rights to try and deal effectively with some of the tradeoff questions which are at the heart of civil liberties politics.

Another important factor will be whether the claimant groups in Canadian politics, groups claiming new racial rights, women's rights, sexual freedom rights or religious liberty rights, manage to project definitions of freedom which are seen by the general mainstream of Canadian politics to be appropriate ways of defining what the Charter is giving and what the Charter ought to give. Much will depend on how interest groups in Canada make use of, and are regarded as legitimately making use of, the Charter in both political debates of the legislature and in test cases in the courts.

In the Charter, I would suggest that Canada is moving to a hybrid system, halfway between the parliamentary supremacy approach of the British tradition and the American written constitutional system. With this shift comes an invitation to develop a new and powerful role for judicial review in the political system. I have been noticing in recent materials that I have read in Canada about the Charter that some people are worried that this will not be a strong synthesis of the two, but rather a weak synthetic. Because there is much that I do admire in Canadian politics and law, I am optimistic that it will work better than that. The kind of prudential sense and the deserving trust in government that has grown up in the Canadian tradition could make possible the use of the opportunities of the Charter to expand the definition of rights and liberties in a way which will be important for Canadian progress.

The ultimate answer, of course, is that time will tell. Every society gets the kind of civil liberties politics that its social realities and its political system deserve and dictate. The ultimate point will be that those things will change which in the deeper currents of Canadian politics are ready to change, and those things will remain the same which are dictated by the major tides of Canadian politics. This mechanism will not act as some kind of magic device that somehow transforms the realities of Canadian politics. It will be a mirror reflection. Just how much the mirror is a pure return or how much it refracts and alters in different ways is where the art of politics comes in, where particular leaders, particular judges, and the particular challenges of Canadian society dictate the direction that the changes take. It is an exciting time for Canadians, and for those of us who study and admire Canadian society.

COMMENTARIES

JAMES PENTON You suggested that it might take a decade or two before one saw a change in the way the courts, the legal profession and society reacted to the Constitution Act, 1982. Could that not be cut down rather quickly by a few quick crucial court decisions? In the United States, had it not been for *Marbury* v *Madison*, and *Barron* v *Baltimore*, then judicial review would not have been such an important constitutional check. Judicial review is not totally unknown to past interpretations, in Canada, of a bill of rights. In Canada, we have people trained in the British tradition. Could tradition, or conventions, not cut off the possible influence of the Constitution Act, 1982 rather quickly?
ALAN WESTIN Regarding your premise about the United States, my own reading for a long time has been that while Chief Justice Marshall was a dramatic figure, even if he had never lived the American Supreme Court would have developed much the same way. The forces of higher law tradition, the separation of powers, issues of federalism, the Rule of Law and the litigiousness of American society are what have brought forth that role in the Supreme Court. If it had not have been Marshall, it would have been Joseph Story. There were other people that were capable of giving the same kind of classic leadership and direction. It might have taken ten years more or thirty years more. But I do not believe that, but for John Marshall, we would have wound up with a departmental theory that each branch of the United States government will decide for itself whether its actions are constitutional.

Applying that to Canada, I do believe that for a reasonable period of time, the assumptions of the judges and the bar, the expectations of the Canadian public, and the style and traditions of the elected and administrative branches will continue to approach civil liberties and civil rights issues in much the same way. You could get a brilliant decision from the Supreme

Court of Canada making some Marshall-like assertion. If it is not acceptable within the Canadian political system, it will either be overriden or it will be avoided. Then there could be a disapproving opinion brought to bear on the justice or justices who wrote the opinion. There could be a feeling that such is not the Canadian way. If so, the Charter will be a flower that encounters soil that is too hard for it to take root and flourish.

DONALD SMILEY I would like Professor Westin to comment on the comparison between Canada and the United States in terms of the natural right / natural law tradition which underlies the American Constitution. Canada, as is the case with other countries who accept the parliamentary tradition, does not 'believe' in natural right / natural law. At any rate, in the debate we had in the last couple of years, there was much mention of that as a *justification* of rights. Is that crucial to what might be ahead for Canadians?

ALAN WESTIN I think it is certainly important historically and contemporaneously in the United States. Edward S. Corwin, the famous constitutional scholar in the United States, wrote a fine pamphlet called the *Higher Law Background of American Constitutional Law*,[11] in which he pointed out that lying in the fertile soil of the American political system was just that idea about a higher law. The Court, in some early decisions, tried to actually use references to a natural law or a higher law as grounds, for example, for striking down laws that would interfere with the obligation of contract. It took a little while for the Supreme Court in the United States to develop the technique of reading into the great clauses of the Constitution (like the due process clause or the obligations of contract clause) the higher law notions they would otherwise have to find brooding in the sky. So the justices developed a technique of taking these large, empty boxes of the clauses that the framers wrote and investing them with natural law vibrations and power.

In fact, that has not ended. For example, one of the things that Justice Hugo Black used to fulminate about in his last decade on the Supreme Court was the fact that his colleagues were appealing to what he liked to call 'natural law traditions' in order to come up with a new right to privacy, and other things which he did not find written in the Constitution.[12] Black did not want to see his colleagues do what, in the 1930s, he thought the 'old' Supreme Court was doing, in finding a natural rights justification for conservative economic and social ideas. That is a very important part of the American tradition, which crossed liberal/conservative lines and cut through the whole history of the Supreme Court.

---

11 Edward S. Corwin, *'Higher Law' Background of American Constitutional Law* (Ithaca, NY: Cornell University Press, 1955)
12 See Black's Dissenting Opinion in *Griswold* v *Connecticut*, 381 US 479 (1965).

The idea remains that the Supreme Court squares positivist law, manmade law, with this notion about what is, in the higher sense, *just and right*. In fact, Charles Black, a constitutional expert in the United States, wrote a book in which he said that one of the key functions the United States Supreme Court has come to exercise is what he called the 'legitimation power.'[13] According to his view, in the United States, when a state legislature or the Congress enacts a law and it is considered to be controversial, in terms of whether it infringes upon basic liberty rights or property rights or whatever, it is almost not considered a law in a totally legitimate sense, until the Supreme Court has either said it is law or they decline to hear it and leave it in the political arena. Thinking about the way in which the American Supreme Court works, I think that is, in fact, a good description of the way many citizens orient themselves.

For example, when President Truman seized the steel mills during the Korean War in order to avert a strike, a lawsuit was filed by the steel companies alleging that this was an abuse of the president's power.[14] Truman had not claimed any legislative right, but said he acted under the inherent powers of the presidency. At this point, the whole country settled down to watch the lawsuit the same way we settle down to watch the World Series. The feeling was that until the Supreme Court said whether that was legitimate or not, one could not decide the issue. That is the way in which the higher law notion – that mere acts of the elected branches in certain situations are not ultimately legitimate until the Supreme Court puts its imprimatur on it – is very much the way Americans approach it.

Now obviously, this is not true in Canada. When Parliament acts and when it has been put to the test of a non-confidence vote or an election, I think that is the point at which the notion of legitimacy attaches. It would take a very different tradition for people to say, 'Well, we won't know until the Supreme Court of Canada tells us whether this is a legitimate way of dealing with affirmative action or dealing with women's rights, or dealing with police practices, and so forth.'

QUESTION Given the force of the Constitution Act, 1982, is it possible then that people's willingness to look for some sort of solution, and their trust in the government, is based on their ability to actually do anything about it? For instance, given the RCMP's proclivity to break the law, people could simply be saying, 'Well, there isn't a lot we can do about it anyway, so why bother about it?' I wonder whether we are left distrustful of power

13 See 'The Legitimating Work of Judicial Review Through History' in Charles L. Black, *The People and the Court; Judicial Review in a Democracy* (New York: Macmillan, 1960).
14 *Youngstown Sheet and Tube Co.* v *Sawyer*, 343 US 579 (1952) is commonly known as the *Steel Seizure Case*.

and authority but then feel that there is little we can do about the abuse of power and authority.

ALAN WESTIN That is a very good question. Let me try to give you two quick reactions. One, you may well be right that people's use of the courts will be directly proportionate to their willingness to be used in terms of standing to sue and what groups are allowed to bring cases. If the Supreme Court of Canada opens the door, there will be many groups and individuals ready to come in. I am sure that this is one way it could develop.

On the other hand, it seems to me that you also have to take account of the fact that if something matters to a group, such as the activities of the RCMP, then going to court is only one of several political mechanisms that one has. One can use the political process and one can create a great deal of protest so that if it matters to people, one would look then at the structure of public opinion as reported in legitimate public opinion polls. One would look for a change in policy to control the RCMP or to set new rules for them.

Just to give you an example, when the FBI engaged in the kind of practices that it did in tapping Martin Luther King Jr's telephone, in putting agents into various black protest groups and leaking information in a wide variety of ways, and when Watergate brought out much of what the CIA and the FBI had been doing in terms of domestic surveillance – that concerned large numbers of Americans. The Supreme Court, I do not think, rules on any of those issues. I cannot think of any time in which the Supreme Court actively became involved in FBI/CIA surveillance and information practices. It was handled through the effort to create greater congressional overseeing of the CIA, through trying to write (and this is still underway in the United States) a charter for the FBI that will be enforced. Congress passed tougher wire-tapping legislation, dealing with national security wire-tapping, by further limiting the effort to do this without a warrant.

All I want to suggest is that if groups feel powerfully about something being done by a government whom they think is overstepping or abusing authority, the Canadian Charter may be a way to get that into a court, and indeed may invite this. But again, try to remember that the same balancing formula that is in the Constitution Act, 1982, can be used just as easily by the Supreme Court of Canada in looking at the problem of the RCMP or the War Measures Act as a consideration of the needs of protection in any civilized society. They might rule that such actions were not unreasonable in a 'free and democratic society.' Courts will still be called upon to look at the justification for what it is that the government does or the police in particular do. Bringing the issue to court is going to be just one part of trying to achieve the result that enhances the 'liberty claim' as opposed to the 'authority claim' in such a case.

QUESTION I wonder if you would comment on the point concerning freedom of information and privacy. The United States has excellent legislation in both these fields. It has existed in Sweden for some two hundred years. Most of the countries of Europe have enacted similar legislation. But it is equally true that to the best of my understanding, no country in the Commonwealth, no parliamentary system based on the 'Westminster style' has ever managed to get around to doing this. I would be interested to know your comments on why this would be.

ALAN WESTIN As I understand it, you are most concerned with freedom of information legislation, not privacy. My instinct would be to choose the explanation that says that parliamentary government is government that was derived from the King's Court and has about it the sense of legitimacy in government action. Freedom of information derives out of the revolution in the United States, out of the public's right to know and of having elected officials that are essentially subject to checks when making abusive use of power. Americans see freedom of information as a way of checking potential government abuse. It comes down to the American attitude toward power and its exercise by government.

An interesting point to note about the United States is that the largest single user of American freedom of information laws is the American business community, which uses freedom of information laws to get information about how the regulatory process is going to affect them. If you look every year at the groups that request information from federal agencies, business is the biggest user. The media comes second, and then a variety of interest groups. That tells you that freedom of information in the United States has a very broad constituency behind it. Americans have defended the freedom of information principles in the last twenty or thirty years against attacks from those who maintain that too much is exposed or that it interferes with confidentiality in government. This occurs because of the lobbying power of those diverse groups, all of whom feel that for their own reasons, freedom of information serves their interest.

The media, for example, obviously sell papers and get big audiences for programs because they know how to pull information out of government through the Freedom of Information Act. Information about foreign policy developments or domestic, economic and social developments make good copy in a democratic society. I would look for the explanation between the general comfort with freedom of information and ideological commitment to it, and the politics that defend it in the United States compared to those kinds of reasons in the parliamentary tradition.

R.G.L. FAIRWEATHER I am interested in the United States Department of Justice as a defender of the Constitution and the Bill of Rights. You mentioned that a ten year hiatus may be ahead for us in Canada. Have you any advice to give our Department of Justice as to how they should respond as enunciators – as the people who were behind the creation of the constitution? The Department of Justice acts as solicitor or counsel to various departments of government who will find – witness the Armed Forces – some of these equality rights very nerve-wracking indeed.[15]

ALAN WESTIN You have captured in your description exactly what I think is the great dilemma for your Department of Justice. It represents the government and is its lawyer. At the same time, it has a role in the rule of law and in the interpretation of the Constitution which is supposed to make it more than just a lawyer representing a client. On the whole, I would not point to the United States Department of Justice as a Galahad that has managed to deal with those conflicting roles very effectively. They would vary a bit from decade to decade because the United States Department of Justice has had some very unusual gyrations over the last forty or fifty years. There have been some points in which divisions within the Department of Justice (such as the Civil Rights Division under Frank Murphy or the voting rights activity of Robert Kennedy and others) have, depending upon the Attorney General, made a powerful commitment to some particular civil liberties or civil rights issue. Often other units of the Department of Justice were at the same time busy defending the government's claims against freedom of information or the like. Since the FBI was under the Department of Justice (not only in Mr Hoover's tenure), there were always other parts of the Department of Justice that were pressing in other directions.

At the present time, I would not myself regard Attorney General William French Smith as the most zealous defender of either the independence of the judiciary or as a defender of some of the kinds of roles for civil liberties and civil rights that lead to justice. Justice should prevail regardless of the Republican or Democrat or liberal or conservative leanings of the Attorney General.

I think you describe the role conflict perfectly to the extent that in a given instance, the Department of Justice could say to a police agency or a tax agency that the Canadian Charter of Rights and Freedoms says this, and as we think about what that command in the constitutional system means, it surely does not allow you to continue to do what you are doing. We would be then enhancing the official definition of the Department as an interpreter, as giving advisory opinions. However, pressure may very well be brought to

---

15 See 'Military to Seek Exemption from Rights Charter,' *Globe and Mail*, 10 March 1982, p 8. The government was quick to react. See 'Forces Won't Get Exemptions from Charter, Ottawa Asserts,' *Globe and Mail*, 13 March 1982, p 11.

bear on the Department of Justice, because those other departments may have political connections that are very important in a parliamentary government.

ARYEH NEIER I invite you to revise or modify what you said about the role of litigation. While clearly you are right in saying that litigation is not playing any role, certainly any significant role in limiting political surveillance, at least in important decisions by the Supreme Court, litigation was very much a part of the arsenal of those who were challenging political surveillance. This is so not because they anticipated that they would ultimately win Supreme Court decisions which tended to limit the activities of the executive branch of government, but because litigation was used as a research tool or as an instrument for obtaining discovery. At other times, it was used as an instrument for public education or as an instrument for exposing abuses that had taken place. I think this suggests something about the role litigation has come to play in Bill of Rights enforcement in the United States. That is, litigation is not always an end in itself but a means towards Bill of Rights enforcement. Very often, litigation is a means of triggering action by the other branches of government because it has the effect of spotlighting certain abuses or eliciting information about other abuses, thereby creating the momentum which brings about action by other branches of government.

ALAN WESTIN I entirely agree. I did not mean to give the impression that the two functions that you mentioned were really not very important, since they are. The courts could easily have been very much less open to discovery had they not considered it legitimate to have asked for information to be produced by the FBI or whatever. If the courts had not felt that these were real questions, the courts would not have given them the dignity of a hearing.

One of the other points you could make about litigation is that it is very good organizational economy, if one is running a group in the United States on behalf of consumers, civil libertarians, egalitarians or business interests, to go to court. They probably get more publicity for the buck by bringing on a lawsuit than by holding a convention and having to pay people to speak, or trying to mount a campaign. 'Dog bites man' is news and 'somebody sues government' is news. In the United States, some groups have actually managed to get far more publicity than their numbers would justify. My best example would be Paul Blanchard, who was the lawyer for a group called Protestants and Other Americans United for Separation of Church and State. He brought a lawsuit calling for every Catholic priest in the United States to be registered under the Foreign Agent Registration Act. That made a lot of news in the United States. But I do not think anybody held their breath for the Supreme Court of the United States to say that every Catholic priest ought to register under the Foreign Agent Registration Act.

PART TWO: THE AMERICAN EXPERIENCE WITH RIGHTS

The Rights of Americans: An Historical View

Paul L. Murphy*

In order to trace the historical record on rights up to the eve of World War II, it is necessary to comprehend what the nature of the founding was in the American context, and some of the legal dimensions of the Bill of Rights as it evolved over time. As the United States was born of revolution, situations emerged in which the considerations of civil liberties became tremendously central.

The Founding Fathers, who met in Philadelphia in 1787, were to some degree the same generation that had been actively involved in the whole revolutionary period. They were caught up in the history of that period. They were also students of English common law. They were students of ancient culture. Madison and John Adams were almost as much at home in ancient Greece and the Roman Forum as they were in the United States and had read, and pondered carefully, much of classical political theory before they ever arrived at Philadelphia. But they were also tremendously cognizant of the fact that the American Revolution had been fought over liberties and freedoms and rights. As opponents of centralized tyranny, they were very sensitive to the fact that not only could kings repress individual rights but so could parliaments.

In reading the Declaration of Independence, it should be noted that the Declaration makes very clear that the purpose of any new government in the United States should be to secure those rights – the rights which the Revolution had been fought to achieve.[1] The rights orientation was a very central kind of focus amongst this group.

---

* Paul Murphy is a Professor of History and American Studies at the University of Minnesota.
1 'We hold these truths to be self-evident: that all men are created equal, that they are endowed by their Creator with certain inalienable Rights, that among these are Life, Liberty and the pursuit of Happiness. That to secure these rights, Governments are insti-

Actually, the states of the United States had begun to write their own constitutions even before any federal government was in the offing. The first state constitution, the one in Virginia, in some ways became the model for a good many of the other states. It was written in 1776 at nearly the same time that the Declaration of Independence was being drafted and submitted to the Congress of that period. Most of the state constitutions included a bill of rights which set forth the usual kinds of guarantees about speech, press and assembly and various procedural guarantees. All were written to protect individuals against the arbitrariness of governments, which was much on the minds of people in this period.[2]

It is all the more incongruous that when the first attempt at setting up a national government occurred with the Articles of Confederation, there was no bill of rights within that arrangement. When the Fathers met in Philadelphia in 1787 to create a more perfect union after the Articles of Confederation had largely led to a decentralized collapse, they also omitted a bill of rights from the final document. The original Constitution itself does not address the question. However, when the document went to the states for ratification, a great many of the states made as a condition for their ratification of that document the addition of amendments which would guarantee citizens protection of their rights *against* the new central government. Thus, we have a rather interesting situation in which entrenchment of a bill of rights in the American Constitution was by the virtual demand of the states, they themselves fearing a central government which was not legally constrained and restricted as far as its power was concerned.

The result was the Bill of Rights, appended to the American Constitution as the first ten amendments. These amendments automatically became an integral part of the original document, making them part of 'the supreme Law of the Land.' It was then actually 'entrenched,' as the phrase is being used in current Canadian terminology. However, the addition of a bill of rights raised almost as many questions as it answered. Who would apply these? It is all very well to say Congress 'shall make no law' restricting free speech. Who enforces that? Where does a citizen go if he or she does indeed feel that a central government is in one way or another restricting rights? And where did the states figure in this particular arrangement?

tuted among Men deriving their just powers from the consent of the governed.' *The Declaration of Independence*, Revised Statutes of the United States, 1st sess. 43rd Cong. 1873–74, 2nd ed (Washington: Government Printing Office, 1878), p. 3.
2 See Richard L. Perry and John C. Cooper, eds, *Sources of Our Liberties* (New York: McGraw-Hill, 1959), pp 301, 323, 341, 352, 358, 368, 379.

James Madison, often referred to as the 'Father' of the American Constitution, very much wanted the original Bill of Rights guarantees to apply to the states as well as to the federal government. Madison wrote at the time: 'A democratic majority can be as repressive as a king. In our government the real power lies in the majority of the community and the invasion of private rights is chiefly to be apprehended, not from acts of government contrary to the sense of its constituents, but from acts in which the government is the mere instrument of the major number of the constituents.'[3] Notice the concern about tyranny, and concern about abusive power. Madison pointed out that he spoke not abstractly, because, as he said, '... in the state of Virginia [his home state], I have seen the Bill of Rights violated in every instance where it has been opposed in a popular current.'[4] When the American Fathers talked about the 'tyranny of the majority' (a phrase often used in this period of history), they were at once concerned to protect the minorities, constitutionally, from zealous majorities engaged in restrictive policies.

But Madison's concept of applying the national Bill of Rights to the states was certainly not what those states had in mind at the time. They were interested in limiting the federal government – they were not interested in limiting themselves, or in having the federal government limit them. Nonetheless, the Ninth and Tenth Amendments of the American Constitution do speak historically to this particular kind of consideration. The Ninth Amendment says that the fact that there are rights in the first eight amendments, and the fact that these rights are enumerated specifically, 'should not be construed to deny or disparage others retained by the people.'

This suggests, apparently, that there were other rights around, and the fact that some are enumerated does not mean that there are others which cannot also be called upon. The Tenth Amendment reinforces this point, in terms of suggesting that there are also powers which the states clearly retain in this interesting three-part structure of federal government – the states, the people, and the unenumerated or reserved rights that both possess.

Madison did not win support for his idea that the federal Bill of Rights should limit the states, even though he at one time had said that he considered an amendment to this effect '... the most valuable in the whole list.'[5]

---

3 Marvin Meyers, ed, *The Mind of the Founder: Sources of the Political Thought of James Madison*, rev ed (Hanover, NH: University Press of New England, 1981), p 173
4 *Ibid*, p 157
5 Bernard Schwartz, *The Great Rights of Mankind: A History of the American Bill of Rights* (New York: Oxford University Press, 1977), pp 168–9

His Proposal XIV, which was rejected, contained protections against the states for speech, press, conscience and the right of trial by jury.[6]

In fact, the question was not resolved formally another forty years. Finally, in 1833, in the case cited as *Barron v Baltimore*,[7] John Marshall, the nationalist judicial activist who ran the Supreme Court for a good many years, clarified it in what many people have felt was a rather incongruous ruling for Marshall, who was an extreme nationalist. He stated that the Bill of Rights of the federal Constitution did not limit the states; that clearly the Bill of Rights of the federal Constitution only limited the federal government. That meant, in practice, that before the American Civil War, if a citizen was being deprived of his or her rights by a state or by an instrumentality of a state government, recourse was only to the state or to the state courts. Thus, one hoped that the state constitution in the state in which a person lived had a bill of rights that was sufficiently entrenched at that level to be able to give them the proper kind of protection.

On the other hand, the question is somewhat academic because prior to the American Civil War, the federal government seldom if ever had actually legislated in a way which would restrict individual freedom. In some respects, to the extent that there was action in the civil liberties/civil rights area prior to 1865, this was largely at the state level where it was handled and of necessity was treated as a state issue.

The American Civil War had a very profound effect upon the American Constitution and upon American constitutionalism generally. The story can almost be reduced, in some ways, to verbs. The average American, prior to 1865, when he spoke of his government said, 'The United States *are*,' and after 1865 he said, 'The United States *is*,' which tells one something about centralizing processes and also something about the degree of states' rights which existed after the 1865 settlement. The Civil War had indeed been fought over a question of states' rights, among other things, and the states' rights interpretation had actually lost and was, to a degree, a casualty of the wartime period.[8] Further, that casualty was swiftly hammered into its coffin by three amendments which were enacted in 1865, 1868 and 1870 – the Thirteenth, Fourteenth and Fifteenth Amendments. The Fourteenth ultimately became the heart and soul of the modern American Constitution. It is a little hard oftentimes to realize that there has been more litigation sur-

---

6 See Edward Dumbauld, *The Bill of Rights and What It Means Today* (Norman: University of Oklahoma Press, 1957).
7 *Barron v Baltimore*, 7 Pet. 243 (1833)
8 See Kenneth M. Stampp, 'The Concept of a Perpetual Union,' *Journal of American History* 65 (June, 1978), pp 5–33.

rounding the Fourteenth Amendment since 1868 than involving all of the rest of the American Constitution put together. This says something about where that particular amendment has come to rest in terms of the American constitutional scene.

Two things about the Fourteenth Amendment should be highlighted. The Fourteenth Amendment for the first time defined citizenship in the United States and made very clear that a citizen was 'a person born or naturalized' – a very simple definition. If you look at the Amendment, it says, 'All persons born or naturalized in the United States, and subject to the jurisdiction thereof, are citizens of the United States and of the State wherein they reside.' What that means is that federal citizenship is *primary*, and state citizenship is secondary. If one goes on it should be noticed that it says, 'No State shall make or enforce any law which shall abridge the privileges or immunities of citizens of the United States.' The amendment then refers to 'due process' and 'equal protection.' What one sees here is the fact that not only is federal citizenship made primary, but the rights of federal citizens have in some way emerged as being a central and overriding consideration. In the relationship of citizen to state to rights, the federal government often became predominant. That is, the relationship between state and citizen became a concern of the federal government because *its citizens* were guaranteed particular rights *as citizens of the United States*, regardless of the state wherein they resided.

These amendments in some ways, then, did what James Madison had been urging in 1791. The Fourteenth Amendment could be used as a tool to apply certain of the guarantees of the Bill of Rights *against* the states.[9] But in the period between 1870, when the last of these three amendments was ratified, and 1900, the Supreme Court of the United States, in one of its most activist periods (and a very conservative activist period), largely dismantled these amendments as far as effective meaning was concerned in regard to the protection of liberties and rights. By 1900, one did not look to the federal government for the protection of his or her speech, press, assembly or, for that matter, for protection of his or her equal rights under the law.

---

9 The theory that the 'due process' clause of the Fourteenth Amendment was meant to include the protections afforded in the first ten amendments is known as the Incorporation Doctrine. The logic of this view is that a resident of a state who is denied protections afforded under the Bill of Rights as a citizen of the United States cannot be legally deprived of those rights by a state, since it would be a denial of 'due process of law' or 'the equal protection of the laws,' which a state, according to the Fourteenth Amendment, is prohibited from denying. [Eds Note]

In this particular period, the Supreme Court made it very clear that it saw its role largely as the protector of property rights – the rights, in other words, of the powerful, the owners, the corporations, the 'haves.' It clearly did not see its role as being that of a broker for the 'have-nots' within American society. In this particular period, if one was clearly outside the mainstream and did not have access to political power or economic power, one did not have much in the way of claimed individual rights at either the federal or the state level.[10] This situation was generally reflective of a variety of American values in this particular period.

World War I, I argue,[11] is a major turning point in this development. During World War I, the federal government for the first time, in any massive kind of way, passed a body of legislation which sharply restricted a variety of bill of rights guarantees. What happened was that the central government – in enacting espionage laws, sedition laws, postal censorship laws, etc. – criminalized, that is, made federal crimes out of, certain forms of expression, certain forms of belief, and certain forms of association which one agreed with, or belonged to, and then set out to prosecute under the espionage and sedition laws. The states followed suit very actively, passed their own sedition laws, their own criminal syndicalism laws, their own red flag laws, punishing criticism of the war, punishing dissent, and punishing opposition to central policy. The war period did not encourage dissent. The federal government prosecuted over two thousand cases involving sedition of some kind or another, usually involving unpopular minorities, German-Americans, Irish-Americans, socialists, agrarian radicals, pacifists, and anti-war people. The states prosecuted a good many also, along very much the same lines. This showed, generally, the frailty of the Bill of Rights guarantees, whether they were in the federal Constitution or the state constitutions, or in the face of wartime exigency, national emergency or national security considerations.

But the period also had the counter-effect of producing the first active civil liberties movement in American history. During the wartime period, the National Civil Liberties Bureau was organized to particularly support pacifists and anti-war protesters. That agency was reorganized at the end of World War I to become the American Civil Liberties Union.[12]

10 See John P. Roche, 'American Liberty: An Examination of the "Tradition" of Freedom,' in *Aspects of Liberty; Essays Presented to Robert E. Cushman*, eds Milton R. Konvitz and Clinton Rossiter (Ithaca, NY: Cornell University Press, 1958), pp 129–62.
11 Paul L. Murphy, *World War I and the Origin of Civil Liberties in the United States* (New York: Norton, 1979)
12 Donald Johnson, *The Challenge to American Freedoms: World War I and the Rise of the American Civil Liberties Union* (Lexington, KY: University of Kentucky Press, 1963)

The wartime period also produced some major shifts in doctrinal thinking as far as lawyers were concerned. For a great many years, Louis Brandeis, who had been an attorney before he was appointed to the bench by Woodrow Wilson, had been increasingly concerned that in American law, the permissible limits of dissent had largely been defined in relation to private property. That is, if dissent, if protest, if criticism tended to threaten private property, then one generally should draw the line in this area. In 1920, in a Minnesota case involving a wartime crisis in which a leader of the non-partisan league had been jailed for protesting against the war, Brandeis said: 'I cannot believe that the liberty guaranteed by the Fourteenth Amendment includes only liberty to acquire and enjoy property.'[13] As the 1920s progressed, an emphasis did indeed shift with the test for the permissible limits of freedom of expression reached when the expression of ideas no longer served the public dialogue. This is a very different test. It says basically that only when ideas no longer contribute to what Holmes once referred to as 'the marketplace of ideas'[14] is one justified in restricting their expression. I was struck recently in reading some opinions by Canadian Judge Ivan Rand in the *Boucher* case,[15] and also in a 1957 case cited as *Switzman* v *Elbling*,[16] that Justice Rand, in those particular cases, expressed a very eloquent kind of marketplace statement regarding the importance of expression serving broader social interests, and those interests being possibly disadvantaged if denied the ideas which such speech contained. Even if those ideas are unpopular or controversial, there is a right to express them if they do indeed contribute to the public dialogue.

But an even larger shift took place starting in 1925 in the United States. Significantly, it began in a free speech case in New York involving a man named Benjamin Gitlow, who was then one of the high officials of the Communist party in the United States.[17] Gitlow had been arrested in the 'red scare' days of 1920 when the United States Attorney General had led raids on radical headquarters throughout the country, fearing 'red' infiltration in American politics. Gitlow had been charged with publishing a journal known as the *Left Wing Manifesto* which was an official paper of the party. The question again was whether or not his publications sufficiently threatened the public interest to warrant suppression. The Supreme Court decided that they did. But at the same time, the Supreme Court also decided a very

13 *Gilbert* v *Minnesota*, 254 US 325, 343 (1920)
14 On Holmes see Murphy, *World War I*, pp 266–7.
15 *Boucher* v *The King* (1951), 1 DLR (2d) 682
16 *Switzman* v *Elbling* (1957), 7 DLR (2d) 337, 357–8
17 *Gitlow* v *New York*, 268 US 652 (1925)

important issue, that is, whether a state law which restricted individual expression was a federal question. It was conceded that this was a legitimate question *to ask*, even though they did not *rule* that way in the *Gitlow* case. What they were saying in 1925 was that when state action does indeed restrict a federal guarantee, such as freedom of speech, there clearly are federal remedies to that particular process.

This process, which American lawyers refer to as 'incorporating the Bill of Rights against the states,' or sometimes as 'nationalizing the Bill of Rights against the states,' began in 1925. It began within a statement of the fact that it is indeed a permissible way to interpret the Fourteenth Amendment, and particularly its 'due process' clause. It suggests that state citizens have federal remedies if the states are restricting their individual freedom.

The Supreme Court, in the next dozen years until 1937, went ahead to incorporate various guarantees against the states through the 'due process' clause of the Fourteenth Amendment. In 1931, freedom of speech was incorporated through a California case.[18] In 1931 also, freedom of the press was incorporated through a Minnesota case,[19] freedom of religion in 1935 through a California case,[20] and freedom of assembly in 1937 through an Oregon case.[21] Both the questions of a fair and impartial jury[22] and the right to counsel,[23] at least in capital cases, were 'nationalized' or 'incorporated' in Alabama cases involving black justice in the American South. By 1937, the question had become not *whether* the Bill of Rights limited the states, but *which* rights should be protected against the states and in what circumstances should these rights be protected against the states.[24]

In 1937, this delineating issue came before the Supreme Court in a case involving a Connecticut law raising the question of double jeopardy – that is, if a state subjects a person to double jeopardy, is this violating the rights of

---

18 *Stromberg* v *California*, 283 US 359 (1931)
19 *Near* v *Minnesota*, 283 US 697 (1931). On *Near* and the general question of 'incorporation,' see Paul L. Murphy, '*Near* v *Minnesota* in the Context of Historical Developments' *Minnesota Law Review* 66 (November, 1981), 95–160.
20 *Hamilton* v *Regents*, 293 US 245 (1934)
21 *De Jonge* v *Oregon*, 299 US 353 (1937)
22 *Norris* v *Alabama*, 294 US 587 (1935)
23 *Powell* v *Alabama*, 287 US 45 (1932)
24 There are four provisions in the Bill of Rights which have not yet been incorporated. They are Second Amendment – the right to keep and bear arms; Third Amendment – the quartering of soldiers without the consent of the owner; Fifth Amendment – the right to indictment by a grand jury for serious crimes; Seventh Amendment – the right of jury trial in civil cases.

federal citizens sufficiently to make it automatically appealable as a federal case. The case was *Palko v Connecticut*.[25] A decision was rendered by Justice Benjamin Cardozo. Cardozo ruled in this particular case that double jeopardy was not a guarantee that should be imposed against the states through the Fourteenth Amendment. Such a ruling suggests some sort of a *selective process*, whereby some rights should be protected and some should not. The question was: which should and which should not, and what rules should be applied? Cardozo in *Palko* said: 'Only those rights implicit in the concept of ordered liberty and so rooted in the traditions and conscience of our people, as to be ranked fundamental, should be nationalized by the court.'[26] Really what Cardozo said in that case was that there are some rights that should exist, there are some rights that should not exist, and the Supreme Court on a case-to-case basis will make the decision as to which it feels are fundamental and which it feels are implicit in the concept of 'ordered liberty.' The case, in other words, virtually directs the Supreme Court by suggesting that it is a duty to go ahead with the process to modernize the Bill of Rights and to do so on some kind of an effective, *selective* basis which makes sense in the process.

Justice Harlan F. Stone was intrigued with this particular distinction. But Stone wanted to go a bit further. In a case in 1938, again involving a state law, Stone said that such 'selective incorporation' is a very complex question because the Court was being asked to say why some state laws restricted liberty too much and others did not restrict liberty too much. Stone wanted the Court to clarify the degree of restriction, because there were also state laws which restricted economic activities, and economic liberty. There should be some rule which would be logical and operational in this area. Stone suggested in a footnote in that case (*United States v Carolene Products Co.*)[27] that there should be a higher presumption of constitutionality for state laws that restrict the economy than for state laws that restrict individual freedom. The Court should look far more critically at a state law which restricts free speech or press than at a state law which restricts certain forms of business activity. It was an interesting kind of standard, a judicial standard, but a standard which Stone felt very clearly might be an operational and justifiable one, at the time. He later admitted that there was a 'power' consideration in his thinking in this particular situation. Clearly, the Court's role in supporting powerless people against state restriction of their rights possibly should be

25 *Palko v Connecticut*, 302 US 319 (1937)
26 *Ibid*, 327
27 *United States v Carolene Products Co.*, 304 US 144 (1938)

more aggressive than their role in restricting business corporations who had the ability through litigation, through a variety of forms of retaliation, to be able to fend off or rationalize that kind of regulation on their own terms.

This is an interesting rule and one which more or less set up a potential role for the Court over the next forty years. I call attention finally, as an historian, to the fact that both of these rulings in 1937 and 1938 (when the Supreme Court was beginning to try to refine what its role should be in the rights area) came at a time when Adolf Hitler was on the move in Germany and Benito Mussolini was on the move in Italy. The Moscow purge trials were occurring in the Soviet Union. The role of central governments in restricting individual freedoms was a very pressing issue in the minds of a great many Americans. Clearly, the rights issue was a very central question, which may also have had something to do with the kind of delineations that were being made at that particular time. As America faced World War II, it did so with a kind of rough civil liberties agenda, which obviously was going to have to be worked on and worked out in subsequent years.

COMMENTARIES

PAUL BENDER At the end of your presentation of both the Cardozo and Stone opinions in the *Palko* and *Carolene Products* cases, you talked about those opinions as if their main effect was to enlarge judicial power – to give the courts more power and discretion. It seems to me that they really were exactly the opposite. The main effect was to limit power. By the time Cardozo wrote the *Palko* decision, and from the enactment of the Fourteenth Amendment, it was clear that there was a due process clause applicable to the states. The question is, what did it mean? It said in the Constitution that no state shall 'deprive any person of life, liberty or property, without due process of law.' Even in the narrower, more literal procedural meaning, that might apply to things like double jeopardy. What Cardozo was saying in *Palko* was that the due process clause does not incorporate every aspect of procedure that the Bill of Rights requires the federal government to observe. It is only those that are so fundamental that a civilized society cannot live without them that are within the meaning of 'due process.'

I see that as a limiting statement, limiting the tendency that the Court had demonstrated prior to World War II to use the due process clause to strike down economic and social legislation because they thought it was unreasonable. There was a reaction against that at that time, and Cardozo's opinion was part of that reaction. Stone's is also. He was trying to justify why the

Court was going to limit its 'strict scrutiny,' its review, its balancing, to certain classes of asserted constitutional rights. Not all rights, not all interferences with freedom were to be subjected by the Court to a strict scrutiny and a balancing, but only those which are really important to the maintenance of a democratic society. Specifically, those that involve oppression against minorities (because those people cannot have their claims properly vindicated in the democratic process) and those issues that have to do with free expression, because free expression is itself necessary to the maintenance of a free and democratic society. This is more of a comment and I would be interested in your response.

PAUL MURPHY It is an excellent comment. I have never been one who has been persuaded that the relentlessness of the incorporation process was such that by 1937, had Cardozo not made these distinctions, we would have moved to total incorporation in a very short time. I think obviously this is an exaggerated claim. *Palko* was reversed, as you know very well, but not until the 1960s in *Malloy* v *Hogan*.[28] We still have not moved all the way to total incorporation. The other point is that Cardozo does say in the *Palko* ruling that speech and the First Amendment rights are indeed the preferred and central rights. He drew a certain distinction, in his mind at least, between what some people at that time referred to as 'preferred freedoms' as opposed to certain other freedoms. This did have the effect, for a number of years, of putting the brakes on further incorporation of procedural guarantees. In some ways, it was the later Warren Court that was expanding – not the Court of the late thirties.

WILLIAM BEANEY I think the last comment, though, illustrates the difficulties we have in reaching agreement on assessing the meaning of a *significant* Court decision. One can certainly argue that if the 1937 Supreme Court 'peaceful revolution' was designed to reduce the Court to a subordinate role with respect to economic matters,[29] one might have assumed that the same principle would concern the Court in dealing with libertarian issues. It seems to me one can interpret the *Palko* decision as the Court's announcement that it was not getting out of the business entirely.

PAUL BENDER There is a tendency to think of the judicial development of constitutional rights and the judicial role in constitutional rights in the United States as one of the Court 'grabbing power,' asserting authority with a compulsion to constitutionalize more and more categories. In fact, for most of the history of the United States, it has been just the opposite. The Court has been very reluctant to do that.

---

28 *Malloy* v *Hogan*, 378 US 1 (1964)
29 *National Labor Relations Board* v *Jones and Laughlin Steel Corp.*, 301 US 1 (1937)

It is true that by the time of the Warren Court, the Court became more aggressive but even then not as aggressive as it sometimes appears to outsiders. Was it the Court's instinct through all that time to enlarge its role? Often, it seems to me, the Court's instinct was precisely the opposite.

R.G.L. ROBERTSON I understand that you do not have a specific recognition of emergency periods in the Constitution, other than the mention in article I, section 9 about the suspension of *habeas corpus*. You do not have the equivalent of the Canadian War Measures Act. Yet it seems that there has not been much litigation concerning emergency powers. I can understand that in World War I where there was only about a year of war. But during the Civil War, why were there no challenges under the Bill of Rights to the broad abrogation of rights by the federal government? Why were there not challenges during World War II? Is it just overwhelmingly assumed that wartime periods permit overriding the Bill of Rights without explicit recognition that such is the case?

PAUL MURPHY Clearly, there was concern about Lincoln's creation of new presidential powers during the Civil War, which he used, among other things, to suspend *habeas corpus*, which the Constitution largely prohibits. Congress eventually got him 'off the hook,' by passing the emergency law which, after the fact, gave him the right to suspend *habeas corpus*. The nature of the wartime crisis was such that people were prepared to place security above particular individual rights.

Nonetheless, in the *Milligan* case,[30] which involved the imposition of martial law during the wartime period and the jailing of a wartime protestor, the Supreme Court, once the Civil War was comfortably over, ruled that the suspension of rights, on martial law argumentation, had been unwarranted. This meant that the law should apply evenly in war or peace. The question is why that particular rule was not used in World War I by those who criticized the war. I am not sure why it was not *effectively* utilized. The National Civil Liberties Bureau, in my own research, made a very serious attempt to try to raise the *Milligan* precedent during World War I as an opposition to some of Wilson's wartime activities. It was simply brushed aside as being a nuisance.

WALTER BERNS The assertion of the power of the executive to suspend the privileges of *habeas corpus* was challenged in the Court, and the opinion by Chief Justice Taney was clearly against the assertion of such power.[31] The plain fact of the matter was that Lincoln, as Chief Executive of the country, ignored the Court. Merryman, without the privilege of *habeas corpus*, stayed

30 *Ex parte Milligan*, 4 Wall. (71 US) 2 (1866)
31 *Ex parte Merryman*, 17 Fed. Cas. 144 (no 9487) (CCD Md. 1861)

in the military prison. The lesson was also confirmed in the Second World War. The lesson was that one had better not test some of these things during wartime emergencies.

What happens when you take the Japanese off the West Coast and the president says this action is essential? (Canadians know all about this too.) The Attorney General of California, Earl Warren, confirmed that this was indeed a crisis and it went to the Supreme Court. The greatest civil libertarians on the Supreme Court confirmed the executive power. There it stands as a precedent that ought to warn us that there are some circumstances where Bills of Rights are best left alone.

ARYEH NEIER In a way, I do not think the *Merryman* case in the Civil War period ought to be lumped together with what happened during World War II. With Taney, one had a Chief Justice who thoroughly discredited himself and the Court in the *Dred Scott* case.[32] The Supreme Court's prestige was probably lower at that moment than at any moment in the history of the United States. Lincoln had no obligation to enforce a decision by a Justice who had helped to bring on the Civil War by his *Dred Scott* decision. If the Supreme Court had ruled the other way in the *Korematsu*,[33] and had the president disregarded the Supreme Court, one might have had some analogy to what took place in the *Merryman* case. We should not be wrapping them together.

In the Steel Seizure case a few years later, the Korean War was underway.[34] The Korean War was a popular war in the United States. The President was not infringing on individual liberties. He was seizing the steel industry, and saying that the steel industry was essential for the maintenance of the war effort. Yet, when the Court ruled against the president, the Court prevailed.

ALAN WESTIN I think I agree. You have to start by saying that we never even had a fully declared war. The country had not girded itself up for the struggle that World Wars I and II represented. That was because the Supreme Court uses intervention in a particular way when the country is locked in 'mortal combat.' During the Steel Seizure, the Supreme Court decided that the war was not much of an emergency. John Roche wrote a good commentary afterwards in which he said that what the Court faced in the Steel Seizure Case was a choice as to whether there was an emergency.[35] If they believed there

32 *Scott* v *Sandford*, 19 How. (60 US) 393 (1857)
33 *Korematsu* v *United States*, 323 US 214 (1944)
34 *Youngstown Sheet and Tube Co.* v *Sawyer*, 343 US 579 (1952)
35 John P. Roche, 'Executive Power and Domestic Emergency: The Quest for Prerogative,' *Western Political Quarterly* 5 (1952), pp 592–618

was an emergency, they would invoke the language of judicial deference to the executive branch of government at a time of great peril to the society. Lacking knowledge about foreign defence policy, they would not intervene. If, on the other hand, they really made the judgment that it was not a great emergency, then they could invoke the great tradition whereby the King is under the law and the executive must be bound by the elected branch of the government. Court will vindicate the rights of the property owner and the liberty-seeker in that kind of situation. As Roche suggested, it was really a question of whether the Court believed that it was facing a true emergency. I think that is a better way to relate the World War II situation to the Steel Seizure events.

DONALD SMILEY It seems very interesting that we are down to emergency powers. Canada really has two constitutions. The one we talk about most of the time, and the 'War Measures Act Constitution' in which the executive can declare in the face of war, invasion or insurrection, real or apprehended, that Canada ceases in a real sense to be either parliamentary or federal. Really it does seem to me, in terms of emergency powers, that there is a distinction between a country with one Constitution, and one with two. That is a pretty different situation in relation to emergency regimes in the two countries.

WILLIAM LEDERMAN I want to draw attention to a forgotten man – John G. Diefenbaker. The Canadian Bill of Rights, the statutory Bill of Rights, does have protections for parliamentary review of a declaration of emergency under the War Measures Act. There is nothing explicit in the Canadian Charter about it. Emergency has to be coped with under section 1, the 'reasonable limits' phrase in the Charter. I think John Diefenbaker was rather worried about the War Measures Act. Part II of the Canadian Bill of Rights, which I hope is going to remain in force alongside the Charter, does have a procedure for parliamentary review.

WILLIAM MCKERCHER I would like to get back to federal state relations in the United States. When talking about incorporation in general terms, it is interesting that it is referred to as 'incorporating the Bill of Rights *against* the states.' Is that terminology common? Secondly, would it historically be the case that with the development of the incorporation doctrine, in terms of the basic freedoms, there are fundamentally no rights retained by the people? In particular terms, one tends to view the American state as one where there are federal powers, state powers and other powers 'reserved' for the people. That is assumed. If one carries incorporation to its logical conclusion, where all the rights that are in the first eight amendments become part of someone's power, in the end no rights are retained by the people that are not *defined*.

PAUL MURPHY The Ninth Amendment is yet undefined, although one of the Justices in a case in 1965 made some attempt to suggest that there were a number of rights some way imbedded in the rights in the Ninth Amendment, which were still retained by the people, which obviously could be invoked and could be developed in the process.[36] What they were and precisely how they would be invoked is another question. Even Hugo Black, who was a rights man in his later years, was a little bit appalled by the suggestion that in some way one could create rights out of this particular amendment and have them emerge as new guarantees and protections.

WILLIAM BEANEY We have in the Constitution the term liberty. There are other rights and aspects of liberty that are in the Bill of Rights. But this is the method by which you can find that there are protective rights not enumerated in the Constitution, both with respect to the national government and to the states. It's the same way the Court back in the early part of the nineteenth century found, in property, all kinds of rights that might not be apparent on the surface. So similarly, liberty has a capacity, if one wishes, to find various rights in it. When you say 'retained by the people,' it can be recognized through the Fifth and the Fourteenth Amendments under the concept of liberty. While in the critical cases like *Griswold*, *Roe* and other privacy cases, it takes on rather strange meanings, such as that funny opinion of Douglas in the *Griswold* case, which produced privacy through 'penumbrance and emanations.'[37] Still I think the majority of them in that case were concerned with this aspect of liberty, which does not find exclusive recognition in the Constitution. It seems to me that the Ninth Amendment and liberty put together gives a Court that wishes it the capacity of finding ways of protecting rights that are not enumerated.

WILLIAM MCKERCHER It seems to me that as the incorporation doctrine proceeds, the power of the federal government seems to be growing in strength by nationalizing rights. What you are effectively doing is allowing the federal government to become the general protector through the definition of the first eight amendments.

PAUL BENDER No matter how much power the federal government has to protect rights, unless the states were to act inconsistently with that there is nothing to stop the states from enlarging upon those rights even further. This can be done by the state judiciary, in interpreting state constitutions, or by state legislatures. That is a common phenomenon in the United States.

36 See Justice Goldberg's concurring opinion in *Griswold* v *Connecticut*, 381 US 479 (1965), which also contains Justice Black's 'reply.'
37 *Griswold* v *Connecticut*, 381 US 479 (1965); *Roe* v *Wade*, 314 F. Supp. 1217 (DCND Tex. 1970)

The fact that litigants today tend to think of litigating in the state forum is in part a reaction to the conservatism of the Burger Court. But I believe you can find, as you go back through history, that there have been some state courts that have been at various times aggressive and firm and creative in interpreting their own constitutions. It is not just a phenomenon of the last ten years. Before the Civil War, that was the *only* guarantee of individual rights against state governments that American citizens had because there was no central guarantee at all.

ALAN WESTIN I think you might also want to distinguish among the issues. In equality legislation and equality decisions, you are really coming forward to protect a variety of groups. The legislative process moves not just hand in hand, but many times ahead of what the Warren Court was willing to do. In responding to equality claims, the state process was much more open and advanced. Correspondingly, in the liberty areas, wherein one cannot use the police practice where procedure violates the process, then the larger picture is one of a federal effort to enlarge the control over state police practices and state criminal procedure matters. That is the dominant pattern.

You cannot take all the rights in the Constitution and treat them as a uniform set. It makes a lot of difference, I would argue, because of the different political realities. In some cases, the groups make their coalitions and are able to get legislatures and judges reflecting dominant public opinion in the states to enlarge equality guarantees. Whereas in the liberty area, you usually have very unpopular minorities, radical political groups and so forth. If they are going to get any protection at the state level, they will get it, if at all, from the state judiciary. They are much *less* likely to get it there than they would from a national Court. In an era like the Warren Court era, that means the protection of those kinds of rights, both substantive and procedural, was part of the Court's liberal defence of civil liberties.

WALTER BERNS When we talk about the relations of people of the United States to the various states, when we talk about this business of incorporation, I wonder if, to be accurate, one does not have to raise the question of the differences between the states.

I think there is reason to believe that the Supreme Court would not have done what it has done in the area of capital punishment if the cases had come from California (whereas as I recall, the Court declared the death penalty unconstitutional under the state constitution) as opposed to state cases coming up from southern state courts. There has really been a difference between states with respect to all kinds of civil liberties matters in the United States. Does Canada have a parallel to the South? Where will the political power in the national government be if that 'Canadian South' happens to be a province where over fifty per cent of a national government's party caucus comes from? The point should be made.

The success of the Supreme Court of the United States in these matters is not simply handing down a decision. Lurking behind it someplace was some political power or a dispersion of power, making it impossible to mount an attack. One wonders whether that will be true under the Charter, given the present configuration of Canadian political power.

PAUL MURPHY This is all beginning to come out now. The early incorporation cases, and particularly the cases involving procedure – fair and impartial jury, right to counsel in criminal cases – were southern cases. They were horrible examples of the total misuse of state power. The Court took them on as a way of looking at whether or not the states could indeed render justice and render fair play. These made the Court's case very eloquently, because when you are railroading poor, ignorant and illiterate blacks to jail with a completely all-white jury and with a total denial of anything resembling counsel, you have made an interesting case for federal intervention in the state court procedures.

DOUGLAS SCHMEISER It is hard to give a Canadian counterpart to what is being discussed here. There are two factors that lead to a possible difference. From the point of view of comparing the American and the Canadian constitutions, one must remember that in Canada, criminal law and criminal procedure are federal matters. In theory, they do not vary according to region of the country where the case arises. We also have a unified judicial system in which our federal judges have power to deal with all matters whether they are considered to be state or federal matters under the constitution. We do not have the diversity that exists in the United States. Having said that, and coming back to criminal law in particular, we have a very unusual situation in the area of criminal law where, in my view, the Canadian Parliament has been much more liberal in the area of police rights than has the Supreme Court of Canada. There are a number of decisions in which our Supreme Court has discussed the rights of the police with respect to powers of arrest. They have clearly changed the intent of the Criminal Code to give the police more powers than intended by Parliament. We have the odd spectacle in Canada of the Court being more conservative in the area of police rights than the Parliament of Canada.

I would refer to two cases in support of that proposition: the *Moore* case, where the Supreme Court utilized the obstruction offence to enforce provincial and municipal by-laws in a way that the Criminal Code never intended;[38]

---

38 *Moore* v *R.*, [1978] 6 WWR 462; 5 CR (3d) 289; 43 CCC (2d) 83; 90 DLR (3d) 112; 24 NR 181; 1979 1 SCR 195

and the *Biron* case, where, in justifying the right of arrest, the Court interpreted the phrase 'found committing an offence' to mean 'apparently committing an offence.'[39] This clearly changes the intent of the legislative provision. In fact, we have the reverse effect in Canada, where our police officers were given rather restricted powers (in fact the term police officer is not used at all in the Code – the phrase is peace officer, which conveys a certain impression). The Supreme Court violated the intent of parliamentary restrictions by adding to police powers in this area.

R.G.L. ROBERTSON I would like to revert, if I may, to Professor Berns' very provocative question for Canadians. Do we have an area where we may have the equivalent to the American South where one cannot rely on the political process or judicial process to mount adequate protections? In Canada, we may have an area that will be a problem – not for the reasons that were prevalent in the South, but for quite different reasons – in relation to Quebec. I do not say this with any thought that Quebec is less vigilant for rights. I think their Charter of Rights is perhaps the best of the provincial charters of rights. But because of two factors Quebec is very special. In the first place, the Charter of Rights is being imposed on Quebec. They have not accepted it, and they did not agree to it being imposed. This is going to create, and has created, an atmosphere of resistance and an atmosphere of suspicion with respect to the Charter of Rights. We must expect in the future not a willingness to see application of the Charter, but on the part of a large part of the population of Quebec a suspicion about the Charter and its objectives and consequences.

The second factor that seems to me to be important is that at least a large part of the francophone population of Quebec feels that it is a defensive minority in danger of being overwhelmed. Some of the things that it has done, and must do, are legitimate defensive measures, not unlike what is done by the United States in a condition of war in mobilizing presidential powers. We will see situations in which the Charter of Rights will conflict with language legislation in Quebec. It will certainly conflict with some provisions of Bill 101. There are also provisions in the Charter, in the mobility rights, that will almost certainly conflict with some of the things that Quebec had incorporated in their law with regard to preferences for employment. They feel that the people of Quebec do not have, *de facto*, the mobility in Canada that the rest of Canadians have because they speak a different language. They will be very likely to feel that the mobility rights operate against Quebecers and create situations of inequality in the country.

39 *R.* v *Biron* (1975), 30 CRNS 109; 23 CCC (2d) 513; DLR (3d) 409; 4 NR 45; [1976] 2 SCR 56

I am delighted that Professor Berns raised that question. I had not really thought about it in his terms, but I think that, at least for some aspects of the Charter in Quebec, we must expect to find what I regard as quite legitimate reasons in feeling that the Charter is not really a Charter in defence of rights that *they* adopted. It is rather a Charter a little bit like unequal treaties imposed on the Chinese, to which they feel a legitimate resistance, and a legitimate sense that they should obey them only if they can.

JAMES PENTON On a more hopeful note, it seems to me that this resistance has certainly appeared in the United States with respect to the rights of blacks in the South, and in Canada in the 1950s, when some of the most important decisions were made by the Supreme Court of Canada, with respect to what was going on in Quebec. However, I think it is interesting to note that while there is a reaction in both instances, after a period of time the communities in question have settled down and more or less accepted the libertarian thrusts of both Supreme Courts. If the political stress and strain that is going on in this country between Quebec and the federal government, and for that matter other areas of the country and the federal government, continues, and the economic situation continues to be bad, I can see this sort of a reaction, but it is in part an incidental reaction. It is like the tomfoolery that is going on in this country with respect to metrication. Where I come from in Alberta, people are as concerned about the fact that they have French printed on their cornflakes boxes, and that there are soon going to be grocery store products measured in kilograms and grams rather than pounds and ounces, as they are about major constitutional precedents. I think that this can be a very serious matter, simply because people think it is serious; not because it really is. If that continues, we can have a Court reaction against the Charter. But I would suggest that if the political situation quietens down and we enter a period in which the provinces and the federal government are not fighting one another consistently, and if the economy improves, I think that Quebec will accept the new constitutional arrangements.

Rights in the
United States Constitution
since 1940

William M. Beaney*

The American experience with constitutionally protected rights since 1940 deserves a longer and more detailed account than is provided here.[1] The growth of governmental intervention in ever more human activities has led to increased opportunities for invoking the written constitution, whose 200th anniversary will occur in 1987.

Whether the American record has great significance for Canada poses a question about which reasonable people may disagree. The entrenchment of rights in the new Canadian Constitution comes after long experience with a system of parliamentary supremacy. The American judicial tradition of treating the written constitution as fundamental law cannot have an instant Canadian counterpart. Thus, it does not follow that the Canadian courts will necessarily claim a role comparable to that of courts in the United States, nor is it clear that the representative bodies in Canada would tolerate such a judicial assertion of power. This paper attempts to note some of the common and distinctive features of the texts of the two constitutions, discuss some of

---

* William M. Beaney is a Professor of Law at the University of Denver and a Visiting Professor of Law (1982–83) at the California Western School of Law.

1 Readers seeking a more detailed account should consult J.E. Nowak, R.D. Rotunda and J.N. Young, *Handbook on Constitutional Law* (St Paul: West Publishing Company, 1978) with 1982 pocket, or L.H. Tribe, *American Constitutional Law* (Mineola, NY: Foundation Press, 1978). The most extensive collection of cases and materials is G. Gunther, *Cases and Materials on Constitutional Law*, 10th ed (Mineola, NY: Foundation Press, 1980) with annual supplement.

A more limited collection of cases and materials is A.T. Mason, W.M. Beaney and G. Stephenson, *American Constitutional Law*, 7th ed (Englewood Cliffs, NJ: Prentice-Hall, 1983).

An excellent annual survey of the Supreme Court's work, including rights litigation, appears in each November issue of *Harvard Law Review*.

the frequently overlooked by-products of judicial review as practised in the United States, and then, in summary fashion, to explain how the Supreme Court has approached some of the major issues involving freedom of expression, equality under law, and the rights of those caught up in the justice system.

While there are differences in the verbal formulations employed, three major classes of rights are protected by both the Canadian and United States constitutions. Freedom of expression, religion, and assembly are safeguarded in part I section 2 of the Canadian Constitution Act, 1982,* and in the First Amendment of the American document. The Legal Rights listed in sections 7–14 of the Canadian Charter of Rights and Freedoms, protecting criminal suspects and defendants by various procedural safeguards, are paralleled by American rights to have counsel against unreasonable searches and seizures, and privilege against self-incrimination, against double jeopardy, excessive bail, etc., which find expression in the Fourth, Fifth, Sixth and Eighth Amendments. Finally, the drive in modern democracies to provide greater legal protection against discriminatory official policies and actions finds expression in section 15 of the Canadian Charter, which bans discriminatory actions and authorizes affirmative action programs to remedy the injuries of past discrimination. The American equivalent, the 'equal protection of the laws' in the Fourteenth Amendment, has served to justify court decisions outlawing segregated schools, unequal treatment of women, and certain forms of discrimination against aliens and other minority groups. But American courts have had to confront legal attacks on government and private affirmative action programs without specific aid from the written document.[2]

---

* The *Constitution Act, 1982*, was proclaimed by Queen Elizabeth II on 17 April 1982, in Ottawa. It is the final Act of the Parliament of the United Kingdom which will extend to Canada and become a part Canadian law. The British cite it as the *Canada Act, 1982*; Canadians, simply as the *Canada Act*. Part 1, Schedule B of the *Canada Act* (Schedule A is the French version) is cited as the *Canadian Charter of Rights and Freedoms* (sections 1–34). The *Canada Act*, which is only part of the written constitution of Canada, should be read in conjunction with Schedule 1 contained within it for a more detailed account of the modernization of the constitution. [Editor's Note]

2 In *Regents of the University of California* v *Bakke*, 438 US 265 (1978). The Court, 5–4, held unconstitutional a state medical school admissions program with an annual specific quota for minority applicants. A majority agreed, however, that race could be taken into account in admissions. A union-employer voluntary agreement incorporating a quota in hiring was upheld in *United Steelworkers* v *Weber*, 443 US 193 (1979), and a congressional act providing that 10% of public works grants should be assigned to minority business enterprises 448 US 448 (1980).

While this paper is not intended to provide a close textual analysis of the two documents, the Canadian constitution has at least three provisions that deserve special comment.

First is the intelligent avoidance of a problem that has occasioned much debate throughout American history: What is the textual source of the power of judicial review? Section 24(1) specifically provides that one whose rights are infringed shall have an appropriate judicial remedy. Chief Justice John Marshall derived a comparable authority for American courts from the nature of a written constitution and the doctrine of the separation of powers, since the constitutional text was silent on the issue.[3] Without clear textual support, defenders of the legitimacy of judicial review of acts of Congress (and the president) have had to battle generation after generation with those who assail it as an usurpation.[4]

A second unique feature to an American reader is section 24(2) where the Canadian framers deal with the exclusionary rule, a frequently invoked American judicial rule penalizing illegal law enforcement practices. This rule was applied after 1914 to federal criminal proceedings and since 1961 to state proceedings.[5] There is a substantial body of opinion to the effect that the rule is not required by the United States Constitution and is simply a judicially-created remedy that could be changed by legislation or court decisions.[6] The Canadian provision is a compromise between the common law rule and the exclusionary rule; evidence obtained by a violation of constitutionally protected right '... shall be excluded if it is established that, having regard to all the circumstances, the admission of it in the proceedings would bring the administration of justice into disrepute.' Thus, technical or good faith official

---

3 *Marbury* v *Madison*, 1 Cranch 137 (1803). Much of the reasoning of Marshall in *Marbury* was anticipated by Alexander Hamilton in *The Federalist*, no 78. In either formulation, the emphasis is on a concept of popular sovereignty, expressed in a written constitution, controlling all of the agents of the people. The Court's role is to decide cases, with the people's constitution treated as fundamental law superior to acts of the people's agents. See William W. Van Alstyne, 'A Critical Guide to *Marbury* v *Madison*,' *Duke Law Journal* 1969 (January, 1969), 1–47 for an appreciation of the 'creativity' of Marshall's analysis.
4 The classic attack on the legitimacy of judicial review of legislative acts is J.B. Thayer, 'The Origin and Scope of the American Doctrine of Constitutional Law,' *Harvard Law Review* 7 (October, 1893), 129–56. An effective modern defence of the doctrine is Charles L. Black, Jr, *The People and the Court: Judicial Review in a Democracy* (New York: Macmillan, 1960).
5 *Weeks* v *United States*, 232 US 383 (1914); *Mapp* v *Ohio*, 367 US 643 (1961)
6 *Michigan* v *Tucker*, 417 US 433 (1974)

actions, though violative of rights, can be distinguished from gross acts of official misconduct.[7]

Third, there is the fascinating puzzle in the Canadian Charter in section 33, the 'notwithstanding' clause, which gives back to Parliament or a provincial legislature the power to declare that a statute shall operate notwithstanding sections 2 or 7–15. While some have minimized this concession to parliamentary supremacy by suggesting that it will be rarely used, it is a constant warning to the judiciary that theirs is not the ultimate power of decision concerning the scope and content of constitutional rights. Its significance may lie less in the possible frequency of its use than in the influence its very existence may exert on the justices in controversial cases of great public concern.

Were the two constitutions identical in their provisions respecting rights, it would not necessarily follow that claims of violation of rights would receive the same response from the courts of the two nations. A proper analysis of why this is so would require a book-length account of the constitutional and political history of Canada and the United States.[8] It would include but would not be limited to the selection and role of judges, the role of legislatures and political leadership, the attitudes and practices of the police and the administrative agencies, and, not least, popular attitudes toward rights, minorities, and government. In short, the whole of a people's way of life. For it is obvious that disputes over rights represent a planned system of testing, in peaceful ways, the never-ending clash of values between authority and legitimacy exemplified by the government of the day and the challenging responses of the less than satisfied governed. From the great variety of factors whose interplay is relevant to an understanding of the role of the United States Supreme Court, three have been chosen to help show the difficulties with any ready transference of the American experience. These are: the concept and practice of the separation of powers and its application, which places the Court in constant tension; second, the tradition of judicial review and its impact on the training of lawyers and the selection of judges; and finally, the extent to which American judges respond to wider currents of opinion outside the legal system itself.

The American system of separated powers, with numerous checks and balances, is frequently attacked as insufficiently responsive to modern problems. It stresses balances that slow down change and weaken leadership. It

---

7 The United States Supreme Court will consider the issue of 'good faith' defences to constitutional violations in the 82–83 term.
8 A.H. Kelly and W.A. Harbison, *The American Constitution* 4th ed (New York: Norton, 1970) is a good short account of the American side.

appears, as a system, to work reasonably well in short bursts, usually in crisis periods of wartime or major depression or on the infrequent occasions when a charismatic president holds office. Even in the latter situation, a president requires loyal and effective lieutenants in Congress. Presidents, traditionally, take a formally respectful view of the Supreme Court and its decisions. Congress, as it has done from the beginning, is certain to react negatively to Court decisions impugning its handiwork. Congress, under the United States Constitution, enjoys an authority to regulate the appellate jurisdiction of the United States Supreme Court, which makes it simple to introduce anti-Court bills to remove or limit the Court's authority to hear certain classes of cases.[9] While few are enacted, they help focus anti-Court opinion. Court decisions, displeasing to individuals or factions in Congress, are the frequent subject of reproachful speeches and insertions of critical materials in the Congressional Record.

On major decisions congressional response is part of the larger media, interest group, and popular response. At the same time, Congress is carrying on its tension-filled relationship with the presidency, a never-ending struggle that partially diverts congressional attention away from the courts. The curious amalgam of political forces constituting each of the major parties helps explain why even presidents with apparent clear majority support in both houses of Congress receive much buffeting. While hostile congressional response to United States Supreme Court decisions may have a partisan basis, ideologues in both parties frequently take issue with Supreme Court decisions.

On rights issues, the normal continuing battle between those of liberal persuasion and their conservative opponents becomes most sharply focused, since controversial rights decisions of the United States Supreme Court invariably represent a threat to the status quo, whether it is greater equality for black or women, new restrictions on the police power of search and seizure, or protection of leftist political expression.

9 There is an ongoing debate with respect to the limits of congressional power under article III to limit or withdraw judicial review power, especially where important rights are involved. This writer's suggestion is that the power to make exceptions to the appellate jurisdiction of the Supreme Court was not intended to give to Congress the potential power to destroy the limitations on governmental power in the Constitution. The concept of entrenched rights is obviously anti-majoritarian. Under a theory of unlimited power in Congress to withdraw judicial review power, right by right, the system is capable of being totally altered. It is depressing to witness so many conservatives, whose long-run interests should lead them to support a system of limited government in the forefront of those who, to achieve short-run gains, would deprive the Court of its review powers. In the long-run, the Court has proved a solid bulwark for property rights, among others.

It is not only Congress, but on occasion the president as well who reprimands the Court. The great Chief Justice Marshall had Thomas Jefferson as his constant critic. Richard Nixon, as president, frequently denounced the Court's liberal decisions and essayed, with considerable success, to appoint judges who would take a more modest view of their vote. While presidents have frequently been disappointed with the judicial product of their appointees, awareness of the power of the president to reshape the Court's posture is an important constraint on judicial behaviour.[10]

The American media and spokesmen for various interest groups are ever ready to point out deficiencies in Court rulings, though the babble of commentators tends to weaken the overall impact of stressing that this or that decision is contrary to the popular will, or to the actions of the political branches of government.[11] The classic example of conflict between the political branches and the Supreme Court occurred after the 1936 presidential election when President Franklin D. Roosevelt, frustrated with Court decisions invalidating important New Deal economic and social legislation, proposed a 'court-packing' bill. The measure purported to add a new member for each current member age 70 and above, thus allowing for a Court comprised of fifteen justices. The explanation offered was that the older justices were unable to keep up with their caseload. This transparent ploy by the president failed to win sufficient congressional support, but did succeed in encouraging some of the older justices with the aid of a generous retirement act to retire, and seemingly helped persuade a few of the remainder to adopt a more tolerant view of social and economic legislation.[12]

Without prolonging this theme further, it is apparent that the distinctive theory and practice of the separation of powers in the United States has necessarily drawn the Court into frequent and vigorous conflicts with the

---

10 Perhaps the most striking example of presidential disillusionment with an appointee's performance was Eisenhower's reaction to Earl Warren's contribution to the Court. 'The worst damn fool mistake I ever made' was Eisenhower's supposed comment.
11 Probably no governmental institution in the world is subject to more professional scrutiny than the United States Supreme Court. Almost every law school has a journal or review, whose editors pick leading decisions for examination and criticism. The November issue of the *Harvard Law Review* provides an annual survey that is both useful and, at times, magisterial in pointing out the shortcomings of judicial analysis.
12 See Robert H. Jackson, *The Struggle for Judicial Supremacy* (New York: A.A. Knopf, 1941), from 1937 through 1941 President Roosevelt, with seven new appointees, was able to reconstitute the Supreme Court.

legislative branch, and into occasional disputes with the president. Public opinion, as expressed through the media, has tended to treat the Supreme Court as one of the principal actors on the national stage. This simple point deserves emphasis: a price must be paid for entry of the highest court into the thickets of public policy-making.

Granted all of the above, there is an important aspect of the American judicial system that is arousing increasing concern. The workload on all courts, including the United States Supreme Court, has grown at an astonishing rate. Frequent references are made to the 'litigious society.' This is relevant to our topic because a large part of the growth of litigation is on the public law side, and is expressed through suits attacking discriminatory legislation and administrative acts, denials of defendants or prisoner's rights, and other individual claims. The growth in litigation at the Supreme Court level is highly conspicuous because several of the justices have complained publicly of the heavy, almost intolerable burden cast upon them. While additional justices have been provided for the two lower federal courts, no similar relief is planned for the highest court. While some of the highest state courts have raised similar complaints, there is statistical proof of the greater burden on the United States Supreme Court, with approximately 4,500 new cases presented each year. While the Court may hand down decisions with full opinions in no more than 150–170 instances, there still is a tremendous burden on the nine individuals composing the Court to sift through the large mass of cases, most of which will be turned away under the Court's authority to choose cases as it deems proper.[13] Although justices are screened for obvious health problems before selection, people of advancing age under excessive case loads may develop health difficulties after appointment. With tenure during good behaviour, justices are reluctant to retire at age 70 even with generous retirement benefits. There is both a charm in retaining a position involving high status and great power and a fear that a president of different outlook will appoint the 'wrong' type of successor. By hanging on for a few additional years perhaps the 'right kind' of appointment will be possible. It is a matter of record that presidents overwhelmingly make appointments from their own party, although, as indicated earlier, this does

---

13 The Freund Report (1972) renamed for the chairman of a seven member study group appointed by the Chief Justice, recommended a new National Court of Appeals to perform a screening function and to decide cases presenting conflicts between circuits. This and similar proposals have elicited little support. See 'Creation of New National Court of Appeals is Proposed by Blue Ribbon Study Group,' *American Bar Association Journal* 59 (February, 1973), pp 139–44.

not guarantee that the appointee's decisions on civil liberties, for example, will comport with the positions assumed by the president.

Presidents commonly do not exhibit an all-absorbing concern with civil liberties issues. Usually the consensus which has elevated a person to the highest office is sufficiently fragile that a president cannot afford to alienate large segments of the public by becoming closely identified with any libertarian cause. President Truman adopted a strong anti-communist stance, although his liberal instincts opposed the crusade by the right. President Eisenhower distanced himself from the Supreme Court's school desegregation decision throughout his two terms, taking positive and supportive steps only when the prestige of the presidential office itself was threatened. Thus, it is not usual for one who seeks and attains the presidency to do so on an agenda of civil rights objectives. Rather, the platform and programs involve foreign affairs issues, budget and taxes, unemployment, and other matters of direct concern to mainstream America.

As a result, judicial appointees, while usually of the same party and assumed to be on the same ideological wave-length as a president, may take positions on rights issues that surprise both their presidential sponsor and the public. Thus, of Franklin D. Roosevelt's eight appointments, Douglas, Murphy, Rutledge and Black tended to be strongly pro-rights while Reed, Byrnes, Jackson and Frankfurter, for various reasons, chose generally to uphold the government's position against libertarian claims.[14] Frankfurter's posture on rights followed inevitably, in his view, from his conception of the role a judge in a democratic-representative system should play – a limited role expressed by straining to uphold the actions of a legislature. Administrative actions might receive less respect because of their lack of a popular base. His long-time colleague, Black, interpreted the Bill of Rights in an almost literal sense. To Black, the Framers had spoken clearly and directly – hence, absolute freedom of speech was guaranteed. The Fourth Amendment protection against 'unreasonable searches and seizures,' on the other hand, gave much leeway to the government. Another colleague, Murphy, probably the most extreme supporter of rights, brought a natural law, universal rights of man approach to his deliberations. Once Murphy identified the underdog, the outcome was certain. Justice Douglas, in a slightly less obvious way, exhibited a persistent suspicion that government was a menace to individual rights. At the other extreme are justices like Reed, who resisted almost to the end in joining the Court majority in outlawing segregation in *Brown* v

---

14 The most revealing picture of the judges at work during the Roosevelt presidency is Alpheus T. Mason, *Harlan Fiske Stone: Pillar of the Law* (New York: Viking Press, 1956).

Board, and Nixon's appointee Rehnquist, whose main philosophical premise, like Frankfurter's, is that the people's government must be allowed to do its worst, as well as its best.

All of this grossly simplifies a very complex ongoing history. One must take into account the subject matter and the specific issues raised. Even the libertarians found constitutional the government's Japanese relocation program in World War II, in which both aliens and American citizens of Japanese ancestry were moved from their houses to inland camps, where they were confined until late in the war. And Frankfurter, the apostle of judicial restraint, was in the forefront of the justices who sought to maintain the separation of church and state.

The jurist who tried to place in broader perspective the role of the judiciary with respect to rights was Chief Justice Stone. In the now famous footnote 4 to the case of *U.S.* v *Carolene Products* (1938),[15] he tried to explain that individual and minority rights issues should find the Court ready to scrutinize with care and even suspicion the basis for the governmental action under challenge. But ordinary economic and social legislation, even though arguably restrictive of property rights, should be upheld if the Court could find any rational basis to justify the legislation. It is fair to say that justices since 1937 have almost universally adhered to Stone's position on economic and social legislation, while differing sharply as to the extent to which the Court should champion individual or minority rights against governmental measures that impinge on these rights.

In one important sense, the movement over time is toward ever greater protection of rights. The conservative nature of the legal system and the courts makes overruling of libertarian decisions unlikely. The current Supreme Court, called the 'Burger Court' after the Chief Justice, has not undone the work of its predecessor 'Warren Court,' but it has refused, in many cases, to extend libertarian precedents in the way that the Warren Court would probably have done. When the Burger Court has broken new ground, such as in cases involving greater protection for advertising and other commercial speech, it is a portion of the business community that reaps the greatest benefit from a new doctrine that has overtones of a *laissez faire* philosophy.

In the brief examination of rights decisions since 1940 that follows, it should become increasingly obvious that while the Court has greatly expanded constitutional guarantees of rights, it has done so in ways that retain for the Court maximum discretion in deciding each new case in the light of its facts and

---

15   *United States* v *Carolene Products Co.*, 304 US 144 (1938)

circumstances. While the Court attempts to give proper respect to the precedents, it is evident that the Court is rarely the prisoner of previous decisions and always retains the continuing capacity to 'judge.'

FREEDOM OF EXPRESSION

Since 1940, American courts have been confronted with a great diversity of issues involving freedom of expression, some of extreme social importance, others verging on the frivolous.

Freedom of expression inevitably suffers during wartime. Because of voluntary censorship and the general support for the war after Pearl Harbour, the occasions when the government had to intervene during World War II were few. A large number of Japanese-Americans, aliens and citizens alike, however, were placed under a curfew, then removed from their homes and relocated in inland camps, where they remained under government control until 'found' loyal, and eventually freed.[16] Apart from this major blot, the administration largely avoided the prosecutorial mania that had been directed toward opponents of America's participation in World War I.

The real test for free expression came in the post-war period, after hopes of good relations with the Soviet Union had vanished. The government brought charges against the principal leaders of the Communist Party in the US and in *Dennis* v *United States*[17] obtained convictions under the 1940 Smith Act banning advocacy of violent overthrow of government and conspiracy to advocate overthrow. The Supreme Court approached the question of the constitutionality of the Act by asking whether teaching Marxist-Leninist doctrines to a receptive audience constituted a 'clear and present danger' to the state, a test developed in the post-World War I era. Recognizing that native communists posed no threat except as part of a larger movement, the Court gave a new twist to 'clear and present danger,' by transforming the test into one in which 'the seriousness of the danger, discounted by the improbability of its occurrence' became the standard. The 'danger' was the Soviet Union, and in a Cold War atmosphere, the Supreme Court was unwilling to oppose the wishes of the elective and executive branches, both of which led and reflected a public opinion harshly opposed to any expression of pro-Soviet sentiment.

---

16 In *Korematsu* v *United States*, 323 US 214 (1944) the Court upheld a presidential order excluding Japanese-Americans from designated West Coast areas. The curfew regulations were upheld a year earlier in *Hirabayashi* v *United States*, 320 US 81 (1943).
17 341 US 494 (1951)

During the continuance of the Cold War, the Court showed a reluctance to confront a Congress set on a course of pursuing communist sympathizers in and out of government. In one case, *Watkins* v *United States* (1957),[18] Chief Justice Warren lectured Congress on the sloppiness and unfairness of its investigations into communist infiltration into various sectors of American life, but the decision actually turned on a rather narrow point – a due process violation, because of failure to inform the witness cited for contempt of the relevance of the questions addressed to him. In a subsequent case, *Basrenblatt* v *United States* (1959),[19] the majority of the Court recanted most of the critical assertions of *Watkins*.

While the Vietnam War policies of the government aroused deep and bitter opposition in the 60s and 70s, especially on the part of young people, the government's response, though harsh in many instances, produced cases reaching the Supreme Court that were concerned mainly with marginal issues. Burning a draft card was held punishable,[20] but burning the American flag was not.[21] Displaying a flag with an affixed peace symbol was permitted[22] as was the wearing of black armbands by public school students.[23] The legality of the war itself, increasingly debated after the prospects of a successful conclusion became ever dimmer, was avoided by the Court, although a minority of justices tried to convince their judicial brethren that the legality of the war presented a justiciable issue.[24] The Court has always shown a reluctance to oppose the elected branches on war-related issues.

Apart from a few of the Vietnam War-related cases, the Court took a strong pro-libertarian position in the 1960s and 1970s. The secondary communist party-leader cases modified and liberalized the *Dennis* decision.[25] In *Brandenburg* v *Ohio* (1969),[26] the Court, in a short *per curiam* opinion, overturned the conviction of a Ku Klux Klan leader, who had made a rabble-rousing anti-negro, anti-semitic speech containing exhortation to action in the future. Applying a test that is clearly more protective of free speech than

18 354 US 178 (1957)
19 360 US 109 (1959)
20 *United States* v *O'Brien*, 391 US 367 (1968)
21 *Street* v *New York*, 394 US 576 (1969)
22 *Spence* v *Washington*, 418 US 405 (1974)
23 *Tinker* v *Des Moines School District*, 393 US 503 (1969)
24 See *Mora* v *McNamara*, cert. den., 389 US (1968), where Justice Stewart, joined by Justice Douglas, dissenting from a denial of *certiorari*, argued that justiciable issues concerning the legality of the Vietnam War should be confronted.
25 *Yates* v *United States*, 354 US 298 (1957); *Scales* v *United States*, 367 US 203 (1961); *Noto* v *United States*, 367 US 290 (1961)
26 395 US 444 (1969)

that adopted in the *Dennis* case, the Court used a two-pronged test limiting state restriction to instances where advocacy is directed to inciting or producing imminent lawless action, *and* is likely to produce such action. Nevertheless, the Court cited *Dennis* as consistent with its *Brandenburg* holding.

A few other developments may illustrate the somewhat inconsistent pattern of Court decisions dealing with free expression. Use of offensive language in public, so long as it falls short of 'fighting' speech, is permissible.[27] Prior restraints on parades and meetings are largely forbidden. Time, place and manner regulations of parades, demonstrations and meetings must be reasonable and fairly administered.[28] Some public places are off-limits to demonstrators.[29] Non-obscene, nude dancing as entertainment is protected.[30]

A remarkable recent development has been the growth in the protection for a formerly unprotected form of expression – commercial speech. Traditionally, corporations and other businesses have been subject to a variety of regulations, some curtailing the use of corporate resources in elections, others prohibiting certain types of advertising. Since 1937, the Supreme Court has shown a general disposition to uphold regulations of business, thus avoiding the difficulties which brought on the Court crisis of that year. In rejecting its 1942 precedent, holding commercial speech outside the protection of the First Amendment,[31] the Court has embarked on an interesting course.

The clash of First Amendment free expression values and the power of legislatures to regulate economic affairs has produced interesting Court alignments. In a 1976 case, the Court invalidated a state ban on the advertisement of prescription drug prices.[32] In 1977, a state limitation on advertising of legal services was overturned,[33] but in the following year, the Court excluded from First Amendment protection in-person solicitation of clients by lawyers.[34] In 1980, the Court rejected a law banning promotional advertising by a state regulated public utility.[35] And in 1981, a badly splintered Court

27 *Cohen* v *California*, 403 US 15 (1971)
28 *Niemotko* v *Maryland*, 340 US 268 (1951); *Cox* v *New Hampshire*, 312 US 569 (1941); *Heffron* v *International Society for Krishna Consciousness*, 452 US 640 (1981); *Walker* v *City of Birmingham*, 388 US 307 (1967)
29 *Adderley* v *Florida*, 385 US 39 (1965), grounds outside a jail. A silent protest within a library was allowed, *Brown* v *Louisiana*, 383 US 131 (1966).
30 *Schad* v *Borough of Mt. Ephraim*, 452 US 61 (1981)
31 *Valentine* v *Chrestensen*, 316 US 52 (1942)
32 *Virginia State Bd. of Pharmacy* v *Virginia Citizens Consumer Council*, 425 US 748 (1976)
33 *Bates* v *State Bar of Arizona*, 433 US 350 (1977)
34 *Ohralik* v *Ohio State Bar Assn*, 436 US 477 (1978)
35 *Central Hudson Gas & Electric Corp.* v *Public Service Commission of New York*, 447 US 557 (1980)

invalidated a San Diego ordinance banning most types of billboards, though the Court seemed to agree that all commercial billboards might be prohibited.[36] In all these cases, the Court made it clear that in order to deserve protection, commercial speech had to be free from fraud and reasonably accurate. The governmental interest in regulation then must be shown to be substantial. The particular regulation must directly advance the governmental interests, and the regulation should not be broader than necessary. Obviously, commercial speech does not receive the full protection given non-commercial speech under the First Amendment, which, as the Court has made clear, is protected regardless of content.

In an important series of cases, the Supreme Court cut back the liability of the media for defamatory publications concerning public officials and public figures. In the seminal case, *New York Times Co.* v *Sullivan* (1964),[37] which grew out of the Montgomery, Alabama racial desegregation struggle, the Court held that a large libel judgment, against the *New York Times*, obtained by Montgomery officials as a result of factual errors in a paid advertisement attacking the pro-segregation activities of Birmingham city officials, must be set aside. The newly announced rule was that when public officials were verbally assaulted, successful libel plaintiffs had to prove that the defendant had shown 'actual malice,' that is, 'with knowledge that it [the published material] was false or with reckless disregard to whether it was false or not.' The same standard was extended to cases involving 'public figures,'[38] and, finally, to private persons caught up in events of a general or public interest. A few years later, the Court cut back this position by holding that the rights of a private person under libel law were definable by the states, so long as they did not impose liability without fault on the media.[39] The vote was 5–4.

Another confusing judicial foray was the Court's efforts to deal with the problem of obscenity. In a 1957 case, *Roth* v *United States*,[40] the Court held that obscene material, defined as 'material which deals with sex in a manner appealing to prurient interests,' was not protected by the First Amendment. In the subsequent efforts to determine what is 'obscene,' the Supreme Court found itself viewing numerous films, books, and art under an elaborate *Roth* test of whether the dominant theme of the material taken as a whole appealed to prurient interests, and whether the materials were contrary to

---

36 *Metromedia, Inc.* v *City of San Diego*, 453 US 490 (1981)
37 376 US 254 (1964)
38 *Curtis Publishing Co.* v *Butts*, 388 US 130 (1967)
39 *Gertz* v *Robert Welch, Inc.*, 418 US 323 (1974)
40 354 US 476 (1957)

contemporary community standards and were utterly devoid of any redeeming social value.

In the later cases, the Court has tried to be more helpful to the states in drafting obscenity laws and convicting those charged with offending these laws. The Burger Court's contribution is a test that concentrates on 'patently offensive representations or descriptions of ultimate sexual acts – [and] patently offensive representations of masturbation, excretory functions and lewd exhibition of the genitals.'[41] 'Hardcore' materials are the target. The 'contemporary standards' are those of a local jury. 'Whether the work, taken as a whole, lacks serious artistic, political, or scientific value' replaces the former test, which casts a heavy burden on the prosecution, as to 'whether the material was utterly without redeeming social value.' Any commercial traffic is prohibited.[42] Special rules apply where minors are involved.[43] In one case decided after *Miller* v *California* (1973), embodying the new standards which went into effect, the Court held invalid a conviction arising from the showing of the film, 'Carnal Knowledge,' because the film did not contain 'patently offensive' material.[44] Thus, the Court made it clear that the 'community standards' must take into account a national standard (i.e., that of the Supreme Court) as to what is legally 'offensive.'

Justice William Brennan, author of the opinion in the crucial 1957 *Roth* case, dissented in the later cases, arguing that, except where minors were involved, or obscene materials are thrust on an unwilling public, the impossibility of defining obscenity with clarity made it undesirable to prosecute on the basis of the content of the materials.[45] In related cases, the Court has protected nudity in drive-in theatre films,[46] and nude dancing against a ban on all live entertainment within a municipality,[47] while upholding zoning measures that required concentration or dispersal of 'adult' entertainment enterprises.[48]

In these and other free expression decisions, the Court has shown a tendency to protect the claimed right unless the state articulates and supports an argument that it was safeguarding a social interest of the highest importance. Time, place and manner regulations are upheld if reasonable, because they

41 *Miller* v *California*, 413 US 15 (1973)
42 *Ginzburg* v *United States*, 383 US 463 (1966)
43 *Ginsberg* v *New York*, 390 US 629 (1968)
44 *Jenkins* v *Georgia*, 418 US 153 (1974)
45 Dissenting, *Paris Adult Theatre* v *Slaton*, 413 US 49 (1973)
46 *Erznoznik* v *City of Jacksonville*, 422 US 205 (1975)
47 *Schad* v *Borough of Mount Ephraim*, 452 US 61 (1981)
48 *Young* v *American Mini Theatres*, 427 US 50 (1976)

help prevent violence. The decision in *Dennis* upheld a government prosecution of leaders of a movement that Congress found threatened the security of the state itself. Yet, a young man with 'fuck the draft' on the back of his jacket was protected in his anti-government stance. The obscenity cases represent a bow to community morals, while at the same time protecting serious works of literature and art. Material is now sold in ordinary bookstores that a generation ago would have resulted in prosecution. As is true with respect to many issues, the Court never moves very far ahead of the *perceived* standards of the people.

EQUAL PROTECTION OF THE LAWS

In the aftermath of the Civil War, three amendments were added to the Constitution. The most important, the Fourteenth (1868), defined citizenship and prohibited states from denying any person due process of law or the equal protection of the laws. As several Supreme Court decisions in the 1870s and 1880s made clear, protection of the rights of the recently emancipated 'new' citizen was the dominant purpose of this and the other two post-Civil War Amendments, [the Thirteenth (1865) abolished slavery; the Fifteenth (1870) safeguarded voting rights]. Without denying this, the Supreme Court destroyed the vitality of the amendments by holding in 1883 that Congress lacked power to prohibit discrimination in places of public accommodation[49] and in 1896 that separate public facilities and treatment of blacks satisfied the requirement of equality.[50] In real life, this Court-approved segregation policy usually meant that blacks and other minorities enjoyed 'separate and unequal' facilities, whether in public schools, military life, or on bathing beaches. But unless the states relied on laws or practices that discriminated in obvious ways, the courts were satisfied with 'substantial' equality for racial minorities.

World War II helped produce a great change in the attitudes of whites and minorities. Even before the United States' entry into the War, the New

---

49 *Civil Rights Cases*, 109 US 3 (1883). The essence of the Court's holding was that the Fourteenth Amendment was directed exclusively toward state action that denied equal protection. Congressional enforcement power, as provided in section 5 of the amendment thus became a judiciary-like authority to supersede unconstitutional state laws of a discriminatory nature.

50 *Plessy* v *Ferguson*, 163 US 537 (1896). Segregated railroad facilities required by state law were upheld. While noting that legislation was powerless to eradicate racial instincts, Justice Brown saw no inconsistency in upholding a law that prevented the operation of 'natural instincts.'

Deal of Franklin D. Roosevelt focused attention on the lower one-third of the nation's ill-clothed, ill-housed and ill-fed, of which racial minorities composed a disproportionate share. Hitler's anti-semitic and racist philosophy made Americans self-conscious about their own discriminatory policies. While segregative policies were followed officially in the military services until the Korean War, many white servicemen in World War II experienced more frequent contact with blacks than their civilian lives had provided. In addition, allied leaders stressed protection of human rights in their statements of war aims, and the United Nations Charter and other documents heavily underscored the universal importance of rights. A policy of discrimination was the antithesis of this growing acceptance of the ideal of a fairer world order.

In spite of these forces for change, elected American officials were reluctant to embrace reforms. The Democratic party had, as always, a powerful southern wing. Republicans of the party of emancipation were strongly resistant to change. In the post-war era, the Supreme Court was the only branch in a position to confront racial apartheid. In the late 40s and early 50s, the Court began to treat seriously litigants supported by the National Association for the Advancement of Colored People who claimed denial of equal rights. Lack of equal treatment of those admitted to graduate study in state universities met Court reproof in a series of cases.[51] The most significant of these arose from a belated effort by Texas to establish a law school for blacks, after denying to black applicants admission to the law school of the University of Texas. In *Sweatt* v *Painter*,[52] the Court for the first time emphasized a list of intangible factors which distinguished the 'new' Texas black law school from the established white school. The next step was the Court's conclusion in 1954 in *Brown* v *Board of Education*[53] that state-imposed segregation in all public schools violated equal protection of the laws. In a second decision, a year later, the Court entrusted to the federal district courts the shaping of appropriate decrees, using their traditional equity powers.[54] Departing from the normal principle that enjoyment of constitutional rights cannot be postponed, the Court commanded the lower courts to proceed 'with all

---

51 *Sipuel* v *Board of Regents*, 332 US 631 (1948); *McLaurin* v *Oklahoma State Regents*, 339 US 637 (1950)
52 339 US 629 (1950)
53 *Brown* v *Board of Education*, 347 US 483 (1954). In a comparison case, *Bolling* v *Sharpe*, 347 US 497 (1954) the due process clause of the Fifth Amendment was applied to the federal government, thus invalidating segregated schools in Washington, DC 'Liberty' was, and has since been, viewed as containing an equal protection component.
54 *Brown* v *Board of Education*, 349 US 294 (1955)

deliberate speed.' As of 1982, cases are still in progress, north and south, though most parts of the country are now free from state imposed segregated facilities. It should be noted that both Congress and the president gave little support to the cause of desegregation until the 60s, when, after the assassination of President John Kennedy, President Lyndon Johnson was able to press through Congress the 1964 Civil Rights Act, banning many forms of private discrimination.[55] Other Civil Rights legislation followed. Since then, presidential support has varied, and Congress has rested on its legislative accomplishments of the 60s. Despite changes of Court membership, the majority has continued to protect racial minorities against discriminatory practices, while upholding at least private and federal affirmative action programs.

Discrimination against other classes has also merited close judicial scrutiny. While Congress has wide latitude in dealing with aliens, states may not bar aliens from essential occupations, such as the law,[56] or the civil service,[57] but under a special 'governmental function' doctrine, states may bar aliens from positions as police officers[58] and public school teachers.[59] Sex discrimination has similarly received judicial attention. While sex is not treated as a 'suspect' class, more than a rational basis must be put forward to justify a law based on sexual distinctions. The somewhat vague judicial criterion is whether the classification is significantly related to an important governmental purpose.[60] One advantage of this test is that the government has a somewhat easier task in justifying legislation favouring women victims of past discrimination.[61] Legislation based on illegitimacy has also received closer scrutiny than in the past.[62] Older citizens have fared less well – age discrimination is

55 In enacting the law, Congress relied principally on its extensive power to regulate 'commerce among the several states,' rather than the power to enforce the post-Civil War Fourteenth Amendment. It was still unclear if Congress could otherwise prohibit private discrimination.
56 *In re Griffiths*, 413 US 717 (1973)
57 *Sugarman v Dougall*, 413 US 634 (1973)
58 *Foley v Connelie*, 435 US 291 (1978)
59 *Ambach v Norwick*, 441 US 68 (1979). The power of the federal government to regulate aliens is vastly greater than that of the states, because of the specific power in article I, section 8, 'to establish a uniform rule of naturalization' plus the more general powers of Congress and presidents in foreign affairs. See *Mathews v Diaz*, 426 US 67 (1976).
60 *Craig v Boren*, 429 US 190 (1976)
61 *Kahn v Shevin*, 416 US 351 (1974); *Schlesinger v Ballard*, 419 US 498 (1975). Later decisions cast doubt on the Court's willingness to extend the doctrine.
62 *Levy v Louisiana*, 391 US 68 (1968); *Weber v Aetna Casualty & Surety Co.*, 406 US 164 (1972). But *Mathews v Lucas*, 427 US 495 (1976) indicates that the scrutiny is less severe than where racial discrimination is involved.

tested by determining if there is a rational basis for the age classification, such as justifying a law prohibiting retention of state police officers over age 50.[63] It is noteworthy that the potentially most revolutionary classification – wealth, or more realistically, poverty – has failed to induce strong action by the Court. Only when indigency prevents enjoyment of an important governmentally controlled function – criminal justice,[64] or granting of a divorce[65] – has the Court subjected the classification to careful scrutiny. Otherwise, the Court accepts a rational basis for analysis in the light of the limited resources that the state has available to aid society's poor and weak.

Finally, the Court has developed a new class of rights which, when limited by legislation, will cause the Court to subject the classification to strict scrutiny. For example, states have typically imposed the residence requirement before a citizen may vote, obtain a divorce or welfare benefits, or receive a lower tuition rate at state universities. In reviewing various measures of this kind, the Court has recognized that such requirements inhibit the right to travel (to relocate) and have insisted that lengthy periods – one year – were excessive, except where divorce was sought.[66] Denying the franchise in certain elections to groups of voters based on property ownership or tax-paying have been held invalid.[67] Access to the courts and the judicial process has been upheld where indigents could not meet fee requirements, although wealth classifications, in general, have been acceptable. Nor has the Court held education to be a fundamental right, where state financing schemes result in sharp differences in the amount of per-pupil expenditures in different localities.[68] In all of these cases, it should be emphasized, the Court has chosen to regard the right – whether to vote or to travel, or to have access to the courts – in a context involving a class of persons deprived of the right, rather than in the more usual form of an individual claiming a denial of free speech, religion or other provisions of the Bill of Rights. Since the Court purports to use the highest level, 'strict scrutiny' test in reviewing all rights violations, the advantages of this equal protection approach are not clear. In any event, the current Supreme Court has resisted the discovery of new

63 *Massachusetts Board of Retirement* v *Murgia*, 427 US 307 (1976)
64 *Griffin* v *Illinois*, 351 US 12 (1956) right to a free transcript to take an appeal. *Douglas* v *California*, 372 US 353 (1963), right to appointed counsel on appeal
65 *Boddie* v *Connecticut*, 401 US 371 (1971)
66 *Shapiro* v *Thompson*, 394 US 618 (1969) for welfare benefits; *Dunn* v *Blumstein*, 405 US 330 (1972) for voting
67 *Kramer* v *Union Free School District No. 15*, 395 US 621 (1969). The basic case denying the dilution of each person's vote was *Reynolds* v *Sims*, 377 US 533 (1964), holding that each house of a bicameral state legislature should reflect one-man, one-vote.
68 *San Antonio School District* v *Rodriguez*, 411 US 1 (1973)

rights deserving treatment under equal protection. Thus, a claim to equal educational programs was not treated as a 'right,' nor was the 'right' to obtain a divorce.

What is remarkable about this expanded role for equal protection is that, as late as 1927, Justice Holmes could term an equal protection assertion as the 'last resort' of a constitutional argument.[69] With the decline of substantive due process in the field of economic and social welfare legislation, the Court seems to have found, in the new equal protection, a doctrine of similar potency. The Burger Court has refused to extend further the egalitarian thrust of the Warren Court, but it has hardly sought to wipe out the progress previously made. All the ingredients are present for further expansion through greater critical scrutiny of classes adversely affected by legislation, or classes whose fundamental rights are denied or unfairly limited. The American lawmaker can never again simply assume that legislative classifications are certain to withstand judicial objections.

THE CRIMINAL JUSTICE SYSTEM

At the present time, the great majority of Americans are critical of the legal system, especially the courts, for being 'soft' on criminals. The chief target in most parts of the country is the Supreme Court. It is charged with having usurped the power of state courts, which presumably would be firmer in dealing with criminal defendants. In a rare event, California voters in 1982 were asked to reject three incumbent justices of their state Supreme Court because of their excessively 'liberal' colouration and especially their overemphasis of the rights of criminal defendants.[70]

The first meaningful intervention by the United States' Supreme Court occurred in 1932, when, in *Powell* v *Alabama*,[71] it held that the due process clause of the Fourteenth Amendment was violated by a trial in which young, ignorant blacks were convicted by an Alabama jury of raping two white women without having an opportunity to retain counsel or being granted free

---

69 *Buck* v *Bell*, 274 US 200 (1927)
70 Although California has been notable by being more liberal in protecting the rights of criminal defendants, other states have also differed with the Supreme Court, and, by relying solely on comparable state constitutional provisions, may afford greater protection to individuals. See the section entitled 'Developments in the Law – The Interpretation of State Constitutional Rights,' *Harvard Law Review* 95 (April, 1982), p 1324, pp 1367–98.
71 287 US 45 (1932). The most useful compilation of case comments as materials is Y. Kamisar, W.R. LaFave and J.H. Israel, *Modern Criminal Procedure: Cases, Comments and Questions*, 5th ed (St Paul: West Publishing Company, 1980).

counsel by the state. With only one dissent, the Alabama Supreme Court had accepted the half-hearted effort of the trial judge to appoint the whole local bar to defend the youths at the time the trial began. This episode captures the essence of the dispute as to the proper role of state and federal courts. Frequently, the state trial record reveals substantial deficiencies, but the state court, concluding that the defendant was clearly guilty, affirms the trial court.[72] The Supreme Court of the United States, applying what its critics regard as overly protective rules, then finds the state procedure or ruling to be faulty.

As might be expected, as counsel for defendants brought more and more cases, many challenging the admission into evidence of confessions, or the denial to suspects of the right to counsel, the Court began to be deluged with appeals from state court judgments. In the 1960s, the Court read virtually all of the procedural protections of the Bill of Rights into the Fourteenth Amendment limitation on the states and applied federal standards: the right to counsel in all felony cases (1963); double jeopardy (1969); self-incrimination (1964); speedy trial (1970); impartial jury (1961); jury trial (1968); confrontation of witnesses (1965); compulsory process (1967); and cruel and unusual punishment (1962).[73]

This movement to federalize the criminal justice system occurred during the chief justiceship of Earl Warren, whose background as a California prosecutor and governor gave no hint of the liberal position he assumed on the Supreme Court.[74] Perhaps the most dramatic and controversial of the criminal justice decisions of his Court was *Miranda v Arizona* (1966).[75] At issue was the admissibility of a confession obtained by a rather normal police procedure – custodial interrogation of an uncounselled suspect until he talked. In previous cases, the Court has used the traditional 'voluntariness' test. Now the Court took a new tack. Taking a hint from the English Judge's Rules, the Court now required that any custodial interrogation must be preceded by a warning that the suspect had the right to remain silent; that anything he said could be used in evidence against him; that the suspect had a right to have his own counsel present before interrogation would take place and that counsel would be appointed if he was indigent. Other comments in

---

72 Both federal and state courts apply the 'harmless error' rule, but quite obviously, that rule invites wide variation in its application.
73 See J.E. Nowak, et al., L.H. Tribe and G. Gunther, *supra* note 1 for accounts of this development.
74 See G. Edward White, *Earl Warren: Paradoxes of a Public Life* (Oxford: Oxford University Press, 1982).
75 384 US 436 (1966)

the opinion stressed that the suspect had a right to stop talking at any time, that where an uncounselled suspect confessed, the burden was on the prosecutor to show that the suspect had knowingly waived counsel and chosen to respond to interrogation. Studies have shown that the warnings have had less than the anticipated effect on suspects – most continue to incriminate themselves.[76] Opponents of the *Miranda* rule have cited it endlessly as an example of improper intrusion by the courts into the world of law enforcement.

Five years earlier, the Court shocked the law enforcement community by imposing the federal exclusionary rule on state proceedings. The federal rule had been adopted in 1914[77] by the Supreme Court on two grounds: the Supreme Court should not appear to be sanctioning police wrongdoing; and exclusion would deter police wrongdoing. This new policy was, of course, contrary to the common law rule that, except for involuntary confessions, the method by which evidence was obtained is irrelevant to its admissibility.

In 1949, the Supreme Court refused to apply the federal exclusionary rule to the states,[78] arguing that while the Fourth Amendment protection against unreasonable searches and seizures was a limitation on the states, it did not carry along the federal remedy. Other remedies – a Tort action against the officer or municipality and a criminal action – were available.

By 1961, the Supreme Court changed its mind. It noted that several states had recently adopted the exclusionary rule (notably, California) and that the failure of the states to observe the Fourth Amendment safeguards made the exclusionary rule necessary. This decision in *Mapp* v *Ohio*,[79] coming at the beginning of the incorporation movement of the 1960s, meant that national, not state, standards would prevail.

It is true that not every defendant whose state conviction was reversed went free. But some did and that, plus the expense of retrying others, produced widespread criticism in the popular press and from special interest groups.

The conservative Burger Court of the 1970s, perhaps because it *failed* to overrule *Mapp* or *Miranda*, harvested continuing criticism as the institutional cause of the weakening of the forces of law and order. In fact, there is a development in several states of a position more protective of rights than the current Supreme Court provides. So long as a state relies on provisions in its

76 See references in Y. Kamisar, et al., *supra* note 71, pp 631–5.
77 *Weeks* v *United States*, 232 US 383 (1914)
78 *Wolf* v *Colorado*, 338 US 25 (1949)
79 367 US 643 (1961)

own constitution, it may choose this more generous role, but, of course, it may not provide less protection than Supreme Court decisions mandate.[80]

What is apparent to most observers is the great difficulty in conveying to the public the nature and complexity of the issues. The criminal justice system involves a rather intricate set of rules designed to protect a citizen against the overwhelming power of the state. The rules never come under attack as a whole but only where violation of one of them serves as justification for reversing a conviction. Some of the rules, such as the exclusionary rule, are designed to deter unlawful police conduct. A violation of the privacy of one's house, or an induced confession in the absence of counsel, may produce a conviction of an obviously guilty person. But the existing rules say that the price for allowing that kind of official behaviour is too high.[81]

---

80 See *supra* note 69.
81 This, of course, is the point on which justices and others may differ. How can one measure in a meaningful way the competing social costs of allowing an occasional guilty person to go unpunished versus allowing the police to act as they find necessary, barring physical violence or other stomach turning methods? As the growing problem of crime frightens ever larger numbers of people, pressure to throw out or weaken rules controlling police conduct increases. It is doubtful whether this response even touches the complex and baffling crime problem, though it is an issue that many political leaders greet with alacrity. Getting tough with criminals is the cheapest and most dramatic immediate reaction to public clamour.

The Legislative Protection of Rights

Walter Berns*

I think it is appropriate, especially for an American, to address the question with regards to the legislative protection of rights by reformulating it as follows: 'How does the Constitution in fact secure rights?' The American people declared their independence with an appeal to 'the Laws of Nature and of Nature's God,' and went on to say that government is instituted to secure the natural rights to 'life, liberty, and the pursuit of happiness,' these being the rights with which all men are by nature equally endowed.

Now, the usual answer to my reformulated question is that rights are secured by the Supreme Court as it enforces the provisions of the Bill of Rights. The former senator from Indiana, Birch Bayh, in a preface he wrote to an official government document (*A Citizen's Guide to Individual Rights* ...), says, for example, that the Bill of Rights is the foundation of America's free and democratic society.[1] That, I think, is a statement most Americans would accept. Yet, if Birch Bayh is right, the Founders were wrong. In the Preamble to the Constitution, they said they were constituting government in order to secure rights – 'to secure the blessings of liberty' – but at that time the Constitution did not have a bill of rights. Not only did it not then have a bill of rights but, in fact, the only time that the word 'right' or 'rights' appears in the original Constitution is in article I, section VIII, the part of the Constitution where Congress gets its powers: 'Congress shall have power ... to promote the Progress of Science and useful Arts, by securing for limited Times to Authors and Inventors the exclusive Right to their respective Writings

---

* Walter Berns is Resident Scholar at the American Enterprise Institute and Professorial Lecturer in Government at Georgetown University.
1 US Congress, Senate, Committee on the Judiciary, Subcommittee on Constitutional Rights, *Citizens' Guide to Individual Rights Under the Constitution of the United States of America* (5th ed), 94th Congress, 2d sess, 1976

and Discoveries.' That is the only time the word 'right' or 'rights' appears in the original Constitution. To secure *national* rights, a government with powers had to be constituted, and the Constitution established such a government. Senator Bayh's statement could be accurate, at most, with respect to *civil* rights, the civil rights delineated in the Bill of Rights.

The Bill of Rights was added to the Constitution in 1791, and the Supreme Court, in *Barron* v *Baltimore*,[2] affirmed the original and common understanding when it held that the Bill of Rights was intended to impose limits not on the states but only on the national government. Did it in fact serve this purpose? We have free speech in the United States, yet it was not until 1967, in *United States* v *Robel*, that the Supreme Court invalidated an act of Congress on First Amendment grounds.[3] ('Congress shall make no law ... abridging the freedom of speech ...') We enjoy freedom of religion in the United States, yet it was not until *Tilton* v *Richardson* in 1971 that the Supreme Court invalidated an Act of Congress on freedom of religion grounds.[4] ('Congress shall make no law respecting an establishment of religion, or prohibiting the free exercise thereof ...') In fact, during the entire course of the nineteenth century, on only nine occasions did the Supreme Court invalidate an Act of Congress as a violation of one of the provisions of the Bill of Rights. One of these was *Dred Scott* v *Sandford*,[5] scarcely a monument to liberty. Until 1925, when the Supreme Court in effect 'nationalized' the Bill of Rights,[6] there were only fifteen cases in which the Supreme Court, on the basis of one of the provisions of the Bill of Rights, invalidated an Act of Congress. There were several reasons for this state of affairs. Congress was not legislating; it was not active. But to say that is not to speak altogether accurately because there were occasions when Congress did enact laws that the Supreme Court might in fact have invalidated on First Amendment grounds. There were, for example, the Alien and Sedition laws of 1798. The lower federal courts had about a dozen opportunities to invalidate the Sedition Act on First Amendment grounds, but did not do so. The Supreme Court never had the opportunity. In the early 1830s there was a great question as to whether the southern states could get away with their practice of not allowing abolitionist literature to be delivered by mailmen, but the Court never had an opportunity to invalidate this practice. Then of course, in 1919,

---

2 *Barron* v *Baltimore*, 7 Pet. (32 US) 243 (1833)
3 *Unived States* v *Robel*, 389 US 258 (1967)
4 *Tilton* v *Richardson*, 403 US 672 (1971)
5 *Scott* v *Sandford*, 19 How. (60 US) 393 (1857)
6 *Gitlow* v *New York*, 268 US 652 (1925)

the Court certainly had an opportunity to invalidate the Espionage Act on First Amendment grounds, but again, it did not do so.

It would seem to be the case that, *politically*, it is much easier for the Supreme Court to invalidate an act of a state than an act of the national government. Yet, on the whole, it seems to me that Hamilton was right in *Federalist* no 84, much of which was devoted to his defence of the Constitution without a Bill of Rights, where he argued that there was no need of a national Bill of Rights. 'The Constitution,' he said, 'is itself in every rational sense and to every useful purpose a bill of rights.' He meant by this it was a bill of 'natural rights,' and it would secure these natural rights *without mentioning them*. Now how would it do this?

To answer this question, let me raise this subordinate question. Who or what threatens rights? In *Federalist* no 51, probably the second most important of the *Federalist* papers, James Madison said, 'If men were angels, no government would be necessary. If angels were to govern men, neither external nor internal controls on government would be necessary. In framing a government which is to be administered by men over men, the great difficulty lies in this: you must first enable the government to control the governed.' The first threat to our rights is other men. He then goes right on to say, 'and in the next place oblige it to control itself.' The second threat to rights is, of course, the government itself.

In the British past, rights were threatened by monarchs who acted outside the law – by prerogative – and who were brought under law beginning with the Magna Carta, and again in 1689 with the English Bill of Rights. One could say that government in the form of a monarch, who acted outside law, was a threat to rights, traditionally understood. But Americans had no cause to fear monarchs acting outside the law. Under democratic conditions, they would, however, have cause to fear the power of the people. Rights would be threatened by an unruly people (when, for example, they act as a mob), and when there are no restraints on democratic majorities. That is how the problem was understood by the men who wrote the American Constitution.

Security for rights would depend, in the first place, on a government with powers, and in the second place, on the various structural devices designed to oblige the government to control itself. The American Constitution does not provide for simple majority rule; its founders would not have accepted Bentham's insidious formulation, the 'greatest good of the greatest number'; that is a very unAmerican formulation. It was understood, and well understood, by the men who wrote the American Constitution that 'the greatest number' was likely to see its 'greatest good' in the deprivation of the minority's rights. The purpose of government is to secure rights, not to permit the greatest number to govern. The structure that would prevent rule by unconstitutional majorities is elaborated in the *Federalist* papers. In *Federalist* no 51, for example, Madison talks of the necessity of 'auxiliary precautions.' They are the separation of powers, checks and balances, a bicameral legislative body; they are the executive veto, the enlarged orbit for the large commercial republic, and so forth. These devices are part of that structure that was intended to secure natural rights; collectively, they embody the American principle of *representation* by which natural rights would be secured and civil rights protected.

One could categorize the American principle of representation in the following simple way. Some distance must be put between the represented, the people, and the representatives. That distance is built into the Constitution of the United States with familiar devices – in addition to those already mentioned, there is the electoral college by which the president is elected, and the creation of large legislative districts. There was a lively dispute over representation during the ratification debates in 1787–88. The anti-Federalists (who opposed ratification of the Constitution) argued that a representative body should be a mirror or a reflection of the people and therefore should be a numerous body.[7] The Federalists disagreed. A representative body should not be a reflection or a mirror of the people, and they therefore supported longer terms of office, larger districts, and, in order to free representatives from a dependence on particular groups, fewer representatives. To the same end, they supported the indirect election of United States senators and the longer terms of office of those senators. This structure of government was intended to prevent rule by simple, one might say, 'Benthamite majorities,' in favour of rule by what I would call 'constitutional majorities,' majorities assembled not in or from the people directly, but assembled in the legislative body.

Following the prescriptions of the founders of liberalism, Thomas Hobbes and John Locke, Americans yielded their natural rights (not all of them, but most of them) to a government in exchange for a fundamental constitutional right, fundamental even though not mentioned in the Constitution itself. This constitutional right is the right, through one's representatives, to be a part of the constitutional majorities necessary to govern. If they are a part of such constitutional majorities, their civil rights and their interests will be protected.

7 Herbert J. Storing, *The Complete Anti-Federalist*, 7 vols (Chicago: University of Chicago Press, 1982)

This, I think, is what Hamilton in *Federalist* no 84 and the other Founders meant when they talked about the structure of government itself being a bill of rights. The failure to grant these constitutional rights to black Americans, or at least the overwhelming majority of them, had profound consequences. In the first place, the consequences were felt by black Americans, most of whom were slaves. Because they were denied the fundamental right to be represented in constitutional majorities, it was impossible for them to secure civil rights. The second consequence was felt by the Constitution. The initial denial of rights to black Americans led to the Civil War, and the Civil War produced not only emancipation but the post-war amendments, the Thirteenth, Fourteenth and Fifteenth. It is the Fourteenth Amendment especially that is responsible for the tremendous growth of the power of the judiciary in America.

As written, the Fourteenth Amendment is very clear; unfortunately, it has never been interpreted as it is written. Section 1 of the Amendment reads as follows:

All persons born or naturalized in the United States, and subject to the jurisdiction thereof, are citizens of the United States and of the State wherein they reside. No State shall make or enforce any law which shall abridge the privileges or immunities of citizens of the United States; nor shall any State deprive any person of life, liberty, or property, without due process of law; nor deny to any person within its jurisdiction the equal protection of the laws.

The clarity of this language was first suggested to me by Professor Michael Zuckert of Carleton College (Northfield, Minnesota). In an as yet unpublished paper, he suggested that one should ask the question: to whom are the three clauses limiting state action addressed? The first one, forbidding laws that abridge national privileges and immunities, is obviously addressed to the state legislatures; after all, they make the laws. The second is obviously addressed to the state courts; after all, it is in the courts that persons are sentenced to death or to prison or to a fine, and the state courts are forbidden to do this except according to the law and its processes. The third is addressed to the state executives who are here enjoined to afford the protection of the laws – and they are the chief law enforcement officers – to everyone within their jurisdictions.

So understood, the only doubtful language is to be found in the first clause. What are the 'privileges or immunities of citizens of the United States'? That, I would argue, is for the Congress of the United States to decide, and if the Fourteenth Amendment had been understood in this fashion, and if Congress had, from time to time, enacted laws defining these privileges or immunities – if, for example, Congress had passed a law providing that it was a privilege of national citizenship to attend racially nonsegregated public schools – the United States would not today be governed by its federal judiciary.

Unfortunately, on the first occasion when the Supreme Court was given the opportunity to interpret the language of the Amendment, which was in the so-called *Slaughter-House Cases* (1873), the privilege or immunities clause was, in effect, nullified and deprived of any effective content.[8] This meant that if the states were ever to be limited with respect to their treatment of racial minorities, it would be as a result of the judiciary's enforcement of the equal protection clause. This, as interpreted, is very unclear. It refers to 'persons' who, as the clause is now interpreted, may not be treated unequally. But aliens as well as citizens, men as well as women, children as well as adults, are persons. Does this mean that, when legislating, states may not draw distinctions between these categories of persons? May states not treat them unequally? The Court has had to answer this question on many occasions, and it can be guided by no principal derived from the clause itself. Hence, the answer is yes and no, and the Court tells us when it is yes and when it is no, and in that telling has assumed powers it was never intended to exercise. The United States is now to a considerable extent governed by its federal judges who, I must point out, hold life appointments. Even the Congress has come to acquiesce in this. When it proposed the Equal Rights Amendment, it suggested only that the 'Equality of rights under the law shall not be denied or abridged by the United States or by any State on account of sex.' What rights? Our judges would decide.

The question of interest to Canada is whether, with the new Charter of Rights, we can expect Canadian judges to follow the examples of their American brethren and seize powers properly belonging to other branches of government. I recall, from my years at the University of Toronto, Chief Justice Bora Laskin on more than one occasion complaining of the lack of attention paid by the press to his court's judgments. But I thought that to be a perfectly rational response on the part of the press. Why should it assume that its typical readers were interested in the Court's reasons for deciding – in the 1957 *Farm Products Marketing* reference – that Ontario may (so long as the transactions are not interprovincial in character) establish a marketing scheme involving a pooling of products and proceeds? But when the Court begins to hear cases involving abortion, the death penalty, a military draft,

---

8 *Slaughter-House Cases*, 16 Wall. 36 (1873)

or – God forbid – a Canadian version of Watergate, then I think we can expect the press to cover it, and, indeed, to hire reporters whose only assignment is to cover the Supreme Court. This is even more likely to happen if Canadian judges prove to be as vain as Americans and covet the attention that comes with 'bold,' 'innovative,' 'creative' adjudication.

When is the last time that the Governor General used the powers under section 56 to disallow an Act of Parliament? It was in 1943. When was the last time that a Lieutenant Governor used the powers under section 90, to 'reserve' an Act of a provincial legislature? It was in 1961, but without success. Is the reason for this political? And if it is for political reasons that these powers are not used, these powers that one might identify as 'executive review of legislation,' why is it that we assume that there will not be political reasons standing in the way of judicial review of legislation? Is that the reason for the *non-obstante* clause? How then does judicial review fit with party government? It strikes me as being important, and it is something we Americans have no experience with. How does judicial review fit with a federal structure where the provinces are not protected, either in the second chamber (because that second chamber does not have any real powers) or in the House of Commons (because they are not really represented in the party controlling the House of Commons)? I ran across a statement by Professor William P. Irving of Queens University in a recent book published by the American Enterprise Institute, *Canada at the Polls, 1979 and 1980*. He says, in his excellent summary article to this volume: 'Canadian governments cannot find in their own ranks spokesmen for the various conflicts affecting Canada.'[9] Now as if to solve the problem, or perhaps to make it worse, Canada has the Charter of Rights and Freedoms. Will Canadian courts prove to be more representative? It will be interesting to learn the answer.

COMMENTARIES

JAMES PENTON Professor Berns, you put your finger on something which is, perhaps, the most serious political defect in our society. The problem arises from the fact that we have a parliamentary system of government in a federal state. We simply have to admit that it is not working very well at this particular time. How one goes about rectifying this has been a matter of speculation for those in political science. We simply have not worked out the answers. I

---

9 Howard R. Penniman ed, *Canada at the Polls, 1979 and 1980: A Study of the General Elections* (Washington, DC: American Enterprise Institute for Public Policy Research, 1981), p 389

feel that in some way the Charter of Rights and judicial review, similar to what exists in the United States, may have the positive effect of neutralizing some of the political abrasion that goes on between the various levels of government in Canada. It will take many issues out of the political arena. Yet there is a serious problem in the way in which the judiciary is appointed in this country. There ought to be some more neutral way of appointing judges and justices so that the provinces will feel involved in the selection process. If that action were taken, it might defuse some of the resentments which are bound to occur if litigation goes forward from Quebec, for instance, in the area of language rights, and the courts do not come down with decisions that are satisfactory to Quebec. I can see the same thing happening with Newfoundland and the western provinces as well. You have managed to identify some real defects in our Constitution. But I tend to be very optimistic about the Charter, and I think it is a step in the right direction.

WALTER BERNS The ability of the Supreme Court to enforce an unpopular decision on a recalcitrant state depends, to some extent, on the manner in which Americans *venerate* the Constitution. The justices speak in the name of the Constitution. We have had the Constitution now for almost 200 years and have prospered under it. We have maintained our liberties under it.

Felix Frankfurter, in *Barnette*, complained about the habit Americans have of identifying constitutionalism with wisdom.[10] That always struck me as a very peculiar thing for Frankfurter to say, as he was talking about traditions all the time. Yet it was *politically* a good statement. The legitimation of the role of the Court depends upon people's understanding that the Constitution is legitimate. The Americans have that kind of veneration for the Constitution because it is old, and therefore venerable, but also because the Constitution is understood to come out of 'the will of the people.' It is *the voice* of the people. It comes *out* of them. Can we foresee recalcitrant provinces in Canada being held up short by a decision of the Supreme Court in the name of a constitution that, in the case of Quebec, has been imposed and it does not come out of the people's will at all? Should *they* accept the Charter?

DOUGLAS SCHMEISER I cannot begin to answer the question that you posed, Professor Berns, but I would like to make a comment on some of the factors that I think are involved in the Canadian situation. Canada is one of the few federal states where there is no protection for regional or provincial interests at the national level. We have nothing similar to the Senate in the United States. There is a feeling of alienation among different regions of the country

---

10 *W. Va. State Bd. of Educ.* v *Barnette*, 319 US 624 (1943)

which have no say in the operation of the national government, particularly when you look at how politics is in fact working in Canada. For example, there is no representation in the federal government at all, politically, from the west of Canada. There is a very great problem in western Canada. There is a problem with the operation of the Supreme Court and the way it is perceived.

First of all, the Justices are selected solely by the national government, as is the case in the United States, while there are large parts of the country unrepresented in the national government. There is a bigger problem with the operation of the Canadian Supreme Court as its jurisdiction is not defined in the Canadian Constitution. As a creature of the federal Parliament, the power to create it is referred to in the British North America Act (Constitution Acts 1867 to 1975). The Court itself has not been given entrenched status in the Constitution, and accordingly it does not have the constitutional veneration which exists in the United States.

There is a further problem in the population makeup of Canada. The central region of Canada, namely Ontario and Quebec, has considerable control over the political process through voting patterns because the bulk of the seats are in Ontario and Quebec. That is starting to change as there now is a population shift in Canada from the central area to the west, as has occurred in the past twenty-five years in the United States. I think that will make a difference. The problem now, in terms of the population makeup, is that the other factors to which I have referred are compounded by the fact that the outlying regions of the country do not have sufficient voting power. This is another source of alienation. There is also a provincial feeling, which is somewhat different than what Professor Penton has expressed. There is a feeling that a Charter of Rights will have a centralizing tendency. A national Supreme Court tends to support national uniform standards, and to impose these standards on a country, as opposed to the acceptance and adoption of imaginative, different and usually provincial approaches to difficult social problems. There is a feeling that much of the advantage of federalism will be lost in the sense that the standards and approaches that will be adopted in the social policy role, which is involved in the entrenchment of rights, will favour these national, and as the system works, central standards rather than provincial ideas and approaches. One can argue at great length about whether or not it is true. I simply wish to suggest that it is a widely held view in many of the provincial areas.

BARRY STRAYER I just want to pick up on a couple of points. I think you have raised a very important question, Professor Berns, about the legitimacy of the Supreme Court, particularly in its newer responsibilities taken on with the adoption of the Charter. This is part of the unfinished business of our constitution that we still have to address. I think that we have been fairly lucky to date in finding acceptance of the Supreme Court over the years. There is no mechanism for the provinces to influence the way the Supreme Court is composed or appointed. Nevertheless, the system has worked and, by and large, the decisions of the Court have been accepted.

The only times when the decisions have not been accepted have been when the political problems were so great that maybe all sides have recognized the good work. I think particularly of the offshore decision in the late 1960s when the Supreme Court held that the federal government should have ownership and jurisdiction over British Columbia's offshore resources. That decision stood for 14 years or 15 years, but in terms of its practical application, it has had practically none. In fact, we have had a continuing dispute over who really ought to control the offshore, not just in BC, but more particularly on the east coast. The difficulties of that decision are recognized on all sides. If the Supreme Court had been appointed by some magic formula involving the Senate or the provinces, it would not have made much difference. The decision would still have been recognized as a difficult one. It is not unknown in the United States. The US Supreme Court has, on occasion, also made decisions which simply did not 'wash.'

I want to also pick up on the point that Professor Schmeiser made about what he called the centralizing tendency of the Charter of Rights. I am wondering if what he really means is not a 'homogenizing tendency.' That is a somewhat different thing and it is maybe better to describe it in that way because one faces up to the real issue of whether there are not some things represented by the contents of the Charter of Rights which ought to be homogenized. When you talk about centralizing, one has this spectre of bold, bad Ottawa drawing everything unto it. But what we are really talking about is the integration of the country through a broadening of shared values represented by a statement in the constitution of fundamental rights common to all Canadians.

ALAN WESTIN Your mention of offshore oil in Canada reminds me of some old issues. The Supreme Court found that the states that have the offshore oil, Louisiana, California and so forth, were not entitled to it. That was made a campaign issue in 1952 by Eisenhower. It opened the coffers of Texas, Louisiana, and numerous other states to the Republican party to an unprecedented degree. When he was elected, Congress passed an offshore oil bill, which because it was not a constitutional law issue but was an interpretive decision involving the meaning of certain kinds of treaties and laws, overturned the decision. That suggests that we have some of the same questions weighing the power of states' rights versus central claims. In this case, it was for revenues of a large amount and whether they should be used nationally or be primarily used in the state from where they were derived.

The American Supreme Court can be overturned in that kind of an instance in a direct way. If Congress felt it did not have the power to do it in one certain way, then it is quite possible for Congress to find another technique by which to do it. Recall, for example, the famous article by Robert Dahl in the *Journal of Public Law*, which gave examples in which the Supreme Court had declared an act of Congress to be unconstitutional.[11] What happened to those programs? Within a period of approximately seven years, Congress had accomplished the purpose of the legislative program that it set out to pursue in the majority of those cases. It took longer and it required some adroitness and some revision of the ways of executing programs. But the analysis was that the Supreme Court had more of a slowdown function than a denial function, even if one looked at something like the national programs that have been struck down as unconstitutional.

WALTER BERNS I think Canadians are not so used to speaking of rights because (and perhaps I had better start running right now) in the formal sense at least, Canadians do not have any rights. They do not have any rights because of what it says on the coin of the realm: *'Dei gratia Regina'* – 'Queen by the Grace of God.' Who governs Canada? The Queen! The Americans revolted against that principle and *that* is what equality means. Nobody governs by the grace of God. The government does not exist by nature. Governments have to be brought into being and legitimate government can be brought into being only when people consent. They consent to secure their rights. I do think that these beginnings have ramifications and radiations that go through history.

DONALD SMILEY I think, as usual, Professor Berns has gotten right to the bottom of this. Canadians, after all, are Hobbesian. In the beginning was government. In the beginning was order, and once order is secured, one can make society more egalitarian, one can have a good deal of freedom, one can have procedures. This is completely contrary to the whole thesis that government exists to protect pre-existing rights.

The notion that there are rights against government is a very foreign idea to the Canadian constitutional system and the Canadian political culture. When the Solicitor General testified before the parliamentary committee, he said that the War Measures Act squares with the Canadian Bill of Rights.

---

11 R.A. Dahl, 'Decision-Making in a Democracy: The Supreme Court as a National Policy Maker,' *Journal of Public Law*, vol 6 (1957)

Now one cannot square that with the notion of pre-existing rights as against government. I do not think any fooling around with the clumsy language of this Charter will help. Nobody has ever become a convert to Christianity through reading the Apostle's Creed. To impose a Charter that one would expect will get embedded into the consciousness of the people, who operate under certain contrary predispositions, will not 'wash.'

WALTER BERNS Let us look at a comparison of the American constitutional debates with the Confederation Debates. The American constitutional debates are collected in the *Federalist Papers* and elsewhere, and now Herbert Storing has brought out the complete anti-federalist seven volumes, which will be the authoritative statement in that area.[12] The debate occurred in newspaper articles, publications, and between the people. The Confederation debates in Canada of course are in the form of Parliamentary debates. If I am not mistaken, in Upper Canada at the time, someone during the debates said 'shouldn't we solicit the opinion of people out of doors?' and someone said, 'Oh no, we don't do that in Canada, we decide these things here because we are governing in the name of the Queen. We do not solicit popular opinion.' Again, these radiations throughout history from these beginnings make a difference.

WILLIAM LEDERMAN We had a very lively newspaper press in Canada all the way from St John's, Newfoundland to Victoria, B.C. There was a very lively debate in the popular press. The editorials of the newspapers were reviewed by Professor Peter Waite of Dalhousie University and published in a book called *Life and Times of Confederation*.[13] One sees there plenty of controversy, far more than one sees in the debates in the parliament of the old province of Canada, which were the only properly published debates. The newspaper press between 1864 and 1867 conducted a very lively debate ventilating all sides of the issues countrywide.

WALTER BERNS My point is that it was understood in the United States that the decision would be made by the people, and in Canada, it was understood that the decision would be made someplace else.

ANDRÉ TREMBLAY We know that one province considers itself not bound by the Constitution Act, 1982. The Quebec Premier René Lévesque said he will not correct provincial legislation to put it into harmony with the constitution. What would you do in the United States with a state that refuses to obey the constitution?

12 Herbert J. Storing, *The Complete Anti-Federalist*, 7 vols (Chicago: University of Chicago Press, 1982)
13 Peter B. Waite, *Life and Times of Confederation, 1864–1867 Politics, Newspapers, and the Union of British North America* (Toronto: University of Toronto Press, 1962)

WALTER BERNS Dwight D. Eisenhower said that he could not imagine the circumstances under which he would send the troops into a state.[14] Within a couple of months, he had sent the 101st Airborne down to Little Rock, Arkansas. In 1976, when the Quebec election results came in, I raised the question at the University of Toronto. Is it possible to imagine a civil war in Canada? It was generally agreed that one could not and then I began to wonder why it was so that in the United States we had a Civil War. In the Canadian context, you would know the answer to that better than I would. Can the Liberal government, which has most of its seats, over half from Quebec, enforce a decision against Quebec? Can a Conservative government, which has one seat in Quebec enforce such a decision? What would be the consequences for the rest of the country in enforcing an unpopular decision?

---

14 US President, *Public Papers of the Presidents of the United States* (Washington, DC: Office of the *Federal Register*, National Archives and Records Service, 1953–   ), Dwight D. Eisenhower, 1957, p 546

The Judicial Protection of Rights

Paul Bender*

To what extent is the judicial protection of 'entrenched' rights consistent with life in a democracy? That is a question that is on the minds of many Canadians as they undertake life, for the first time, under a judicially enforceable charter of constitutional rights. Americans, as is well known, have had extensive experience with judicial enforcement of such rights. I will try to offer some observations on the general nature of the American system and the way it has worked in practice – observations that, I hope, will be of some relevance in forming a judgment about the democratic – or anti-democratic – tendencies of a system of judicially enforced constitutional rights.

One should bear in mind, of course, that what the American experience has been is not by any means necessarily what the Canadian experience will be. The Charter of Rights is similar, in many respects, to the American constitutional protections, as they have been elaborated by the courts, but there are also some potentially important textual differences. (Two of these are the 'notwithstanding' provision (section 33 of the Charter), which has no direct counterpart in the American system, and section 1 of the Charter, which states a single standard, applicable to all of the rights set out in the Charter, for judging the legitimacy of governmental justifications for limiting rights. United States law has a variety of standards for judging the adequacy of governmental justifications, for limiting constitutional rights, depending on the nature, strength and history of the particular right.) Canadian politics and judicial traditions are also different in potentially important ways. Most importantly – and this is a theme that I cannot emphasize too strongly – it is simply impossible to tell, at the beginning of life under the Charter of Rights, how things will work out over time. The American system of rights today is

* Paul Bender is a Professor of Law at the University of Pennsylvania.

vastly different from what it was one hundred years ago, and even more vastly different from what it was one hundred and twenty-five years ago, before the adoption of the Fourteenth Amendment. I suspect that it may be equally as different one hundred years from now. The Civil War, the Great Depression, and World War II had an enormous impact on the judicial enforcement of individual rights in the United States, to say nothing of the influence of individuals like John Marshall, Earl Warren, and others in between and perhaps since. The events and personalities that will shape the system of judicially enforceable rights in Canada are unknowable now. The Charter provides a framework, but only that; many of the most important decisions about the Canadian system of rights remain to be made, and they will not all be made in the next year, or the next several years, or even the next several decades.

I think it only fair to state at the outset that I do not think that the system of judicially enforced constitutional rights in the United States has proved, overall, to have been fatally anti-democratic in nature, or even to have been dangerously anti-democratic in the long run. It is, of course, true that whenever, in a particular case, a court holds an act of a democratically elected legislature to be unconstitutional, that is, in some meaningful sense at least, an anti-democratic decision. American courts have held legislative acts unconstitutional on several hundred occasions. Many of these judicial decisions have involved isolated pieces of state and local legislation relatively unimportant to the quality of life in the country; but some have certainly had a much greater impact and significance. American courts have, at times, invoked the individual rights guarantees of the United States Constitution against important legislative programs that, in retrospect, appear to have been perfectly legitimate programs to implement 'in a free and democratic society' (to borrow a phrase from section 1 of the Charter). Perhaps the most well-known examples of this were the decisions of the United States Supreme Court in the early part of this century that applied the due process clause of the Fourteenth Amendment to strike down some important social welfare measures, such as certain minimum wage and maximum hour laws.[1] Some people think, although I am not among them, that the Court's more recent decisions in the areas of abortion rights[2] and school prayer[3] may also fall into this category.

Nevertheless, my belief is that judicial enforcement of rights has, overall, not had a dangerously anti-democratic influence in the United States. Indeed, I

1 See e.g., *Lochner* v *New York*, 198 US 45 (1905).
2 *Roe* v *Wade*, 410 US 113 (1973)
3 *Engel* v *Vitale*, 370 US 421 (1962); *Abington School Dist.* v *Schempp*, 374 US 203 (1963)

believe that our system of judicially enforceable rights has actually significantly *enhanced* the democratic quality of American society. I hold this belief, in part, because the Supreme Court has, at least until now, been relatively restrained in the manner in which it has confronted the legislative will in most areas where important legislative policies are at stake. Secondly, it seems to me that when the Court is not restrained – where the battle-lines between the Court and legislature exist over a substantial period of time (as they did, for example, over the application of the due process clause to some kinds of social welfare legislation) – the Court is bound to lose to the democratic will in the end, unless the country ultimately becomes persuaded of the correctness of the Court's viewpoint. Even though they have life tenure, United States federal judges do respond to persistent scholarly and popular criticism. In all events, even judges with life tenure are eventually replaced. New Supreme Court Justices are the product of a democratically controlled selection process that pays a good deal of attention to the basic attitudes of prospective nominees toward current constitutional issues. In the United States, new Court majorities are not bound to follow precedent, but can and do over-rule important constitutional decisions that they consider harmful and wrong. But, perhaps most importantly I think that the American system of judicial enforcement of rights has enhanced the democratic process overall simply because some of the most important rights that the judiciary has enforced (contrary to the will of legislative majorities) have been decidedly *pro*-democratic rights. I refer here primarily to rights of free expression, rights of free political association, and to equality rights that help to ensure equal access to education, to the marketplace, and to the political process. For example, it is clear to me that American society is definitely *more*, rather than less, democratic in nature today because the Supreme Court, after years of indecision, decided to over-rule itself in 1954 and hold unconstitutional 'democratic' legislative decisions requiring racial segregation and supporting doctrines of white supremacy.[4]

That is my own general view of the overall relationship between judicial enforcement of rights and democracy in the United States. It is by no means the only view that may be rationally entertained on the subject and I do not wish this paper to play the role of an advocate in other circumstances, of the American system. But in talking with Canadians about the American experience and its possible lessons for Canada, it has seemed to me that some of the opinions I have heard about the possibly dangerous anti-democratic

---

4 *Brown* v *Board of Education*, 374 US 483 (1954), overruling *Plessy* v *Ferguson*, 163 US 537 (1896)

qualities of judicially enforceable constitutional rights flow from a certain degree of misunderstanding about what actually transpires in the United States when courts enforce fundamental rights. It is to some of these possible misunderstandings that I would now like to turn.

The principal potential misconception that I will address is the view, held by some people, that the system of judicially enforceable rights in the United States has meant that the judiciary has, to a substantial extent, 'taken over' the government of the United States; that in enforcing rights, the judiciary finally decides a vast range of important and controversial questions of social policy. The United States judiciary certainly does some of that, but by no means is it the principal organ of government in the United States. Americans do not have anything approaching government by judiciary, except in some relatively limited areas. Even in these areas, there remains a considerable degree of legislative authority. I am going to try to describe what it is about the way we engage in judicial review in the United States that may help to moderate the anti-democratic impact of the role of the judiciary.

I will begin with the term 'entrenchment.' I think that is an unfortunate word to use when talking about judicially enforced constitutional rights, and I think Canadians should banish it from their vocabularies as soon as possible. 'Entrenchment' suggests a static situation: 'We will entrench certain rights and there they will remain, as fixed barriers to the will of the majority, no matter how urgent the situation or compelling the governmental need.' That is not at all the way the process of judicial enforcement of rights has worked in the United States, and I doubt very much that it is the way it will work in Canada.

Consider first, from the 'entrenchment' standpoint, the substantive content of American constitutional rights – the rights that American courts will meaningfully enforce when an appropriate case is presented to them. The fact is that the substance of the rights of Americans, even those rights that have been explicitly recognized in the Constitution from the beginning, has changed substantially over the course of time, even when the constitutional text has remained completely unchanged. The substantive scope of constitutionally protected free expression in the United States today, for example, is quite different from the scope of constitutionally protected free expression at the time of the adoption of the First Amendment. I think, for instance, that it was well understood at the beginning that libel, slander, profanity, obscenity and blasphemy were all forms of expression not subject to First Amendment protection.[5] Except for obscenity, however, all of these kinds of speech

---

5 See *Chaplinsky* v *New Hampshire*, 315 US 568 (1942).

are now protected by the First Amendment,[6] and the concept of unprotected obscenity has also shrunk very considerably in scope in the United States since 1800.[7] Commercial advertising – held to be unprotected by constitutional free expression guarantees as recently as forty years ago[8] – is now substantially protected by those same guarantees.[9] Perhaps the most dramatic developments in the meaning of constitutional rights guarantees in the United States have occurred in connection with the Fourteenth Amendment. Once deemed by the Supreme Court to be an amendment whose 'one pervading purpose' was 'the freedom of the slave race,'[10] the Fourteenth Amendment, through subsequent judicial interpretations, nevertheless was used to protect a wide range of private economic activities on grounds that had nothing to do with race. That meaning of the Fourteenth Amendment was then largely abandoned[11] and replaced by an interpretation that now, among other things, fastens freedom of expression guarantees upon the states,[12] prohibits states from 'establishing' religion,[13] subjects states to a code of constitutionally required criminal procedures,[14] prohibits some gender-based and other forms of non-racial discrimination,[15] and forms the basis for the important right of personal privacy.[16]

By using the word 'entrenchment,' a sense is conveyed that the substance of rights remains more or less the same and that is not, I suggest, an accurate message. What a judicially enforceable charter of rights like the United States Bill of Rights really does is to give life to a continuous and somewhat cyclical process of judicial development that is guided, but not really constrained, by the text.

It is guided as well by strong currents of non-judicial thought, by economic and social realities, by developments in technology, by logic, and by the argument of litigants. What we now think of as very important rights in the United States did not come into being in any substantial, significant form

6 See e.g., *New York Times* v *Sullivan*, 376 US 254 (1964); *Gertz* v *Robert Welch, Inc.*, 418 US 323 (1974).
7 See *Roth* v *United States*, 354 US 476 (1957).
8 See *Valentine* v *Chrestensen*, 316 US 52 (1942).
9 E.g., *Virginia State Bd. of Pharmacy* v *Virginia Citizens Consumer Council*, 425 US 748 (1976).
10 *Slaughter-House Cases*, 16 Wall. 36 (1873)
11 See *Ferguson* v *Skrupa*, 372 US 726 (1963).
12 See *Palko* v *Connecticut*, 302 US 319 (1937).
13 *Everson* v *Board of Educ.*, 330 US 1 (1947)
14 E.g., *Duncan* v *Louisiana*, 391 US 145 (1968)
15 E.g., *Craig* v *Boren*, 429 US 190 (1976)
16 *Roe* v *Wade*, 410 US 113 (1973)

until the last thirty years, and yet we have been enforcing some of these rights for almost two hundred years. Other rights, such as freedom of contract, have risen and fallen during this period. I suspect that other rights, including some that may have been rather important to the original Framers of the United States Constitution, have been allowed to fall by the wayside. A charter of rights is a live, changing, evolving document that both teaches to and learns from the society around it. It is not a system of entrenched, static fortifications against the democratic will.

'Entrenchment' is also a misleading concept, as applied to the American system of rights, because it suggests a one-sided process where only the content of rights, but not the governmental justifications for seeking to limit those rights, is significant. There are, perhaps, some United States constitutional rights that are relatively absolute in nature. But most rights – and certainly many of the most important rights – have not been thus formulated by the United States courts. In the case of some rights, the need to take governmental and societal justifications into account is apparent from the text of the Constitution itself. Thus, the Fourth Amendment prohibits only 'unreasonable' searches and seizures; the phrase 'due process' also suggests the relevance of practical considerations. But whether or not such words are used in the constitutional text, the United States Supreme Court has incorporated various rules of reason and necessity into its formulations of rights at almost every opportunity. This is true even with regard to some of our most highly protected rights. It is not accurate, for example, to say that there is a right to be free from governmental prohibitions on the content of speech in the United States, or a right to be free from governmental interference with freedom of religion, or from racial or gender classifications. Rather, one has these rights only if government fails to establish in some cases that a 'clear and present danger' supported its prohibition,[17] or in other areas that the challenged law was 'necessary' to serve a 'compelling' governmental interest,[18] or in others that the restriction was 'substantially' related to an 'important' governmental objective.[19]

These 'balancing-type' rules have become a very prominent feature of American constitutional rights jurisprudence. The flexibility that they afford is not an unmixed blessing. It is possible for important rights to be 'balanced away,' as Justice Hugo Black used to warn with regard to the rights of free speech.[20] Parts of the 'balancing' process – e.g., the determination of whether

17 See *Dennis* v *United States*, 341 US 494 (1951) (prohibition on subversive advocacy).
18 See *Shapiro* v *Thompson*, 394 US 618 (1969) (penalty on the right to travel).
19 *Craig* v *Boren*, 429 US 190 (1976) (gender classification)
20 See e.g., *Konigsberg* v *State Bar of California*, 366 US 36 (1961) (dissenting opinion).

a governmental objective is sufficiently 'compelling' – are enormously subjective and may require a court to make judgments that often seem more legislative than judicial in nature. But flexible protections of rights, whatever their defects, plainly do not constitute impenetrable, completely entrenched barriers to the will of the majority. The legislature can make its case, and if it acts responsibly, if it shows a sensitive awareness to minority concerns and to the constitutional values at stake, it may well properly prevail.

Another potential misunderstanding about the American system of judicial enforcement of rights has to do with the way in which the courts (I speak here of the United States federal courts, although the same essential point could be made about the United States state courts) obtain the authority to enforce constitutional rights in the first place. It is common knowledge that in *Marbury* v *Madison*[21] and subsequent cases, the United States Supreme Court has held that, with regard to most litigatable constitutional issues, the judiciary has the last word on what the Constitution means and can thus enforce constitutional limitations – including individual rights provisions – against legislative and executive action. But what makes a constitutional question litigatable? How does a court get hold of a dispute so as to be able to supply the *Marbury* role of judicial supremacy? I think that it is very interesting – and very important – to recognize, in considering the democratic or anti-democratic quality of judicial review, that federal judicial enforcement of constitutional rights in the United States has occurred *through affirmative grants of power given to the courts by the Congress*. There is, for example, no explicit, constitutionally fixed, minimum appellate jurisdiction of the Supreme Court of the United States in this area. Indeed, Article III of the United States Constitution provides that 'The Supreme Court shall have appellate Jurisdiction ... *with such Exceptions, and under such Regulations as the Congress shall make.*' No one knows for sure the extent to which Congress, by making such 'exceptions' and 'regulations,' could effectively withdraw jurisdiction from the Supreme Court over constitutional questions, including alleged violations of individual rights. That is a major constitutional question in the United States that has never been authoritatively resolved. The important point for present purposes is that the question has not been resolved because Congress has not, in fact, sought to withdraw jurisdiction but has, on the contrary, affirmatively and continuously acted to confer jurisdiction on the Supreme Court to decide virtually the full range of cases involving constitutional rights. It is true that almost every time, in recent years, that the Supreme Court has made an important unpopular indi-

---

21 1 Cranch (US) 137 (1803)

vidual rights decision, there have been proposals in Congress to limit or abolish Supreme Court jurisdiction over cases dealing with that subject. Such proposals were generated, for example, by the school prayer decisions, by the reapportionment decisions, by certain Supreme Court obscenity decisions, by its abortion decisions, and so on. Those proposals, however, have not been successful within the national legislature, although some of them have come close to succeeding.

The same situation prevails, believe it or not, with regard to the jurisdiction of the lower United States federal courts. Although Article 3, section 2 of the United States Constitution provides that the judicial power of the United States 'shall extend to all Cases, in Law and Equity, arising under this Constitution,' that language has not generally been read to require that the judicial power *must* extend to all such cases, but only to mean that it *may* extend to those cases. To what extent Congress could withdraw or refuse to confer jurisdiction on the lower federal courts in particular classes of constitutional cases – for example, in segregation cases or reapportionment cases – or indeed in all constitutional cases, no one knows for sure. Again, we do not know the limits, if any, on Congress' authority in this area because Congress has, for many years, voluntarily conferred very broad jurisdiction on the lower federal courts to consider cases raising alleged violations of constitutional rights. Congress has, in addition, enacted and re-enacted a well-known statute,[22] that creates a cause of action and right to relief in the most controversial of individual rights cases – those where persons acting under colour of state law are alleged to violate 'rights, privileges or immunities secured by the Constitution.' This statute was the basis of suit in, among others, the Supreme Court's school segregation, reapportionment and abortion cases.

One of the reasons why, in my view, judicial enforcement of constitutional rights in the United States has been successful, is that it has proceeded with both the acquiescence and the active cooperation of Congress. Despite many controversial federal court decisions, Congress has not attempted substantially to limit the jurisdiction of those courts. Instead, there has been a fairly wide consensus, even among people who strongly disagree with particular Supreme Court decisions (or with whole generations of Supreme Court decisions) that the basic system of judicial enforcement of fundamental rights in the United States is a wise system that ought to be preserved.

What have the United States federal courts done with the jurisdiction that is so broadly conferred upon them? An impression may exist that American judges hunger for power and reach out to decide as much as they possibly

---

22 Now 42 USC s 1983

can. That may, perhaps, be an individual characteristic of some of the judges, but it is hardly a central part of the institutional personality. Perusal of decisional law and practice relating to the exercise of federal jurisdiction in the area of constitutional adjudication – including cases involving individual rights – could easily lead one to conclude, quite to the contrary, that United States courts confront important issues only when they are forced to – and that they may not even confront them then. This judicial reluctance is one of the tempering factors that has made judicial enforcement of rights more acceptable than it might otherwise be within the context of American democracy.

The United States Constitution permits federal courts to exercise jurisdiction over 'cases' and 'controversies.' The Supreme Court decided quite early that these words had a limiting significance – that they were not equivalent to 'issues' or 'questions,' but required instead that disputes, including constitutional disputes, arise in the context of relatively traditional lawsuits. Thus, the federal courts, including the Supreme Court, do not give 'advisory' opinions to the executive branch regarding the legality (or constitutionality) of proposed actions; nor can they accept legislative references. Even with regard to proceedings that do closely resemble traditional adversary lawsuits, the Supreme Court has developed a wide variety of doctrines that it may and often does invoke to preclude judicial consideration of the merits of constitutional disputes. Some of these doctrines appear to be constitutionally required by the limiting significance of the 'case' and 'controversy' language; others may be court-made self-supervisory rules that may be (but usually are not) countermanded by Congress. Some of these jurisdictional rules are meant to safeguard the quality of judicial decision-making; others are meant to preserve the separation of powers between the executive, legislative and judicial branches; still others are designed out of respect for an appropriate degree of state autonomy. In practice, all of these rules can be used to delay, narrow, or even totally avoid difficult or controversial questions – to avoid, that is, immediate and direct confrontations with the democratic process.

It would be impossible for me to catalogue all the relevant jurisdictional rules and practices in this area. Let me give a few examples to impart a flavour of the kinds of limitations to which I refer. The Supreme Court has, for many years, adhered to the doctrine that plaintiffs do not ordinarily have sufficient 'standing' to challenge the constitutionality of federal legislation merely because they are citizens or taxpayers.[23] Challenges must instead be

---

23 E.g., *Frothingham* v *Mellon*, 262 US 447 (1923); *Schlesinger* v *Reservists Committee to Stop the War*, 418 US 206 (1974)

brought, if they are to be brought at all, by parties who are more particularly and substantially adversely affected by the legislation. If the challenged legislation is a federal benefit program, the result may be that no judicial challenge at all is possible, even though there may be a fairly strong case for its unconstitutionality.[24] There is also a doctrine of 'ripeness' – that constitutional challenges may not be brought until it is clear that there is, in fact, an irreconcilable dispute between the parties. When the constitutional controversy over anti-contraception laws came to the Supreme Court in the early 1960s, the Court first avoided decision on the merits by holding the case 'unripe'; it was not sufficiently clear, said the Court, that the state involved (Connecticut) would, in fact, actually enforce its statutory prohibition on contraceptive use.[25] A birth control clinic was subsequently opened, its operators were charged and convicted by the state for aiding and abetting the use of contraceptives by married couples, and the Court was forced to decide *Griswold* v *Connecticut*,[26] a case which gave birth to the modern right of privacy and which led to the 1973 abortion decisions.[27]

At the opposite end of the spectrum is an active judicial doctrine of mootness – a doctrine of 'overripeness,' if you prefer. The Supreme Court has, at times, invoked this doctrine to avoid dealing with highly charged and difficult questions that are anything but moot as issues, although they may be moot if one refers only to the immediate interests of the specific parties involved. That is precisely what happened, for example, with regard to the issue of the constitutionality of race-conscious affirmative action programs in the United States. The issue first came to the Court in a case involving a challenge to a law-school minority admissions program by a disappointed white applicant.[28] The plaintiff, who ultimately lost in the lower courts, had nevertheless been permitted to attend the school in question while his constitutional challenge was being litigated. When the case finally arrived in the Supreme Court, he was in his last semester and it was fairly clear that he would be permitted to finish school, whatever the Supreme Court's decision. For this reason, the Supreme Court consequently held the case to be 'moot.' The issue, of course, did not disappear and came back to the Court four years later in the famous *Bakke* case.[29] Even then the Court, as a whole, displayed anything but enthusiasm for deciding the basic constitutional issue of whether

24 See e.g., *Valley Forge Christian College* v *Americans United*, US (1982).
25 *Poe* v *Ullman*, 367 US 497 (1961)
26 381 US 479 (1965)
27 *Roe* v *Wade*, 410 US 113 (1973); *Doe* v *Bolton*, 410 US 179 (1973)
28 *DeFunis* v *Odegard*, 416 US 312 (1974)
29 *University of California Regents* v *Bakke*, 438 US 265 (1978)

a 'preference' for minority applicants violates the equal protection clause. Four Justices[30] in *Bakke* sought to dispose of the case on statutory grounds. When their statutory argument was rejected by the majority, they nevertheless dug in their heels and refused to go on to consider the constitutional question. The remaining five Justices divided, four to one, on both the proper constitutional standard by which to judge affirmative action programs and on the ultimate constitutionality of the particular challenged program. As a result, there was no opinion of the Court in *Bakke* and the basic constitutional issue has, even now, still not been authoritatively resolved by the Court.

Moving from matters of timing to matters of substance, the Supreme Court has made clear that, despite some broad language in *Marbury* v *Madison* and other cases, not every constitutional provision is, in fact, amenable to judicial enforcement.[31] One such provision that the courts will probably not enforce is Article IV, section 4 of the Constitution, providing that the United States 'shall guarantee to every state ... a Republican Form of Government' and protect them against 'invasion' and 'domestic violence.'[32] Nor will the United States courts likely review judgments in impeachment cases. In many contexts, it is also doubtful that they will determine whether a 'war' has properly been declared by Congress pursuant to the Constitution.[33] The so-called reapportionment cases,[34] deciding that both state and federal legislative districts must be based primarily on population equality, are an extremely important and well-known line of decisions in which the courts have repeatedly come into conflict with legislative action or inaction. It is perhaps not as well known that, for many years, United States courts refused to adjudicate claims of gross legislative malapportionment on the ground that these claims raised 'political questions' that were not justiciable.[35]

The United States Supreme Court has even, and more than occasionally, exhibited a reluctance to assert itself – and to permit the lower federal courts to assert themselves – in the area where it is perhaps most often criticized for its anti-democratic 'activism,' i.e., the enforcement of constitutional rights in state criminal proceedings. (In the American model of federalism, most criminal law is of state or local origin and law enforcement takes place prima-

---

30 Chief Justice Burger and Justices Stewart, Rehnquist and Stevens
31 See *Powell* v *McCormack*, 395 US 486 (1969).
32 See e.g., *Pacific States Telephone & Telegraph Co.* v *Oregon*, 223 US 118 (1912).
33 See *Mora* v *McNamara*, 389 US 934 (1967).
34 E.g., *Reynolds* v *Sims*, 377 US 533 (1964)
35 See *Colegrove* v *Green*, 328 US 549 (1946), overruled in *Baker* v *Carr*, 369 US 186 (1962).

rily in state courts.) Thus, although the Supreme Court decided as early as 1914 that illegally obtained evidence was not admissible in federal prosecutions,[36] it was not until 1961 that the Court applied this 'exclusionary rule' to require states to bar unconstitutionally obtained evidence in their prosecutions.[37] By the time the Court adopted this constitutional exclusionary rule, the majority of states had, in fact, adopted the exclusionary rule for themselves. It had also become clear that other methods of enforcing the constitutional restraints on police conduct simply were not working, and that without a federally-imposed exclusionary rule those constitutional restraints would largely become a nullity in jurisdictions that still had not adopted the rule for themselves.

One other aspect of Supreme Court self-imposed restraint in the area of federal-state relations bears mentioning. Suppose a person stands accused of a statutory crime in a state court. The statute employed in the prosecution, however, is a rather clearly unconstitutional invasion of their rights of free speech. Given the broad authority to protect and enforce constitutional rights that has been conferred on the United States federal courts by the Congress,[38] that person might expect to be able to obtain federal judicial relief from the necessity of standing trial under such an unconstitutional statute. Such a trial, it might be alleged, would not only cause expense and great inconvenience (as most criminal trials do), but might also act as a powerful deterrent upon the defendant and others, effectively preventing him (and them) from exercising free speech rights during the (sometimes protracted) period when the state criminal proceeding would be pending. Here, it might seem, is a fairly appealing case for the judicial enforcement of constitutional rights. For some years, the United States federal courts intervened in such cases on appropriate occasions.[39] But in 1971 the Supreme Court decided that considerations of 'comity' in state-federal relations required that the federal courts not exercise their jurisdiction in such cases; the Court held that, once state proceedings have begun, federal judicial enforcement of constitutional rights must await final conviction and exhaustion of all state appeals.[40]

The picture that emerges from even this brief examination is of a United States judiciary that, as often as not, seeks ways to avoid rather than to pre-

36   *Weeks* v *United States*, 232 US 383 (1914)
37   *Mapp* v *Ohio*, 367 US 643 (1961), overruling *Wolf* v *Colorado*, 338 US 25 (1949), which had expressly refused to fasten a broad exclusionary rule upon the states.
38   E.g., 42 USC s 1983, mentioned above
39   E.g., *Dombrowski* v *Pfister*, 380 US 479 (1965)
40   *Younger* v *Harris*, 401 US 37 (1971)

cipitate collisions with the democratic process. I do not mean to suggest that I agree with all of these Supreme Court decisions and doctrines. It seems clear, however, that judicial enforcement of rights becomes significantly more acceptable from a democratic perspective when a judiciary generally reserves its intervention for situations that urgently demand it.

Let me end with three related observations about the nature of the Supreme Court's business in circumstances when it *does* decide to act judicially to enforce constitutional rights – observations that bear directly upon the compatibility of judicial enforcement of constitutonal rights with democratic government. Many people assume that when a court enforces constitutional rights, there is inevitably going to be collision between its will and that of the legislature. That, however, is not always the case. Indeed, in most of the cases where the United States federal courts have ruled governmental activity unconstitutional, there has probably been no collision at all with the legislative will. These cases have involved judgments, not about the constitutionality of legislation, but about the constitutionality of either the individual acts of governmental officials, or of the acts of administrative bodies. Such acts are often neither required nor affirmatively authorized by legislation; they may indeed be acts directly prohibited by the legislature. Thus, a policeman may conduct a search, arrest or interrogation in violation of both the Constitution and the applicable statutes.[41] (More United States constitutional cases probably fall into this single category than into any other.) At the other end of the spectrum, a president or cabinet officer may exceed both constitutional and statutory limits on his behaviour.[42] It seems difficult to attribute any anti-democratic quality at all to the institution of judicial review in such circumstances. It does not appear to be dangerously anti-democratic for a court to fashion a remedy for unconstitutional behaviour in circumstances where no legislative remedies have been forthcoming. That, for example, is precisely what transpired in the case of the Supreme Court's reluctant adoption of an exclusionary rule barring unconstitutionally obtained evidence from state criminal trials.

Secondly, when a court does rule legislation unconstitutional, thus presumably conflicting with the decision of *some* democratic majority, that does not always mean that it will have acted contrary to the will of the majority when the issue is viewed from a *national* perspective. (Federal legislation is rarely held unconstitutional in the United States for individual rights reasons; when it is, the aspect of the programme that is struck down may be

---

41 E.g., *Monroe* v *Pape*, 365 US 176 (1961)
42 Cf *Youngstown Sheet & Tube Co.* v *Sawyer*, 343 US 579 (1952)

relatively tangential to the central legislative – and democratic – purpose.[43]) The cases in which the United States Supreme Court has frustrated important legislative purposes for individual rights reasons have mostly involved state or local legislation. The segregation cases, the reapportionment cases, and the contraception and abortion cases are all examples of this. In almost all of these cases, however, the legislation struck down clearly did *not* represent the views of the majority of the country. In the school segregation cases, for example, the Supreme Court was, in reality, enforcing the fundamental values of the United States majority, rather than its own peculiar constitutional views, on a minority of the country that was seriously and harmfully out of step with the rest of the nation on a matter of basic importance to the quality of national life. And even in the abortion area, the individual rights position adopted by the Supreme Court in 1973 was, so far as public opinion polls reveal, wholly consistent with the views of a majority of United States citizens. Moreover, the Supreme Court's decision was basically similar, in effect, to the trend of recent state legislation and to authoritative reform proposals, such as that of the American Law Institute in its Model Penal Code.

My final observation also draws on the 1973 abortion decision. That Supreme Court case is often cited as an important example of illegitimate judicial lawmaking in an area that, it is said, ought to be governed by more democratic decision-making processes. I am not at all sure, however, that I can agree that the Supreme Court's 1973 abortion decision is accurately viewed as one that supplanted truly democratic decision-making in those states that sought to continue to criminalize all abortions. As I mentioned at the beginning of this paper, one of the reasons for my belief that the judicial enforcement of rights in the United States generally enhances democracy is that many individual rights decisions enforce basic democratic equal protection principles. The abortion case is not ordinarily thought of as an equal protection case, and the Supreme Court's opinion was certainly not written from an equality perspective. But the fact is that the abortion laws struck down in *Roe* v *Wade* were patently *not* equal in their practical application. I am not primarily referring here to the fact that anti-abortion laws have their most direct impact upon women, a group that has been vastly under-represented in the American political process (although that is certainly a fact that

---

43 E.g., *Frontiero* v *Richardson*, 411 US 677 (1973), striking down, as unconstitutional gender discrimination, a federal statute that permitted male members of the armed forces – but not female members – to obtain dependents' benefits for their spouses in certain circumstances. I cannot imagine that this gender discrimination was an important part of the legislative program.

needs to be conjured with in considering the constitutionality of anti-abortion laws). In addition to that aspect of inequality, it was also well known at the time of *Roe* v *Wade* that relatively affluent people in the United States could get safe abortions when they wished, even when they lived in states where abortions were illegal. This situation had become more marked as some states repealed or changed their strict abortion laws (thus permitting women, with the means to do so, to travel to another state to obtain abortions) and as enforcement of existing criminal laws against abortions performed by private physicians in private facilities became increasingly lax. The real impact of the laws struck down in *Roe* v *Wade* was on poor people, and even here the result of the laws was more often to cause illegal, unsafe abortions than to eliminate abortions or substantially reduce their incidence. This situation is not unique. For example, the real impact of the anti-contraceptive laws struck down by the United States Supreme Court in *Griswold* v *Connecticut* was, similarly, to prevent the establishment of birth control clinics primarily serving the poor; contraceptives and contraceptive information were quite available to more affluent people, even in states where they were technically illegal. When judicial enforcement of fundamental rights primarily achieves equal application of those rights, so that the rights of the disadvantaged come more into line with those of the affluent, it is difficult, in my view, to characterize the resulting situation as undemocratic.

Enforcing a Bill of Rights

Aryeh Neier*

It is not easy to enforce a bill of rights. It is not easy because it means, necessarily, that one is confronting those institutions which have the power, and have used the power to deprive people of their rights. It means that one is confronting the executive branch as well as the legislative branch of the government. Those are the branches of government that have power. Alexander Hamilton, writing in the *Federalist Papers*, noted that courts – to which those who try to enforce the Bill of Rights in the United States frequently repair – lack control over the sword or the purse; all they have is judgment. They have to use their judgment to confront those institutions in society that deprive other people of rights. Ordinarily, when deprivations of rights take place, it is not because a legislative or executive branch of government has been careless. It is because it *matters significantly* to the executive branch and to the legislative branch of government to deprive people of their rights. One does not go up against the executive and legislative branches of government with either the sword or with the purse. One has to use judgment. The important question is: how to get that judgment respected by the branches of government that have the power to deprive individuals of their rights? That is a central question, with which anyone who tries to enforce a bill of rights must be concerned. There are some fairly obvious answers, but I think that they are worth enumerating.

First, those who try to enforce rights against those who have power must have at least prestige in order to confront power. If courts are going to be the instrument for enforcing rights against those who control the sword and the purse, prestige is the very least that they can use as a weapon on their behalf. In

---

* Aryeh Neier is Vice-Chairman of the United States Helsinki Watch and Americas Watch Committees in New York.

the history of the United States, courts have sometimes been prestigious, and they have been able to enforce their decisions on rights because of this. Sometimes they have lacked prestige and have inflicted wounds upon themselves, which have made it impossible for them to enforce their decisions on rights.

During the Civil War in the United States, President Lincoln ignored a decision by the Chief Justice of the Supreme Court in a case involving rights. The reason that President Lincoln was able to ignore a decision by the Chief Justice of the United States Supreme Court attempting to enforce rights is that the Chief Justice completely lacked prestige. He had so damaged himself by a decision with which he is identified in history that he had no moral suasion over the president of the United States, and was unable to secure compliance with his decision.[1]

The Chief Justice of the United States, Justice Taney, had been the architect of the United States Supreme Court's decision in the *Dred Scott* case.[2] In this case, the Supreme Court said that the principal question that was involved in a case involving a slave was a denial of the rights of the slaveholder to his property, namely, the slave. The *Dred Scott* decision overturned an effort by the Congress of the United States to avoid the kind of confrontation, which ultimately helped to bring on the Civil War. The decision deprived the Supreme Court, over which Chief Justice Taney presided, of the prestige that was needed to enforce rights during the Civil War. Justice Taney himself, as the personification of the Supreme Court, was the person most lacking in the prestige needed to enforce rights.

This question of the prestige of the courts, and their ability to use prestige to enforce rights, has been a recurring question in the history of the United States. One of the most familiar areas deals with the controversy over the role of the United States Supreme Court in enforcing its decisions on school segregation. The United States Supreme Court was very frequently in the position of confronting recalcitrant governors, state legislatures, and school board administrators. Time and time again, the Court had to rely on its prestige in order to secure compliance with its decisions.

In these instances, the Supreme Court had enormous prestige but it did not necessarily reflect the popularity of its decisions. In the areas of the country in which the Supreme Court was trying to enforce its decisions requiring

1 See *Ex parte Merryman*, 17 Fed. Cas. 144 (no 9487) (CCD Md. 1861). Lincoln's actions regarding the suspension of habeas corpus were subsequently authorized by Congress. See George C. Sellery, *Lincoln's Suspension of Habeas Corpus as Viewed by Congress*, Bulletin of the University of Wisconsin, no 149. History series, v 1, no 3 (Madison, Wis: University of Wisconsin, 1907), pp 213–86.
2 *Scott* v *Sandford*, 19 How. (60 US) 393 (1857)

the desegregation of the schools, to say that the Supreme Court was unpopular would be a vast understatement. And yet, despite its unpopularity, it had prestige.

It is important to note that prestige and popularity are entirely separate phenomena. It is possible for enforcers of a bill of rights to be simultaneously extremely prestigious and, at the same time, extremely unpopular. What is required is a sense that the institution deserves respect. It may be an extremely grudging respect, but the institution earns respect because there is an apparent or perceived morality to its decision-making. There is an apparent rightness about its involvement in the making of decisions. Making certain that there is that apparent morality and apparent rightness in making a decision, even though it may be enormously unpopular, has been essential in building prestige for those who try to enforce a bill of rights.

It is also necessary for those who enforce a bill of rights to be persuasive. If they are not persuasive, they do not have a chance. Those who try to enforce a bill of rights must make it plain what the interests are that they are trying to protect, and whether those interests are worthy of protection. If they fail to do so, they risk disregard or circumvention of their decisions. The number of examples available could be multiplied endlessly, but two will suffice.

One very important decision of the United States Supreme Court came in 1961, when the Supreme Court held that it was improper for the states to use illegally obtained evidence – that is, evidence obtained in disregard of the laws which regulate search and seizure – in prosecuting criminal defendants.[3] Up until that time, it had been improper for the federal government to use illegally seized evidence in criminal prosecutions. In 1961, for the first time the United States Supreme Court held that the states could not use illegally seized evidence. That decision was extremely controversial and, unfortunately, the proponents of that decision, including the Supreme Court itself, were extremely unpersuasive in trying to explain why that was a just decision. I think the decision could have been explained persuasively but it was not. There has only been token compliance with that decision since it was handed down. Anyone who is familiar with the day-to-day practices of the lower criminal courts in the United States is well aware that there has never been significant compliance with it.

A phenomenon that developed about a year after that decision has acquired a peculiar name in the lower criminal courts of the United States. An enormous number of criminal defendants suddenly developed a new disease that became known as 'dropsy.' Dropsy had these symptoms. Every time a police

[3] *Marcus* v *Search Warrant*, 367 US 717 (1961)

officer approached a criminal defendant in a gambling case or a narcotics case, the criminal defendant became extremely apprehensive and reached into his pocket and proceeded to drop an envelope to the ground, which the police officer promptly found. The police officer, having found this envelope, never had to conduct a physical search of the person who was afflicted with this disease; or at least that is the way police officers testified when they came into criminal court. They circumvented the prohibition on using illegally seized evidence in order to obtain convictions. In the United States, in more recent years, in the enormous number of prosecutions that involved possession of marijuana, most arose out of a mobile variety of the dropsy case.

Here is how it has worked. Police officers stop cars and, if they see young people, they say that they smelled marijuana smoke. This avoids the need for a search in order to determine that there is cause to believe that the person might have had marijuana. Alternatively, the police officer says that, as the motorist was identifying himself to the police officer, the motorist reached into this pocket to pull out his driver's licence and managed to pull out the marijuana and hand it to the police officer at the same time. Sometimes the police officer testified that the marijuana was lying in plain view on the seat. This is 'mobile dropsy,' the up-to-date version of what was invented about 1962, a year after the Supreme Court's decision on illegally seized evidence.

The ingenuity of police officers in circumventing this particular decision has been very great. What is involved here is a perception by police, and a perception by judges who listen to these stories told time and time again, that, after all, the right thing to do is to convict the person, if the person was carrying some kind of contraband. This rule about illegally seized evidence is, after all, a technicality that need not be obeyed. That reflects a failure on the part of the proponents of the rule that illegally seized evidence should not be used in order to convict a criminal defendant. Their constitutional arguments about rights were nor persuasive; they were not persuasive to the police; they were not persuasive to state court criminal judges; they were not persuasive to most of the people in the United States. Though there is a Supreme Court decision from on high saying that this illegally seized evidence cannot be used, those who try to enforce the Bill of Rights ought not to fool themselves. They have not succeeded in enforcing the provisions of the Bill of Rights which prohibit illegal searches and seizures. They have only managed to enforce that provision of the Bill of Rights in name; they have not managed to enforce that provision of the Bill of Rights in practice.

There are similar problems that arise in enforcing the Bill of Rights in many of the large institutions to which American courts have tried to apply bill of rights principles. A large number of prisons, mental hospitals, institutions for the mentally retarded and juvenile institutions in the United States have been targets of litigation because of abhorrent practices that have taken place within those institutions. In some instances, courts have succeeded in dealing with the most severe abuses that take place in those institutions. Very often, they have acted under the provision of the Bill of Rights which prohibits 'cruel and unusual punishment.' When the circumstances of confinement get to be particularly bizarre, American courts say, 'That is cruel and unusual punishment – You may not deal with a human being in this way. Even if you must confine the person in an institution because the person is mentally ill or because the person is a criminal or because the person is mentally retarded he does not lose all rights.' Unfortunately, a great many of the decisions that courts have handed down, trying to enforce the Bill of Rights in those circumstances, have been ignored or circumvented. This also represents a failure to be sufficiently persuasive. Those who become aware of what actually takes place in those institutions are persuaded that this kind of enforcement of the Bill of Rights is necessary. But to the public as a whole, that message has not 'gotten through.' Accordingly, the public is not persuaded that it is right for courts to interfere in the administration of these institutions. The consequence is that the enforcement is often lacking.

In trying to enforce a bill of rights, it is very important that the would-be enforcers engage in political opportunism. That is, there are moments when it is more likely that they will succeed in enforcing the Bill of Rights. They should not allow those moments to pass because they may not have another chance to do so. Perhaps the most famous example of an attempt to enforce the Bill of Rights (and here I am using the term 'bill of rights' in an extended sense to encompass the post-Civil War amendments that guarantee equal protection under the law) was the decision of the United States Supreme Court in *Brown* v *Board of Education* in 1954.[4] That is an extraordinary case from many standpoints. One standpoint from which it is extraordinary is that at no time prior to that in the history of the United States, or perhaps in the history of any country, did a court try to take unto itself the responsibility for dealing with so vast a social problem.

We do not think of courts, or at least we did not think of courts prior to the time of *Brown* v *Board of Education*, as capable of taking on such large enterprises as desegregating the schools. The number of people directly affected was very large. In the south, there were some three million black children and nine million white children who were directly affected by the United

---

4 *Brown* v *Board of Education*, 347 US 483 (1954)

States Supreme Court's decision in *Brown*. The Court made it clear, in the way in which it went about deciding the case, that it understood that it was not dealing with one school and the set of circumstances in one school. It dealt with cases simultaneously from four states and the District of Columbia to make it plain that it was trying in one stroke (subsequently it became many strokes) to end segregation of the schools in the United States.

The political opportunism that was involved in *Brown* (I am presenting a revisionist view of *Brown*) seems to me to be reflected in the editorial reactions that appeared in newspapers throughout the United States immediately after the decision. The year was 1954, the height of the Cold War period. One of the great concerns of the United States was a Cold War competition with the Soviet Union for the loyalties and affections of the newly independent non-white nations of the world. If one reads the editorials that appeared in American newspapers in the immediate aftermath of the decision in *Brown*, there was much more concern about how the decision would affect the Cold War struggle than how the decision would affect what happened in the schools.

The *New York Times* editorial was typical. It said, 'When some hostile propagandist rises in Moscow or Peking to accuse us of being a class society, we cannot do better than cite the courageous words of yesterday's opinion.'[5] The *Washington Post* and *Times-Herald* said, 'It will help us to refurbish American prestige in a world which looks to this land for moral inspiration ...'[6] The *San Francisco Chronicle* said, 'Great as the impact ... will be upon the states of the South ... still greater, we believe, will be its impact in South America, Africa and Asia, to this country's lasting honor and benefit.'[7] The Minneapolis *Tribune* said, '... the words of Chief Justice Warren will echo far beyond our borders and may greatly influence our relations with dark-skinned peoples ... the world over.'[8] The *St. Louis Post-Dispatch* said, 'The greater significance is the affirmation in the eyes of millions of people in India, Pakistan and Africa, in China, Japan, Burma, in Indo-China, Thailand and Indonesia that the pledge in the United States of the worth and the dignity of the humblest individual means exactly what it says. Had this decision gone the other way, the loss to the free world and its struggle against Communist encroachment would have been incalculable.'[9] The *Hartford*

5 'Editorial Excerpts from the Nation's Press on Segregation Ruling,' *New York Times*, 19 May 1954, p 19
6 *Ibid*
7 *Ibid*
8 *Ibid*
9 'Editorial Excerpts on School Bias Ruling,' *New York Times*, 19 May 1954, p 19

Courant said, '[The decision] ... may have even deeper and more encouraging impact outside our borders.'[10] The Chattanooga *Times* said, 'Internationally, opinion will benefit this nation in a time of great crisis countering one of the most effective talking points of ... Communist propaganda.'[11]

Curiously, black newspapers echoed the same theme. The *Pittsburgh Courier* said, 'This clarion announcement will also stun and silence America's communist traducers behind the Iron Curtain. It will effectively impress upon millions of colored people in Asia and Africa the fact that idealism and social morality can and do prevail in the United States ... regardless of race, creed or color.'[12] The *Chicago Defender* said, 'Neither the atom bomb nor the hydrogen bomb will ever be as meaningful to our democracy.'[13] The *Atlanta Daily World* said, 'It will strengthen the position of our nation in carrying out the imposed duties of world leadership.'[14] The *Boston Chronicle* said, '... it strengthens incalculably the diplomatic efficiency of our Government.'[15] The tersest summation of this point of view was from congressman Adam Clayton Powell, perhaps the best known black leader in the United States at the time. He called it 'communism's worst defeat ... democracy's shining hour.'[16]

This was not an accidental consequence of the Supreme Court's decision in *Brown*. I think that the Truman administration, which took part in the initial presentation of the case to the United States Supreme Court, by filing an *amicus* brief in 1952, was very plain in telling the Court of the importance of deciding this case in order to serve foreign policy needs. The Truman administration's brief had a seven-page section, which stated the interest of *amicus*. Of those seven pages, five pages were devoted to the foreign policy reasons for desegregation, including a two-page letter from the Secretary of State telling the United States Supreme Court how important it was for United States foreign policy that the Supreme Court end segregation of the schools.

At that moment in history, this was a pre-eminent concern of the nation. The Truman administration had told this to the Supreme Court in several other 'friend of the court briefs' that it filed with the United States Supreme

10 'Editorial Excerpts from the Nation's Press on Segregation Ruling,' *New York Times*, 18 May 1954, p 19
11 *Ibid*
12 *Ibid*
13 *Ibid*
14 *Ibid*
15 'Editorial Excerpts on School Bias Ruling,' *New York Times*, 19 May 1954, p 20
16 'Civil Groups Hail Anti-Bias Ruling,' *New York Times*, 19 May 1954, p 21

Court between 1950 and 1952. The problem of segregation could not be dealt with by any other institution of the United States government. The executive branch of the federal government lacked the power to deal with desegregation of the schools because the schools were controlled by the states. The Congress of the United States would not act because the Congress was dominated by members from the deep south. The southern state legislatures, which had direct control over the schools, would not act because they were committed to segregation. Yet the executive branch of the federal government had a foreign policy problem – this Cold War competition. It had no way of dealing with this foreign policy problem except by going to the United States Supreme Court.

Prior to the Supreme Court's *Brown* decision, the Court had heard a series of cases that involved less sweeping challenges to segregation. They were cases very carefully chosen by the NAACP Legal Defense Fund. The cases involved black students who were not allowed to attend graduate schools in their own states. Separate but equal graduate schools did not exist. The Supreme Court decided that, in those individual cases, desegregation was required.[17] But those cases involved a handful of graduate students. It was an enormous jump to go from admitting a handful of graduate students to previously all-white institutions to deciding that schools attended by nine million white children and three million black children had to be desegregated and where several hundred thousand teaching jobs were involved that would also be affected by school desegregation.

The enforcement of the Bill of Rights was made possible by the politically opportune circumstances of the moment: the Cold War competition with the Soviet Union for the affections of the newly independent non-white nations. Therefore, it was possible to persuade the Supreme Court to act. The Supreme Court decision was viewed, as indicated by the newspaper editorials, to be a triumph for the United States in the Cold War competition. The apparent morality of the decision was enormously enhanced. At that moment in the history of the United States, it was very important to Americans that they see their system as a moral system in confronting the challenge of world communism. The *Brown* decision, perhaps more than anything else that took place at that junction in American history, confirmed to Americans the morality of their system. 'See, we have dealt with this overwhelming problem on our own. We have solved it through the legal process.' In my view, the Supreme Court enormously enhanced its prestige by the *Brown* decision. As a direct consequence it became, in the decade, two decades, and even

---

17 *Sipuel* v *Board of Regents*, 332 US 631 (1948)

three decades beyond *Brown*, a far more effective instrument for enforcing the Bill of Rights than it had been at any time previously.

In the last decade, the Supreme Court has been dominated by justices who seem intent on turning back the clock on many of the decisions of the era associated with Chief Justice Earl Warren. Yet they have not done so to any significant extent. The momentum the Supreme Court acquired at the time of *Brown* was carried forward up to now, and may still be carrying forward.

There is another element to this enforcement process which is very important: resoluteness. In the period following *Brown*, despite the enormous prestige of the Supreme Court, there was considerable defiance of Supreme Court decisions. For a decade and more following *Brown*, the Supreme Court did not waver in the face of defiance. During that period, the Supreme Court was always unanimous in its decisions on school desegregation matters.

Max Weber has suggested that one of the forms of authority is charismatic authority. In my view, the Supreme Court, as an institution, acquired charismatic authority during the decade following the *Brown* decision. This charismatic authority was transformed over time into what Weber would describe as traditional authority: that is, it is this way because it has always been this way; this authority is deciding in this way because this authority has always decided this way. That is the way it came to appear. Very much was achieved by the Supreme Court's resoluteness in the face of the defiance inspired by *Brown*.

When the *Brown* decision was handed down, Dwight Eisenhower was president. Eisenhower had not participated in the effort to persuade the Supreme Court to decide *Brown* in the way it was decided. Yet the Supreme Court may have received a wrong signal because *Brown* was re-argued in the first year of Eisenhower's presidency. Re-argument focused on one question: the historical meaning of the Fourteenth Amendment. Eisenhower did not himself play any significant part in determining the way in which the executive branch of the federal government took part in that proceeding. He left it to his Attorney General, Herbert Brownell Jr, who took a very strong position, stronger in some ways than the NAACP Legal Defense Fund. The Attorney General's position was that the Fourteenth Amendment required the school desegregation decision and was *intended* to require it. The Supreme Court ultimately said that the history of the Fourteenth Amendment was not conclusive on this point, but it must have had the impression from the role played by Eisenhower's Attorney General that Eisenhower was on the same track as the Truman administration. The Court must have been very disappointed subsequently by the fact that Dwight Eisenhower denied the

Supreme Court the public expressions of support that it probably thought it was entitled to after the decision. But even Dwight Eisenhower, who was at best unenthusiastic about the *Brown* decision, was compelled to send troops to Arkansas in order to enforce compliance with the Supreme Court decision. This happened shortly after he insisted that he would never do such a thing.[18] Ultimately, the prestige the Court acquired because of its resoluteness, because of the moral authority of the decision – enhanced enormously by the moral authority it gave the United States in international competition with the Soviet Union – made it necessary for Dwight Eisenhower to use the power of the sword in order to back up the decision that resulted from the Supreme Court's judgment.

In conclusion, one must consider those aspects of enforcement that I have mentioned as being all of a piece. They relate to each other. Sensitivity to what is taking place politically is an essential ingredient of enforcement. Resoluteness contributes to the prestige of the institution of enforcement. The prestige of the institution engaged in enforcement contributes to its persuasiveness. Persuasiveness is essential if enforcement is not to be token but is to be real. Persuasiveness is impossible without sensitivity to political circumstances – which brings one back full circle.

COMMENTARIES

QUESTION I would suggest to you that the Supreme Court is merely a manifestation of those who you referred to as 'holders of the sword and the purse,' the elites who gave us our inalienable rights. At times when economic prosperity abounds, the decisions of the Court reflect that. The courts are being looked after by those who carry the sword. Are the courts able to hand out decisions on the enforcement of the Bill of Rights in a fair and just manner? I would suggest to you that in times of economic hardship in either the United States or Canada (we will soon see how Canadian courts respond), courts, particularly the Supreme Courts will tend to be more conservative in their outlook as it is not in their best interest to become embroiled in the political process. Rockefeller and his Trilateral Commission suggested something similar to that: as economic times became hard, so infringement of individual rights would become greater. I was wondering how you felt about such issues.

18 US President, *Public Papers of the Presidents of the United States* (Washington, DC: Office of the *Federal Register*, National Archives and Records Service, 1953–), Dwight D. Eisenhower, 1957, p 546

ARYEH NEIER In a very broad sense, I think there is something to that, because when times are difficult, the pressures are greater and it is more likely that the rights will be abridged. But I am not an economic determinist and I do not think it is accurate to say that a court necessarily reflects the other institutions of government because it responds to different pressures. One of the pressures that it responds to is its own previous decisions, its own traditions. Such decisions have an impact on the way in which a court acts. I will use the example of the way in which the Supreme Court of the United States has performed during the past decade. Certainly at the beginning of the last decade there was no special economic difficulty within the United States. The early 1970s were very good times economically for the United States. Yet, during that period, there were a number of people appointed to the Supreme Court who had far more restricted views of rights than was characteristic of the Court as a whole in the previous decade and a half. I think that their predilections may have been to cut back on individual rights. At the same time, the momentum of the previous decade and a half had a great impact on them. The Court had established traditions during that period. The Supreme Court of that period was not particularly damaging to individual rights. There were cases which set back the cause of individual rights, and those that advanced them. Now the economic climate in the United States is much worse, but there is no discernible impact on that deterioration of economic circumstances on the decisions of the United States Supreme Court.
COMMENT You yourself mentioned though, that the Supreme Court today has been trying to turn back some of those decisions.
ARYEH NEIER I said it has been ineffectual in turning them back because, if one were an economic determinist, this would affect not just the justices on the Supreme Court but also the justices on the lower courts. As it happens, one of the major reasons why the Supreme Court of the United States is ineffectual in cutting back on the enforcement of rights is the fact that the lower federal courts in the United States continue to be extremely aggressive in enforcing rights. Some of them are extraordinarily good at finding those places within decisions of the current Supreme Court which still permit them to enforce rights very effectively. I do not see that the economic circumstances of the country have had an effect on the judges of our lower federal courts.
QUESTION In the Canadian context, I am curious as to how rights can be enforced when we have a Charter of Rights with a 'notwithstanding' clause which will enable certain provinces, if they wish, to opt out of certain rights which will go unrecognized in their jurisdictions. How do you enforce a

charter that applies only in some areas of the Court's jurisdiction and not in others? How do you gain this respect for your moral authorities when people in one part of the country can look across the provincial boundary and see that people in the next province have more or fewer rights?

ARYEH NEIER I think that is a very serious problem. One of the important characteristics of the *Brown* decision was its universality. It applied everywhere and the Supreme Court had to go to considerable lengths to apply that decision to Washington, DC because it decided that the equal protection clause of the Fourteenth Amendment required school desegregation in the states. The Fourteenth Amendment does not apply to Washington, DC, which is not a state. Therefore, the Supreme Court had to stretch quite far, in effect, to read that guarantee of equal protection into the 'due process' clause of the Fifth Amendment. The universality, the fact that it applied everywhere, was part of the apparent morality of the decision, and part of what secured respect for it. The notion that rights are *not* different from one place to another is an important part of the process of gaining respect for the idea of rights. That is not the only way that one gains respect for the idea of rights and for the enforcement of rights. Respect for the Court has a lot to do with the cases which the Court chooses as the vehicles for its important decisions on rights and the way in which the courts conduct themselves in handing down the decisions. Much depends upon what they say in their opinions, the rationale that they provide, and whether that rationale is persuasive. I do not believe that it is possible to predict whether the courts in Canada will be successful in inculcating respect for decisions without actually seeing how they go about the process. There may be more fortuitous factors, which help to determine how successful they are in inculcating respect for rights.

QUESTION In the Canadian political context, we have a province where there are serious disagreements between the French majority and the English minority. Which right becomes salient, under the Charter of Rights, as to whether or not Quebec can protect its language against erosion by ensuring that French becomes the official language in Quebec? Do you give salience to the individual person, who may choose to speak English and therefore may be undermining the French language, over a long period of time, in that province? Does the province of Quebec or does the individual become salient?

ARYEH NEIER I would guess that ninety per cent of the people in this room have thought about that question more than I have so I really do not feel that I should hazard a response to it. The only thing I want to say is that we do have some analagous problems in the United States. One of those involves the Indian Bill of Rights Act, which imposes certain due process requirements on the way in which punishments are meted out in Indian tribal courts. It has been argued by a number of Indians, and others, that in the process of protecting the rights of the individual against the Indian tribe which could impose punishment on him, tribal authority has been undermined, and in the process has helped to destroy tribal culture. If we think of one of the values that is inherent in a bill of rights, the value of diversity, the value of pluralism, then the Indian Bill of Rights Act helps to destroy exactly that which it says that it intended to protect. There are no easy answers to questions of that sort. The answer to which I incline is that when the burden on the individual is very severe, it is the individual who ought to be protected. When it is possible to promote cultural diversity without imposing severe burdens on the individual, then I would move in the direction of trying to support cultural diversity. Individual cases, though, can get horrendously complicated.

QUESTION In the United States, several situations have arisen where clauses have been put into the Constitution due to civil disobedience. What is your view of using this tactic to promote the expansion of rights? What other means are available to the electorate to shape or to get their opinions through to the people who actually make the decisions?

ARYEH NEIER All of the means that are available to deal with any other issue in a democratic society. One speaks, one organizes, one acts politically, one acts through interest groups, one uses the machinery of communication. Sometimes that involves efforts to do dramatic things in order to attract more attention to one's point of view. If one uses the example of civil disobedience that is an example of an attempt to use a dramatic method. The drama occurs because one is doing something against the law and, therefore, one is inviting punishment of oneself as a way of expressing strongly the way one feels about something. Civil disobedience is an effective way of expressing oneself if one is willing to take that punishment that is provided by the law. It becomes very ineffective if the person both violates the law and then tries to avoid the punishment that comes from transgressing the law. At that point, it very often produces a backlash in popular opinion.

QUESTION You have had considerable experience in connection with the New York and the American Civil Liberties Union as a strategist in promoting human rights and civil liberties. If you reflect on the prospective situation in Canada with the Charter of Rights and Freedoms, and drawing upon the experience you have had in the 1960s and 70s, what kind of advice would you give to interest groups such as the Canadian Civil Liberties Association as to how to go about seeking to promote implementation of the Charter of

Rights and Freedoms for the promotion of civil rights, human rights and civil liberties in Canada?

ARYEH NEIER One of the lessons from the United States relates to the fact that when campaigns to provoke rights were carefully planned, and litigation strategy was thought out and accompanied by public education efforts, the chances of success were greater. When some effort was made to coordinate what was done in litigation efforts with what was done in legislative efforts, there was far more success in promoting rights than if cases involving rights came up haphazardly to the courts. If they came up haphazardly, they very often did so with incomplete factual evidence, which tended to invite bad decisions. They came up without the arguments having been thought through and without the information that needed to be presented to courts having been assembled effectively. The careful planning of litigation seems to be enormously important, and it is especially significant that litigation not be considered as something separate unto itself. If it is to be used effectively to promote rights, it must be coordinated with efforts to promote rights in other forums through public education and through legislative efforts.

QUESTION You pointed out that in enforcing a bill of rights, the ability of the Court to enforce those rights is directly related to its prestige. In Canada, where the Supreme Court has not as much prestige as in the United States, and where the political parties have far more power, how do you see the role of the Supreme Court? Will its decisions be enforced?

ARYEH NEIER A court only acquires prestige as a consequence of the things that it does. It does not start out with prestige. The United States Supreme Court acquired enormous prestige by deciding *Brown* v *Board of Education* at the time that it did. That prestige made it possible for the United States Supreme Court to become an infinitely greater instrument for enforcing the Bill of Rights in the period thereafter than it could have been except for that decision. At other times, the United States Supreme Court has done things which have diminished its prestige and have made it an ineffective instrument for promoting rights. A court to a very large extent controls its own prestige, the quality of its own thinking, and the quality of its persuasiveness. The adherence to principle and the apparent morality of its decisions are the ingredients of prestige. They must also possess sensitivity to the political winds that blow in the country.

QUESTION Do you think that the Supreme Court ought to be sensitive to the dominant or ruling political party?

ARYEH NEIER No. What I certainly do not mean is that the Court ought to go with the political party or the political movement that is strongest. That would be a betrayal of the responsibility of a court. But there are times when enforcing rights, in what would ordinarily be difficult circumstances, is made easier because there is great public concern over something which coincides with a move to enforce rights. At a moment when there has been a great scandal about electronic eavesdropping, it is easier for a court to deal with the problem of political surveillance than it might be on some other occasion. When I say that a court ought to be sensitive to the political wind, that is what I have in mind. I certainly do not have in mind that a court ought to be deferential to partisan political forces or those forces that happen to have political strength in a country.

QUESTION Let us take the discussion one step further and ask you as an active participant in Watch Committee functions that operate in other countries: how would you respond to the criticism that the United States is overstepping its boundaries by trying to impose its values and ideals about human rights on other countries?

ARYEH NEIER One, it is true. Beyond that, I am very much in favour of the United States trying to promote individual rights beyond its own borders. The question is *how* does it promote individual rights beyond its own borders? Does it invade a country or destabilize a country because it believes that country is engaged in some abuse of its rights? Does it try to influence a country in other ways, such as selling arms to a country that is systematically abusing the rights of its own citizens? There are benign ways of trying to promote human rights and I very much endorse those. There are also malevolent ways of trying to promote conformance with the values that happen to be held by the United States and I oppose those equally strongly.

PART THREE: THE CANADIAN PERSPECTIVE ON RIGHTS

Rights and Constitutional Change in Canada: A Roundtable Discussion

S.J.R. NOEL I am struck by the repeated emphasis on the part of our American colleagues on the extent to which rights in the United States are involved in the political process. Rights, it has been stressed, have to be seen within the political framework. Also, we have been constantly reminded that the American conception of rights entails primarily those rights which are *individual* rights. This conception is, of course, by no means alien to people in Canada, but it is not the *main* conception of rights in Canada as I understand it. The stress here has been always primarily on rights conceived as *collective* or *community* rights. The only rights embodied in the BNA Act, for example, are rights of this kind. There is no mention whatsoever of individual rights.

Now, in the Constitution Act, 1982, individual rights have found a place. But historically, in the Canadian political process, conflicts over rights have revolved not so much around differing conceptions of individual rights as around differing conceptions of collective rights – such as language rights, education rights, and, more recently, rights to the control of natural resources. By embodying individual rights in the Canadian constitution, we may well be ensuring that they will become a more important focus of political conflict than they have been in the past. Hence, I think, the relevance of the American experience to us. We will increasingly be taking note of American precedents and comparisons will naturally be made between judicial decisions in Canada and those in the United States. I do not think the tension within the Canadian political system over collective or community rights and individual rights is going to disappear. We are going to have, I think, considerable discordance arising from them. With these few observations, I thought perhaps we could make some further comparisons of rights in the Canadian and American systems.

WILLIAM MCKERCHER I would like to address a question to our American colleagues with regard to legislating for or against rights in relation to the question of legislative jurisdiction. In Canada, there are two jurisdictions of legislative authority, provincial and federal. These jurisdictions, under a 'divided' parliamentary sovereignty, may define, enhance, or restrict the individual rights of Canadians. In the American system, there are two jurisdictions as well, but there also seems to be an area wherein *no* government may legislate.

Pierre Trudeau has suggested with an eye towards the American experience that if Canadians adopted a charter of rights and freedoms, they too would be protected from zealous governments and no government would be able to infringe upon their entrenched rights. Is there any merit in the belief that an area of human endeavour can be thus constitutionally removed from the legislative area, and does the American Constitution in fact attempt to do so?

PAUL BENDER It is very hard to make absolute, unqualified statements about this, but in general I think it is true in the American system. The qualifications are that none of the rights in the American system are absolute. None of them that I know of are such that they exist independent of governmental justifications. Speech, for example, is a very highly protected right, but if there is sufficiently strong governmental justification it can be made a crime to utter certain phrases. Therefore, subject to the qualification that there is almost always the possibility of a sufficiently strong overriding interest, there are areas where government may not legislate. They may not, in this sense, legislate on thought, conscience, or freedom of religion, or on certain aspects of privacy. Neither the federal nor the state nor the local governments can make regulations or prohibitions in these areas. They can legislate only in the sense of giving remedies to individuals when those rights are impinged upon. For example, in the case of freedom of religion, the federal government has the power, under the enabling clause in section 5 of the Fourteenth Amendment, to give civil or criminal remedies for violations of that right. If a policeman violates my freedom of religion by arresting me for going to church, or for wearing a religious symbol, I can bring a civil action against that policeman. The right to take civil action is given to me by the federal government. In that sense, they can legislate. But neither the federal nor the state nor the local governments can legislate or interfere with the exercise of that right unless there is an enormously strong governmental justification.

PAUL MURPHY Let me add an historical note. The original Constitution did not include a Bill of Rights. One of the justifications which was given at the time when criticism was raised was that since the federal government has only enumerated powers, the states presumably have everything that is left. There is no need to limit the federal government since its power is specifically delegated and it obviously cannot do things that it is not given the power to do in the original charter. A lot of people were concerned about this and the Tenth Amendment of the Constitution reinforced this particular line of argument. Presumably, the federal government does not have the authority to legislate in an area like freedom of the press.

QUESTION I wonder if Professor Bender would be good enough to address the matter of the civil rights injunction as a technique for enforcing rights. Is that something which is within the original jurisdiction of the courts in the United States or is it an authority granted through legislation, and how effective is it?

PAUL BENDER An action by a private individual to restrain the government is very common in the United States, especially in the last twenty or thirty years. The principal statute creating the cause of action is Title 42, the United States Code section 1983 (at the present time, the designation has changed over the years). The more difficult technical problem has been what happens when a federal official, for example, an FBI agent, violates your rights. That is what the *Bivens*[1] case was about. There, there was no statute creating a cause of action, and the *Bivens* case said we will imply cause of action from the Constitution. I think the Supreme Court was influenced there by the feeling that if there were a federal cause of action only against state officials who violate the Constitution, it would not make much sense. So we now have a system where you can sue for injunction against any governmental official in the United States whom you believe is violating your constitutional rights. The chances of getting such cases decided on their merits are quite good.

It applies even in criminal cases, even to enjoining the operations of criminal statutes. I just represented, for example, in the State of Pennsylvania, a newspaper publisher who was subjected to a new ordinance that stopped him from distributing papers the way he wanted to, and instead of violating it, he obeyed the statute and sued for an injunction against the operation of the statute and he got his injunction. He is now free to violate the statute because there is an injunction enjoining the enforcement of the statute on the grounds that it was unconstitutional.

S.J.R. NOEL That, I think, illustrates one important difference between our two political systems. Such procedures in the United States are seen as a

---

1 *Bivens* v *Six Unknown Named Agents of the Federal Bureau of Narcotics*, 403 US 388 (1971)

means of enforcing a right, establishing a right, or expanding a right. But consider the reaction to a similar procedure in Canada, for example, if used by an English-speaking individual against the language legislation of Quebec. This might be seen, from the individual's point of view, as a means of obtaining his rights, but for the French-speaking majority in the community, it might be seen as an infringement of their rights. There is a fundamental difference of perception over procedures of this kind. I think Americans generally approve the successful use of such procedure. But there is a great deal of division over it in Canada.

ANDRÉ TREMBLAY Perhaps I could interject at this point to make a few comments about collective rights or group rights in Canada. There are, as you know, a few constitutions in the world that do recognize collective rights. One is the Belgian constitution, another the Canadian constitution. Canadians have collective rights in section 93 of the BNA Act, which concerns denominational schools and civil law. Section 133 deals with linguistic rights. The questions we can ask are the following: Are those rights, as recognized, still justified? They were recognized in 1867 because it was a precondition to Confederation. Quebec would not have participated in the federal union if those rights were not protected. As to their justification, obviously they are still justified, and I would say even more necessary. It is when they become suspect that the minority feels that federalism is not a good way to protect them. To my mind, collective rights mean justice for minorities who want to survive, who want to develop. I am not against the protection of individual rights, but Quebec's legitimate demands for collective rights have yet to be met. It is very hard to meet them because the leaders, who represented the majority in the recent constitutional negotiations, went too far in their demands. What worries me is that this constitution is the product of confrontation and means fewer collective rights, less justice for minorities, and more bitterness in Quebec. There will also be more confrontation. The Court of Appeals of Quebec or the Supreme Court of Canada will rule Bill 101 unconstitutional. It is contrary to section 23 of the Charter. The question is, to what extent is the minority bound to respect a decision which will remove its collective rights?

JAMES PENTON We could not only have conflict between collective rights and individual rights, but between different groups' collective rights. Look at the two sections of the BNA Act that you mentioned, section 93 and section 133. They do have collective rights for French-speaking Canadians, but they also have collective rights for English-speaking Canadians in Quebec. I think we are not really talking so much about individual rights versus collective rights, as different collective rights which come into conflict.

DAVID FLAHERTY Professor Tremblay, I do not understand exactly what you mean by collective rights.

ANDRÉ TREMBLAY Group rights or minority rights may be called collective rights – rights that are given to a specific community. It is not always the same minority that is protected in the BNA Act. The minority, which is protected in section 92, subsection 13, is the *whole* of Quebec. The minorities, which are protected in section 93, are mainly the Catholics outside of Quebec and the Protestants inside Quebec. The minority protected in section 133 is the Anglophone in Quebec.

JAMES PENTON I want to defend the Charter a bit. I have some objections to it, particularly section 15, and I have much more negative feelings towards the idea of collective rights than most Canadians, because my own personal experience as well as my studies lead me to believe that, when collective rights are stressed, they are the collective rights of the major entities within society at the expense of both individual rights and the collective rights of smaller groups. We live in a society in which Anglo-Saxons and French-Canadians, within their own respective bailiwicks, have been God. I hope that there will be some remedy under section 15 for some injustices. In Quebec, after something like seventy years of existence as a religious community, Jehovah's Witnesses still cannot solemnize marriages. In Ontario and Alberta, Scientologists cannot solemnize marriages. It is left to the entire discretion of the provincial governments. In Alberta, an official in charge of vital statistics determines who can and cannot solemnize marriages, and when one talks to him he says 'It is entirely up to me and I do not have to give any answers to anybody.'

It should also be noted that property rights fall entirely within provincial jurisdiction. The Communal Property Act of Alberta was recently upheld. A similar Act, apparently based on it in South Dakota, was declared unconstitutional. The Alberta Act was aimed specifically at Doukhobors and Hutterites. Others could set up a commune if they wanted to, but not Doukhobors and Hutterites. This is why I am hopeful of some dramatic changes on the basis of section 15.

WALTER BERNS Much of the mystery of the United States can be traced to the notion of collective rights which, for a long time, have gone under the name of 'states rights.' Most Americans understand this to be a code term for something else, namely the right to deny black people their rights. This notion of collective rights is advantageous to states rights advocates. Last summer, I served as the American representative in the United Nations Seminar on Human Rights, Peace and Development. There I encountered two arguments in combination that illustrate the problem. First, there was a demand on the part of economic development. The United States has consistently resisted that demand because they know what it means. It means that, where there is a right, there is a duty, and the Third World has the right, and the United States the duty. The other argument was that the right of economic development should be a collective right. One would have to say that there is a tendency for collective rights to be exercised by those who speak in the name of the collectivity – which means the government. So the government exercises its right, which the United Nations is supposed to recognize, to determine the *means* of that economic development. Many decided that economic development requires the collectivization of agriculture. There are some people who are going to stand in the way of this. They are known as kulaks. And when they stand in the way of this collective right, you kill them. If the United Nations recognizes this right, then the United Nations justifies the destruction of the kulaks. That is why one should not play this game.

I am not suggesting that what we have here in Canada is a facsimile of that, but finally, perhaps it is, because one will have to recognize that the community rights of Quebec would be exercised by the government of Quebec, which may be all right if everybody in Quebec were part of that community. The trouble is that there are some people in Quebec who insist that they have a 'trump,' and they point to the Canadian Charter of Rights and Freedoms. How does one resolve it without civil war?

S.J.R. NOEL Professor Berns points out the difficulties with a bill of rights in culturally segmented societies. Are these difficulties inevitable?

WALTER BERNS We had them in the United States and we know how it came out. More Americans were killed in the Civil War than in all American wars, if one excludes Vietnam.

S.J.R. NOEL But, unlike the United States, Canada has never had a civil war. One could reasonably argue it has not precisely because collective rights have been so widely recognized in this country.

JAMES PENTON Is that really true? What about French Canadians and French language groups in Anglo Canada? Up until very recently, the pattern has been to ignore them and to assimilate them. The Métis in Canada and the Indians and the Inuit were, at least until recently, ignored. When we talk about them, we realize that the rights of certain collectivities have been recognized because they have the political power to say, 'You must recognize us.' One cannot ignore the French in Quebec, but the French in Manitoba have long been treated as though they did not exist.

WALTER TARNOPOLSKY I do not doubt that the Charter and the whole constitutional resolution are going to continue to run into opposition in Quebec.

But it is not really correct to say that there is a conflict between individual and collective rights. The rights that we have in section 23 of the Charter are *group rights*. When we are talking about the right of an English-speaking parent, who is a citizen of Canada, to send his or her children to an English-speaking school, that is not an individual right, it is a group right. It is a group right of the English. We are not saying 'Every parent can send his or her children to whatever language school he or she wishes.' Once one recognizes a language for purposes of a school education, one is recognizing a group right. There *is* conflict between individual and group rights. What section 23 does is protect an English-speaking minority in Quebec (group rights) against an overriding majority, as well as a French-speaking minority elsewhere. There are no individual rights involved in that. There is no conflict with individual rights. It is between two different group rights.

If one goes through the whole Charter, I do not see that what the Charter does is a contradiction of the Quebec Charter of Human Rights and Freedoms. The Quebec Charter is the most extensive in Canada, and most of its provisions are duplicated in the Canadian Charter. There are also quite a few provisions in the Quebec Charter which are not in the Canadian Charter and which will obviously continue to operate. The Canadian Charter does not revoke the Quebec Charter. The Quebec Charter provides not only for the right to contact counsel, but also the right to inform the next of kin. I do not see why, under the Quebec Charter, that right does not continue. It is not touched by the fact that the Canadian Charter has a more limited right upon arrest or detention. Whatever might be considered in conflict with the federal Charter would also be in conflict with the Quebec Charter, except for the language provisions.

BARRY STRAYER It seems to me that there is only one likely conflict with Bill 101, and that is with the education clause in it which prevents Canadian anglophones moving into Quebec from sending their children to an English school unless the parents were educated in English in Quebec.

WILLIAM LEDERMAN However it comes about, our life in Canada is going to be a mixture of individual rights and collective or group rights of one kind or another. The tensions in the Charter between collective rights and individual rights are bound to emerge. Every time you prescribe reasonable limits for equality rights, every time you prescribe election machinery, every time you operate an affirmative action clause, you are going to get tension between some group right and some individual right – every time.

WALTER BERNS Why has Canada adopted this Charter of Rights, given the problems that seem to be on the horizon as a result of it? What do you hope to gain by it, or who will gain?

WALTER TARNOPOLSKY Ever since Prime Minister Trudeau made a submission to the Tremblay Commission in 1956 urging the inclusion of a charter in the constitution, it has been one of his fundamental principles. He said it at the beginning, and he said it again in 1967 when he was Minister of Justice, before he became Prime Minister. It was clear that there would not be a patriation of the constitution while he was Prime Minister that did not include a charter. It is as simple as that.

DAVID FLAHERTY An impression that may have been left with our American friends is that Quebec is opposed to the Charter. It might be worth clarifying what the situation is. What we apparently have is the current Quebec government being opposed to, but the overwhelming number of federal MPs from Quebec in support of, patriation *with the Charter*. Have there been public opinion polls in the province showing how people generally feel, given the fact that they have a provincial government which feels one way, and a federal government which feels the other? Is there a split in opinion in Quebec over the Charter?

ANDRÉ TREMBLAY We are good citizens of Canada. Last week, there was a seminar of judges in Montreal, and more than 150 of them came. They were very enthusiastic about the constitution and the Charter. We respect individual rights in Quebec. The point I made with regard to Bill 101 was that, because we voted 'No' in the referendum, our expectations were raised in the hope of a better form of accommodation for Quebec within Canada. When I meet with my students and we have a conversation, the feeling that we all have is that we have demands for collective rights which have not been met. We do not ignore individual rights, but Trudeau answered with individual rights only. The feeling is that individual rights have been used as a weapon to diminish collective rights.

DOUGLAS SCHMEISER Perhaps the problem is not one of individual versus collective rights. I think that is perhaps a red herring. Nor is it simply a problem of a national majority and a national minority having to work out some sort of balance between them. Rather, it is a problem of an overlapping national majority and national minority, a national majority which is English, and a national minority which is French. But we also have a French and Catholic provincial majority with an Anglo-Canadian minority in Quebec. It is an old problem, and an old question. How do you protect the English-Canadian minority in Quebec, or the French-Canadian minority in Alberta or Manitoba, while at the same time allowing the provincial majority to exercise its collective right?

The traditional solution has been a political one. But now we are looking for a legal solution through the Charter of Rights and Freedoms. The question we have to address is, is that the best way to go about it? Among other things, will the Court's judgments be accepted as legitimate? Will they be respected, or must we always fall back on political solutions in these matters? That is what we must think about. If the Court does strike down certain provisions of Bill 101, for example, will the government or the people of Quebec refuse to implement or obey the decision?

S.J.R. NOEL I would like to say one brief word on that. We should learn from our American colleagues who, from the beginning, have repeatedly stressed the involvement of rights in their political process. It is not realistic to think that they can somehow be taken out of the Canadian political process. Yet that process revolves around, and is driven by, collective concerns with the politics of accommodation between collectivities. If that is the case, where in that process will the Charter of Rights fit?

GORDON ROBERTSON I agree completely with what Professor Tremblay said about the high regard that the people of Quebec have for the Rule of Law. There is little question but that the general attitude of the population will be one of respect for what the courts decide. However, we have to recognize that the Charter of Rights was not accepted by the Government of Quebec. That fact is the more important because the Charter imposes certain limits on powers of the Assemblée nationale of Quebec that were previously unlimited. The powers of the Assemblée have traditionally been very jealously guarded by Quebec governments. There is cause to wonder, then, how the conflicting loyalties of the people will work out: loyalty on the one hand to the Rule of Law, and loyalty on the other to the provincial powers that have traditionally been seen as a prime guarantee of the security of the French culture and language of Quebec.

A further uncertainty is introduced by the conflicting claims of elected legislators to represent the true wishes of the people of Quebec. The government of Quebec, supported by the majority of the Assemblée nationale, has invariably been regarded as the 'spokesman' of the people of Quebec on all things relating to provincial jurisdiction and the position of the province as the political embodiment of the Quebec community. The Charter affects provincial jurisdiction so the provincial government would normally be seen as the voice of Quebec with regard to it – in that context at least. However, many Canadians, both in Quebec and in other provinces, have grave doubts whether the present Parti Québécois government, representing a party dedicated to the achievement of political sovereignty for Quebec, can be regarded as a valid spokesman on areas of constitutional change where the underlying assumption is the continuation of Canada as a federation of which Quebec would be a member. Such a continuation is obviously in conflict with the objective of taking Quebec out of confederation. The Lévesque government is clearly the government of Quebec, duly elected and supported by a majority in the Assemblée nationale. However, since it was defeated in the referendum of May 1980 on its basic constitutional proposition, is it genuinely representative of the people of Quebec when issues about the constitution of the federation are under review? The seventy-four Liberal members of Parliament elected from Quebec out of a total of seventy-five members from the province say it is not. They claim that they are at least as much, if not much more, the real voice of the Quebec people on such issues.

What it amounts to is that a cloud hangs over the Charter of Rights so far as Quebec is concerned. For all Quebeckers, it is a cloud of uncertainty. For some Quebeckers, it is a cloud of illegitimacy. These clouds may darken when conflict arises between the Charter and the Quebec Language Law, commonly known as Bill 101, with respect to the language of education.

Under the Quebec law, the governing provision for English-speaking parents embodies what is called the 'Quebec clause.' Such parents have the right to have their children educated in English, if either parent was educated in English in a Quebec school. Many English-speaking Quebeckers, who came to Quebec from other provinces or from outside Canada, are strenuously opposed to that narrow limitation of this right. The Charter of Rights states more broadly the right of parents of a linguistic minority, such as the English-speaking people of Quebec. They are, under the Charter, entitled to have their children educated in their own official language if they themselves were educated in it anywhere in Canada. This is referred to as the 'Canada clause.' It is clear that Bill 101 and the Charter are in conflict on this fundamental point. There are many English-speaking parents in Quebec, who were not educated in English in Quebec, who will want their children to be able to go to English language schools. In the circumstances, a challenge to the Quebec Language Law is inevitable.

There could not be a clash on a more sensitive issue in Quebec. The security of the French language and culture in the province is seen as fundamental. It has been thought to be seriously at risk for the future. The Quebec birth-rate has dropped sharply in recent years and is now the lowest of all the provinces of Canada. Immigrants to Quebec have tended to identify with the English-speaking community and to become English-speaking. The proportion of French-speaking people in Quebec accordingly dropped from 1951 onward. Successive governments tried to devise laws to stop the shrinkage of the French-speaking element of the population, and Bill 101 was the solution finally and laboriously achieved. It is widely accepted by the francophone population as necessary. It is also regarded as being at least as generous in result for the English-speaking of Quebec as are the situations of fact in the other provinces for their French-speaking minorities.

In all this complex of circumstances, it is very difficult to know just how the people of Quebec will react to a conflict between the Charter and the provincial language law.

As far as the point about collective rights is concerned, it seems to me that it would be a mistake to assess the protection of collective rights only in terms of clauses like section 92(13) or section 93 or section 133 of the BNA Act, that formally and directly protect specific rights. The powers of the government of Quebec are seen in Quebec as being in themselves important protections of the collective rights of the French-speaking people of the province. Those people in Quebec constitute eighty-five per cent of the French-speaking people of Canada. Their continuity as a vibrant, healthy, French-speaking society is seen as a *sine qua non* for the survival of French-speaking communities in the rest of Canada. In short, the rights and powers of the government of Quebec become a very important instrument of protection for the entire French-speaking minority of Canada.

At the time of the referendum in May 1980, the argument on the part of the Parti Québécois was that to vote 'No' was to vote for the *status quo*. Most of what the government of Quebec wanted was a modification in the distribution of powers so as to clarify or to increase the powers of the province. This would better protect the position and permanence of the francophone population of Quebec, who are the *de facto* dominant community in Quebec.

The response on the federalist side was to deny the proposition that a 'No' vote would be a vote for the *status quo*. Federalist leaders from Ottawa and from other provinces assured the voters of Quebec that 'A vote no will *not* be a vote for the *status quo*, it will be a vote for the renewal of federalism.' The only renewal of federalism we have so far is a provision – the Charter of Rights – which *diminishes* the powers of the Assemblée nationale of Quebec. This runs exactly in the opposite direction to what the people of Quebec thought they were being promised as the result of a negative vote in the referendum.

My own assessment would be that the likelihood of our getting back to the constitutional bargaining table at any early date is very slim. The country is fed up with the constitution. Economic problems are first and foremost on people's minds. The likelihood of more constitutional negotiation in the near future is almost zero.

If and when constitutional negotiations are resumed, the obstacles to agreement will be enormous. I lived through many years of constitutional negotiations and was an observer and commentator during the last two constitutional conferences. At various stages, the negotiators had fourteen items of powers for discussion and could not agree on one. In 1980 and 1981, there were twelve items for negotiation, and again there was no agreement on any single item involving the distribution of powers. The prospect of agreeing is remote at this stage of our constitutional development, and yet we do have a commitment to the people of Quebec about a renewed federalism.

I mention all of this to say that the government of Quebec and a lot of people in Quebec have been interested in the better protection of collective rights. Professor Tremblay is absolutely right in that. They wanted not just formal clauses for rights, they have also seen protection in more effective provincial powers. They have not got them yet and the question is whether they will get them at all.

What the consequences of this will be, of an imposed Charter that will be in conflict with a highly popular law in Quebec, is something that should give us pause. It may not lead to serious trouble. It may well be that Mr Trudeau will win his gamble. However, it would be a mistake to think that we do not have a potential powder-keg here that could blow up with devastating consequences to the Charter of Rights and perhaps to confederation.

The Canadian Charter of Rights and Freedoms: An Ontario View

Hon R. Roy McMurtry, QC*

In 1982, Canada entered upon a new and very challenging phase of its constitutional development. The patriation of our basic constitutional document and the acquisition of an amending formula will make it possible to adapt our constitutional structures more readily to new needs and problems. Equally significant and of more immediate practical concern are the challenges and the opportunities afforded by the advent of the Canadian Charter of Rights and Freedoms.

We have all heard the argument that the Charter represents a major break with our tradition of the sovereignty of parliament – that by entrusting to the courts the definition and protection of individual rights, we have transferred willy nilly to an appointed judiciary too much of the policy-making function, which is properly the domain of elected legislatures. In a word, we have 'Americanized' the Canadian constitution. It was fitting and timely then that an international conference on 'The United States Bill of Rights: Implications for Canada' should have been organized by the University of Western Ontario in March of this year. It was a privilege to have participated in the conference proceedings. I am doubly honoured that the editor of this publication of papers arising out of the conference has afforded me this opportunity to commit to writing some of the thoughts which I endeavoured to convey on behalf of the government and people of Ontario.

Essentially my message to the conference was three-fold. First, I sought to emphasize the critical importance, at the threshhold of this new era, of attempting to understand what we have tried to accomplish as a nation by adopting the Charter. Next, I argued that the Charter which we have embraced is not the United States Bill of Rights. Last, but not least, I expressed my

---

* The Hon R. Roy McMurtry is the Attorney General of Ontario.

profound concern that in taking justifiable pride in our accomplishments as Canadians, we should not lose sight of the promise which we have made to our brothers and sisters in the Province of Quebec, that the 'renewed federalism' will better accommodate their needs as a part of Canadian society. The first two points are inextricably tied together, the conclusion about the second flowing from the exposition of the first. Accordingly, I will deal with them together.

It behooves us to pause at this initial or threshhold stage of the new Charter era to think carefully about the nature of the Charter which has been put into place. It is only *after* we have attempted to understand what the Charter was intended to accomplish that we should hazard conclusions about the content of any of its individual provisions. Of course, it will be the courts which will render the authoritative interpretations of the Charter. However, I have had some direct personal involvement in events which led ten of Canada's eleven governments to accept the proposed Charter. I trust then that you will permit me to suggest to you, from that perspective, what I believe to be the nature of our Charter and what we have sought to accomplish through its enactment.

May I say quite emphatically that the Charter is not the United States Bill of Rights. That the American Bill was an inspiration, and even that some of its notions and language were borrowed and adapted, is undeniable. But the Charter is not the reflection of a state which was created by revolution and refined in the crucible of a long and bloody civil war. It is rather a further evolutionary development of a state which evolved peacefully from colony to fully independent state. In the process, our law and institutions have evolved also, so that today they are better adapted than they ever have been to protect civil liberties. In virtually every province and at the federal level, special legislation has been enacted to promote civil rights. It is fair to say that although we have suffered some notable lapses, Canadians have enjoyed an enviable level of freedom. Nevertheless, the entrenchment of a charter of rights in our constitution was the response to a widely felt need in our society.

Several of the distinguished Americans who addressed the conference urged Canadians to develop indigenous solutions to our particular problems. They have cautioned us against seeking pre-packaged instant solutions by resorting to the jurisprudence on the American Bill of Rights. This wise counsel is grounded in the belief that constitutions, like nations, are unique and reflect different realities. It will not surprise you that I cite these arguments in support of my thesis.

We have not embraced the extensive regime of judicial review which one obtains under the Constitution of the United States of America. We have not 'gone all the way' but have settled for a compromise. We have traded away some sovereignty of the legislatures for some judicial review. In the difficult and seemingly impossible balancing act whereby the many competing interests and perceptions of the eleven governments involved were reconciled, we sacrificed some uniformity and elegance of expression. This makes more difficult the task of interpreting the document. But if there is one common thread in the Charter, it is that the legislatures and the political process can continue to play the *dominant* role in resolving the great issues of public policy.

It would serve us well to examine the evidence.

Rather than rely on the courts to imply that there are reasonable limits to the sometimes absolute terms in which rights are expressed, we have developed section 1. Section 1 specifies that the rights and freedoms in the Charter are 'subject only to such reasonable limits prescribed by law as can be demonstrably justified in a free and democratic society.' This explicit recognition of the role of legislatures would appear to give them broader scope to limit and define the rights and freedoms than would be the case if section 1 did not exist. In addition, the Mobility Rights and Equality Rights sections are subject to legislation which makes provision for affirmative action programs. Finally, Fundamental Rights, the entire range of the Legal Rights section, and the Equality Rights section have been made subject to the controversial 'notwithstanding' clause, section 33.

Two additional indications of our wish to retain a prominent role for the elected branch in policy-making in this area are sections 37 and 59. Section 37 requires that a federal/provincial conference of First Ministers be held within one year after the Constitution Act, 1982 comes into effect. By virtue of section 37(2) that conference: 'Shall have included in its agenda an item respecting constitutional matters that directly affect the aboriginal peoples of Canada, including the identification and definition of the rights of those peoples to be included in the Constitution of Canada, and the Prime Minister of Canada shall invite representatives of those peoples to participate in the discussion on that item.' The full operation of section 23 of the Charter concerning Minority Language Education Rights depends, in Quebec, upon the authorization of either the Legislative Assembly or Government of Quebec required by section 59 of the Constitution Act, 1982.

I indicated, however, that we have traded some sovereignty of the legislatures for some judicial review. In so describing this development, I do not seek to minimize its significance. Our courts will have a much expanded jurisdiction to review legislative and administrative action to ensure that such action complies with the constitutionally-imposed requirements of the Charter.

Obviously, it is difficult to predict with certainty how Canadian courts will interpret their new mandate. There has been already much healthy speculation and debate on this question. One possibility is that they will continue their tradition of self-restraint evident in the judicial interpretation of the Diefenbaker Bill of Rights. The other possibility is that the courts will respond to the advent of a constitutionally entrenched charter by abandoning, in whole or in part, the tradition of self-restraint. There are some clues, both in the text of the Charter and outside, which merit examination and which may aid speculation on the scope of the new mandate of the courts and how they will interpret it.

Section 24(1) provides that: 'Anyone whose rights or freedoms, as guaranteed by this Charter, have been infringed or denied may apply to a court of competent jurisdiction to obtain such remedy as the court considers appropriate and just in the circumstances.' Initially, this provision would appear to contemplate proceedings not only against governments, but by one individual against another. Some observers are of the view that the Charter forms the foundation for a new variety of claims in tort based upon the violation of rights which it guarantees. If this were so, it would have an obvious bearing on the extent of the involvement of the courts in applying the Charter.

Such a result was not intended, however, by the authors of the document. I can assure you that consideration was given to that issue and care was taken to make clear the intent that the Charter is to apply to the activities of legislatures and of governments *only*. In this regard, section 32 entitled 'Application of Charter' provides that the Charter applies to the Parliament and Government of Canada and to the legislature and government of each province in respect of all matters within their respective authority. Furthermore, section 24(1) itself speaks of rights and freedoms 'as guaranteed by this Charter,' a phrase referable, arguably, to section 32 of the Charter. In addition, section 52 of the Constitution Act declares the primacy of the constitution of Canada in these terms: 'The Constitution of Canada is the supreme law of Canada, and any law that is inconsistent with the provisions of the Constitution is, to the extent of the inconsistency, of no force or effect.' Section 31 declares that nothing in the Charter 'extends the legislative powers of any body or authority.' Finally, section 26 provides that the guarantee in the Charter of certain rights and freedoms 'shall not be construed as denying the existence of any other rights or freedoms that exist in Canada.' Read together, these various provisions should serve to remove any residual doubts on this question. In Ontario, therefore, the Ontario Human Rights Code and the Ontario Human Rights Commission will continue to be the principal agencies through which human rights issues are solved between individuals. The judgment of the Supreme Court of Canada on 22 June 1981 in the *Bhadauria* case [*The Board of Governors of the Seneca College of Applied Arts and Technology* v *Pushpa Bhadauria*] will continue to be good law after the Charter comes into force.[1]

A factor external to the Charter, which can have the tendency of enhancing the role of the courts, is the attitude of governments to section 33(1) of the Charter. Section 33 is the much-debated 'notwithstanding' clause intended to preserve, for certain specified matters at least, the principle of the supremacy of Parliament. It applies to section 2 (Fundamental Freedoms) and to sections 7 to 15 (Legal Rights and Equality Rights), and makes it possible for legislatures to have the final say in establishing policy on these matters.

Section 33 raises the policy issue of whether or not it can be invoked without violating the 'spirit' of the rights and freedoms guaranteed by the Charter. Clearly, there will be significant *political* implications for any government, which invokes section 33 in circumstances where to do so would violate that 'spirit.' Section 33, therefore, imposes its own discipline.

It has been and continues to be the opinion of the Government of Ontario that section 33 is a safety valve provision to be resorted to only in the most exceptional circumstances, such as where the courts may feel compelled to interpret the provisions of the Charter in a manner offensive to the overwhelming sense of right and justice in the community on a particular policy issue. It is difficult indeed to conceive of such circumstances.

Accordingly, Ontario would look to section 33 only where there is no practical alternative and only where the public interest might demand such action. Frankly, I would be very surprised indeed if such circumstances were to arise. Standard operating procedure will be to amend statutes or practices to bring them into conformity with the requirements of the Charter.

To summarize, I am urging that we look behind the rhetoric which has been levelled at the Charter. We have not elevated the judiciary to the status of a parallel power to the legislatures in policy-making. Indeed, the potential to have the final say in establishing policy in the most vital areas of rights and freedoms rests with the legislatures. I have referred to the internal evidence in the Charter to demonstrate that the scope of judicial review depends in large measure upon the will of the legislatures. This is what I mean when I say that we have fashioned a compromise – a compromise admittedly with some flaws – but an honourable compromise which will lead to a better Canada.

1 *The Board of Governors of the Seneca College of Applied Arts and Technology* v *Pushpa Bhadauria* (1981) 37 NR 455

I have suggested that the Charter is not the American Bill of Rights in another guise, even though some of the language of the Charter was inspired by the American document. Certainly, the preference of the federal government was for a charter which would resemble more closely the American model. But we have been through a period of intense federal/provincial negotiations, controversy, and litigation which culminated in the agreement of 5 November 1981. The Charter approved by the Parliament of Canada in December of 1981 enjoys the support of ten of Canada's eleven senior governments because it embodies the compromise which I referred to earlier. It will be our duty now to ensure that that compromise works and that the agreement from which it emerged is honoured.

I am still enough of a lawyer to know that once these matters have been committed to writing in a statute or in a written constitution, it then becomes open season. Lawyers advising clients can, and no doubt will, urge any reasonable interpretation of the Charter which will advance their client's interests. In fact, they have a clear duty to do so. As one noted jurist has observed: 'Over the centuries what we call ... freedom for the individual has been won partly on the field of battle, partly in legislative halls, but for the most part in the courts of law.'[2] I say, however, that we break faith if we ignore the 'legislative history,' that is, the events leading up to the agreement of 5 November 1981. We do the community a disservice if we pass hasty and rash judgment on the Charter, if we seek to interpret rights and freedoms in the abstract and out of context, or if we invoke the judicial process to advance our own views of what the Charter *ought to be* rather than to seek clarification and confirmation of its scope.

Thus, my message to you is, above all, that the Charter will demand of us all imagination, caution, and sound judgment. It will change the practice of law in many ways. It will make the government's job of securing the general benefit more difficult and more sensitive. But I am convinced that it will also result in a better Canada, a more open and humane community.

The Constitutional Accord will not end the task of constitutional reform. The pressing problem of Quebec, the unfinished agenda with Canada's native peoples, and the continuing demands for re-allocation of constitutional jurisdiction will require us to continue our efforts toward reform. Quebec represents the most immediately urgent and difficult issue. We must not underestimate the danger to national unity of a continuing perception of

---

2 Arthur T. Vanderbilt, *The Challenge of Law Reform* (Princeton, NJ: Princeton University Press, 1955), p 36

betrayal within Quebec, a sense of betrayal that is not confined to members of the Parti Québécois.

We cannot allow the Accord of November to become a new *status quo*; we cannot rest self-satisfied. I look forward to the day when Quebec returns to the bargaining table, eager to share in fashioning a new model of Canada. This new model must permit each region to make and nurture its own special identity and culture; it must maintain a strong central government fully able to define and pursue Canada's national interest. The challenge is to accommodate diversity in unity.

It is to our credit that we have come so far in a civilized and democratic fashion. Remember it took revolution, secession and a civil war to fashion a nation in the United States. The way is open to us to give content to Canada's nationhood, to resolve our residual problems, to find strength in diversity. Canada has lessons to teach a divided and conflict-ridden world. Our drama is still continuing to unfold. It is a drama of law, and of politics, and of commitment too. A commitment to something intangible yet real – a spirit – something called Canada. The distinguished historian from Quebec, Jacques Monet, put it best when he said: 'The challenge of brotherhood, of an experiment that bursts through the limits of nationalism to embrace men of diverse ways and diverse tongues, is what it means to be a Canadian. You see, it is not a question of economics or common sense: it is a question of the heart.'[3]

---

3 Jacques Monet, *The Last Cannon Shot: A Study of French-Canadian Nationalism, 1837–1850* (Toronto: University of Toronto Press, 1969)

Entrenchment Revisited: The Effect of the Canadian Charter of Rights and Freedoms

Douglas A. Schmeiser*

INTRODUCTION**

The issue of constitutional entrenchment of a bill of rights was a matter of political controversy in Canada for over a quarter of a century. The question was extensively debated in the late 1950s, prior to the enactment of the Canadian Bill of Rights,[1] but the federal government of the day bowed to political reality and adopted a legislative rather than a constitutional bill. The question resurfaced at various constitutional conferences in the 1960s and 1970s because of federal proposals to place a bill of rights in the Constitution. The debate heated up markedly in 1980, when the federal government tabled a proposed Resolution in the Senate and House of Commons concerning the Constitution of Canada. The Resolution provided not only for patriation of the Canadian constitution,[2] but also included a Canadian Charter of Rights and Freedoms. The federal government insisted that, upon approval by both Houses of the Parliament of Canada of the Resolution requesting amendment of the British North America Act, 1867, the British Parliament had no choice but to pass the requested legislation. The proposed Charter undoubtedly affected provincial rights, powers and privileges, and all provinces but Ontario and New Brunswick stoutly opposed the federal unilateral concept of constitutional amendment. The opposition resulted in reference questions being presented to the Courts of Appeal of Manitoba,

* Douglas A. Schmeiser is a Professor of Law at the University of Saskatchewan.
** Some of the ideas contained herein were discussed in an article previously published in *Alberta Law Review* 19 (1981): 375–83.
1 Assented to on 10 August 1960; presently found in RSC 1970, Appendix III.
2 Then called The British North America Act, 1867 (UK), 30–1 Vict., c 3; now called the Constitution Act, 1867.

Newfoundland and Quebec concerning the validity of the proposed federal action. Ultimately an appeal was taken from the divergent provincial appellate decisions to the Supreme Court of Canada. On 28 September 1981, the Supreme Court ruled in a split decision that provincial consent to constitutional amendment concerning their powers was not required as a matter of law but was constitutionally required as a matter of convention. No view was expressed as to the quantification of provincial consent.[3]

Consequent upon the judgment of the Supreme Court, the federal government found itself constrained to return to the bargaining table. A further First Ministers Conference was held in Ottawa on 2–5 November 1981, and an agreement[4] was arrived at on a constitutional package which included the Charter of Rights and Freedoms. This agreement was embodied in a Resolution addressed to the United Kingdom Parliament and adopted by the Canadian House of Commons and Senate on 2 and 8 December 1981, respectively. The Resolution was passed by the British Parliament on 29 March 1982 as the Canada Act 1982.[5] It was proclaimed in force by the Queen in Ottawa on 17 April 1982.

The political controversy concerning entrenchment of the Charter of Rights is over. The legal controversy concerning its meaning and effect, however, is just beginning. The Canadian Charter contains some unique features, which can be interpreted in widely divergent fashion. The key sections are:

1. The *Canadian Charter of Rights and Freedoms* guarantees the rights and freedoms set out in it subject only to such reasonable limits prescribed by law as can be demonstrably justified in a free and democratic society.
24. (1) Anyone whose rights or freedoms, as guaranteed by this Charter, have been infringed or denied may apply to a court of competent jurisdiction to obtain such remedy as the court considers appropriate and just in the circumstances.

    (2) Where, in proceedings under subsection (1), a court concludes that evidence was obtained in a manner that infringed or denied any rights or freedoms guaranteed by this Charter, the evidence shall be excluded if it is established that, having regard to all the circumstances, the admission of it in the proceedings would bring the administration of justice into disrepute.

---

3 *Reference re Amendment of the Constitution of Canada* (1981), 1 SCR 753; (1981), 6 WWR 1; 39 NR 1; 125 DLR (3d) 1 (SCC)
4 The agreement was supported by the federal government and by all provincial governments except Quebec.
5 1982, c 11 (UK)

52. (1) The Constitution of Canada is the supreme law of Canada, and any law that is inconsistent with the provisions of the Constitution is, to the extent of the inconsistency, of no force or effect.

In addition, there is the override provision allowing for legislative paramountcy over the Charter:

33. (1) Parliament or the legislature of a province may expressly declare in an Act of Parliament or of the legislature, as the case may be, that the Act or a provision thereof shall operate notwithstanding a provision included in section 2 or sections 7 to 15 of this Charter.
(2) An Act or a provision of an Act in respect of which a declaration made under this section is in effect shall have such operation as it would have but for the provision of this Charter referred to in the declaration.
(3) A declaration made under subsection (1) shall cease to have effect five years after it comes into force or on such earlier date as may be specified in the declaration.
(4) Parliament or a legislature of a province may re-enact a declaration made under subsection (1).
(5) Subsection (3) applies in respect of a re-enactment made under subsection (4).

An analysis of some of the interpretive problems of these sections will be attempted later. For the moment it is suggested that the interpretation and applicability of these provisions will be influenced by the views of judges, lawyers and politicians concerning entrenchment. Accordingly, consideration of the purported advantages and disadvantages of entrenchment is still relevant.

REASONS FOR ENTRENCHMENT

The fundamental argument in favour of entrenchment is that entrenchment is necessary to protect the freedom of the individual from encroachment by capricious majorities. Special reference is usually made to the position of minorities, and to the stresses in time of emergency. A typical expression of this view is the following statement found in *Constitutional Reform: Canadian Charter of Rights and Freedoms*, a federal government paper issued under the authority of the Honourable Otto E. Lang in 1978.[6] It states that 'Only by

---

6 Canada, Department of Justice, *Constitutional Reform: Canadian Charter of Rights and Freedoms* (Ottawa: Canadian Unity Information Office, 1978)

placing such a guarantee in the Constitution may individuals and minorities be assured that their rights and freedoms are adequately protected against arbitrary action by others, be those others individuals, majorities, governments or legislators.'[7] Similarly, in 1978, the Committee on the Constitution of the Canadian Bar Association recommended entrenchment, stating that: 'In the absence of guaranteed rights, a transient majority in Parliament or a legislature can do incalculable harm to a minority or an individual.'[8]

Closely allied to the protection argument is the position that human rights are so basic, necessary and everlasting that they must be elevated to an immutable status. The Supreme Court of the United States stated in *West Virginia Board of Education* v *Barnette*:

> The very purpose of a Bill of Rights was to withdraw certain subjects from the vicissitudes of political controversy, to place them beyond the reach of majorities and officials and to establish them as legal principles to be applied by the Courts. One's right to life, liberty and property, to free speech, a free press, freedom of worship and assembly, and other fundamental rights may not be submitted to vote; they depend on the outcome of no elections.[9]

This passage was quoted in *A Canadian Charter of Human Rights*, another federal government document, issued under the authority of the Honourable Pierre Elliott Trudeau in 1968.[10] This document argued that 'Language in this form would possess a degree of permanence and would override even unambiguous legislation purporting to violate the protected rights.'[11]

Similarly, the Lang document stated that the first main justification for enshrining basic rights was 'because certain human rights are so basic to our society, they should be given a permanence, which can only be assured by placing them beyond the reach of the ordinary legislative process.'[12]

Other supporters of entrenchment are more moderate in their assessment of the degree of protection which it affords; their position is that entrenchment operates as a brake on precipitous government action, forcing a sober

---

7   Canada, *Constitutional Reform*, p 1
8   Canadian Bar Association, Committee on the Constitution, *Towards a New Canada* (Toronto: Canadian Bar Foundation, 1978), p 15
9   *West Virginia State Board of Education* v *Barnette*, 319 US 624 (1943), per Jackson J. at 638
10 Canada, Department of Justice, *A Canadian Charter of Human Rights* (Ottawa: Queen's Printer, 1968), p 11
11 *Ibid*, p 14
12 Canada, *Constitutional Reform*, p 2

second thought to changes affecting fundamental rights. The Special Joint Committee of the Senate and of the House of Commons on the Constitution of Canada, 1972, recommended entrenchment on the following more limited basis:

> What democracy requires is that a continuing popular majority must prevail, and it is by no means inconsistent with democracy to erect safeguards to ensure that a majority is a continuing one before it may be allowed to interfere with certain long-established rights. Democracy cannot lose by being forced to have second thoughts on some matters of great moment; in fact this is the rationale of the power which our system of government gives to opposition parties to delay government legislative programs ... In reality courts in a democratic society always eventually accept what the majority wants, if only because the political representatives of the majority will ensure that judicial appointees share their philosophy. Moreover, the legislative process of reversal of judicial interpretation through constitutional amendment, though cumbersome, is also assured to the majority.[13]

The Canadian Bar Association report took a similarly restrained approach:

> This is not, as some would argue, a denial of the democratic principle that the majority rules. Sustained majority opinion must and will prevail. Courts will eventually accept the consistent views of the majority as expressed in the legislature. What a Bill of Rights ensures is that fundamental freedoms will not be set aside by a transient majority. As the Joint Committee of the Senate and House of Commons on the Constitution noted, it ensures second thought by society through the courts of legislative and executive action that infringes individual freedoms.[14]

An entrenched bill of rights undoubtedly has educational and inspirational value for a nation. It stimulates interest in rights, fosters their acceptance, and leads to a greater public awareness of human rights problems. In some circumstances, it serves as a statement of national goals, and in other circumstances, it serves as an authoritative standard by which to judge governmental action.

Other arguments supporting entrenchment arose in a distinctively Canadian context. One contention, at odds with Canada's federal structure, was that entrenchment was required to achieve a greater uniformity of rights

---

13 Canada, Parliament, Special Joint Committee of the Senate and the House of Commons on the Constitution of Canada, *Final Report* (Ottawa: Queen's Printer, 1972), p 18
14 Canadian Bar Association, *Towards a New Canada*, pp 15–16

throughout Canada. The 1968 Trudeau paper, after acknowledging divided legislative competence over fundamental rights, stated that: 'Only by a single constitutional enactment will the fundamental rights of all Canadians be guaranteed equal protection.'[15] The 1978 Lang paper gave as its second main justification for entrenchment that 'these human rights should be common to all Canadians whatever may be their place of residence within Canada ... The rights enjoyed should not be dependent upon the particular place where an individual chooses to reside.'[16]

The claim was also made that an entrenched bill of rights will contribute to Canadian unity. The Task Force on Canadian Unity,[17] co-chaired by Jean-Luc Pépin and John P. Robarts, concluded, 'on balance,' that some key individual and collective rights should be entrenched, since 'entrenchment would perform an educational and inspirational function by making Canadians more aware and more proud of the wide range of freedoms they do have. Above all, a sense of individual and collective confidence in the security of their rights would contribute to a positive attitude to Canadian unity.'[18] The Canadian Bar Association report also suggested that 'A clear statement in the Constitution of the fundamental values all Canadians share would, we think, have an important unifying effect.'[19]

Another Canadian argument has arisen out of the frustration experienced by civil libertarians with the Canadian Bill of Rights. The decision of the Supreme Court of Canada in *R.* v *Drybones*,[20] holding that the Bill rendered inoperative any law of Canada inconsistent with it, was a monumental decision, since it was by no means clear what effect the Bill was intended to have. However, the high hopes generated by *Drybones* were shattered by the subsequent decision in *A.G. Canada* v *Lavell, Isaac* v *Bedard*,[21] upholding s. 12(1)(b) of the Indian Act.[22] Civil libertarians expressed the hope that the Supreme Court of Canada would take a new and sympathetic approach to the protection of fundamental rights under an entrenched bill, and would reject the sterile interpretation given to the legislative bill.

15 Canada, *Canadian Charter of Human Rights*, p 14
16 Canada, *Constitutional Reform*, p 2
17 Canada, Task Force on Canadian Unity, *A Future Together: Observations and Recommendations* (Ottawa: Department of Supply and Services, 1979)
18 Canada, Task Force on Canadian Unity, *A Time to Speak* (Ottawa: Department of Supply and Services, 1979), p 108
19 Canadian Bar Association, *Towards a New Canada*, p 15
20 (1970) SCR 282, (1970) 3 CCC 355, 10 CRNS 334, 71 WWR 161, 9 DLR (3d) 473
21 (1973) 38 DLR (3d) 481, 23 CRNS 197, (1974) SCR 1349 (SCC)
22 RSC 1970, c I-6

A substantial benefit accrues to the legal profession under entrenchment. What entrenchment really offers is a right to litigate, and it does not require much imagination to find a seemingly plausible ground to challenge socially significant legislation. In addition to increased legal activity, there may also be an increase in professional status, for the lawyer may pose as the champion of liberty and the defender of the constitution, even when he is defending selfish interests.

Support for entrenchment has also been predicated on the assertion that entrenchment is required for compliance with Canada's international obligations. Reference is usually made to the Universal Declaration of Human Rights and the International Covenant on Civil and Political Rights. The preamble to the Universal Declaration recites that member states of the United Nations have pledged themselves to achieve 'the promotion of universal respect for and observance of human rights and fundamental freedoms.' Article 2, section 1 of the International Covenant stipulates that 'each State Party to the present Covenant undertakes to take the necessary steps, in accordance with its constitutional processes and with the provisions of the present Covenant, to adopt such legislative or other measures as may be necessary to give effect to the rights recognized in the present Covenant.'

Finally, the ancillary argument is raised that any limitations on the principle of parliamentary sovereignty caused by entrenchment are justified by democratic concerns. The Special Joint Committee Report gave the following rationalization:

We admit that an entrenched Bill of Rights would limit legislative sovereignty, but then parliamentary sovereignty is no more sacrosanct a principle than is the respect for human liberty which is reflected in a Bill of Rights. Legislative sovereignty is already limited legally by the distribution of powers under a federal system and, some would say, by natural law or by a common-law Bill of Rights. The kind of additional limit on it which would be imposed by a constitutional Bill of Rights is not an absolute one, for a Bill of Rights constitutes rather a healthy tension point between two principles of fundamental value, establishing the kind of equilibrium among the competing interests of majority rule and minority rights which is in our view of the essence of democracy.[23]

The Canadian Bar Association report goes further, suggesting that there is no conflict between entrenchment and parliamentary supremacy,[24] but its

---

23 Special Joint Committee on the Constitution, *Final Report*, 1972, pp 18–19
24 Canadian Bar Association, *Towards a New Canada*, p 16

argument can hardly be described as convincing. The rationale given is that 'It is a prerequisite to the proper operation of the principle of the supremacy of Parliament that the courts apply principles of natural or fundamental justice.'[25]

REASONS AGAINST ENTRENCHMENT

While many arguments have been advanced against entrenchment, most of them stem from the proposition that words describing fundamental rights are general words of varying and uncertain content, and that decisions as to their meaning primarily involve matters of social policy, better left to the legislative process than to the courts. No right can be interpreted in an absolute fashion; it must be subject to the dictates of national security, public order, health and morality. The freedom of one is necessarily subject to the freedom of others, and freedom can only exist under the law. Indeed, rights on occasion conflict with each other. Policy choices must be made in the recognition of fundamental rights, and these choices are best made by legislatures because of their representative character, their accessibility, and their superior abilities with respect to fact-finding, awareness of public needs, formulation of national goals, compromise, timing and economic resources. The adversary system of judicial proceedings, restricted to the facts of a particular case and limited by rules of evidence and procedure, is ill-equipped to create universal solutions to complex social problems.

At the outset, it should be noted that it is difficult to avoid some degree of generalization in a discussion of entrenchment. Courts are often influenced by public policy considerations, especially in their roles as arbiters of federal-provincial conflicts. They have, on occasion, effectively protected fundamental rights by rejecting the legislative authority of the body that was attempting to deal with them. In some situations, they clearly create law. It is also incorrect to suggest that there are no entrenched rights in the Canadian constitution. Democratic rights are clearly guaranteed by part IV of the British North America Act, denominational education rights by section 93, and the use of English and French by section 133. Various judges have also suggested the existence of an implied bill of rights in our constitution,[26] at least until the recent rejection of that doctrine by the Supreme Court of Canada in *Attorney-*

---

25 *Ibid*
26 See, for example, *Reference re Alberta Legislation* (1938) SCR 100, 2 DLR 81; *Saumur* v *City of Quebec* (1953) 2 SCR 299, 4 DLR 641; *Switzman* v *Elbling and A.G. Quebec* (1957) SCR 285, 7 DLR (2d) 337.

General of Canada v *Dupond*.[27] Accordingly, the Canadian dispute never solely concerned the presence or absence of the power of judicial review, but the extent of its operation. What was at issue was whether courts should be invested with power to openly invalidate the political decisions of Parliament or of the provincial legislatures acting within their jurisdictional competence. With respect to some entrenched rights, such as educational and linguistic rights, the courts may be required to move beyond constitutional invalidation to judicial legislation and to direct administrative supervision.

If most human disputes in a democratic society involve policy choices, then judges exercising a power of judicial review necessarily will be imposing their personal values and biases on the legislatures, sometimes frustrating the popular will. Consider the following examples, all borrowed from American law. American courts have held that a convicted criminal must be released because his trial was delayed too long; that illegally obtained evidence is admissible;[28] that a woman has a constitutional right to an abortion;[29] that school attendance laws violate religious freedom;[30] that school children have a constitutional right to wear black arm bands as a form of political protest;[31] that school boards must bus pupils to desegregate a school system, even specifying the number of buses which a system must purchase. They have grappled with capital punishment and the circumstances under which it constitutes cruel and unusual punishment,[32] electoral boundaries, the conduct of voting, and the ward system. From a Canadian perspective, many people would prefer a political, rather than a judicial, determination of these issues.

A topical Canadian example may highlight the political difficulty under entrenchment. The Canadian Charter guarantees equality before the law without discrimination because of age. In Canada, we are becoming more conscious of the position of the elderly, and we are concerned whether mandatory retirement constitutes age discrimination. This issue has great implications for such matters as employment opportunities and advancement, employer-employee relations, union negotiations, health care, safety standards, pension plans, and the like. Under entrenchment, a court might be constrained, in a dispute involving only two persons, to hold that all mandatory retirement is unconstitutional. Critics of entrenchment would suggest

27 (1978) 2 SCR 770, 84 DLR (3d) 420, 19 NR 478
28 *Mapp* v *Ohio*, 367 US 643 (1961)
29 *Roe* v *Wade*, 410 US 113 (1973); *Doe* v *Bolton*, 410 US 179 (1973)
30 *Wisconsin* v *Yoder*, 406 US 205 (1973)
31 *Tinker* v *Des Moines Independent Community School District*, 393 US 503 (1969)
32 *Furman* v *Georgia*, 408 US 238 (1972)

instead that the legislatures, as the representatives of the people, should pass final judgment on this issue.

If it is correct that policy matters are better decided by the legislatures, then judicial decisions invalidating legislation will be wrong on occasion. Critics of entrenchment point to the American experience as supporting this allegation, since many Supreme Court decisions originally nullified welfare legislation, but were eventually reversed by the Court itself. In the process, needed social reform was unnecessarily delayed. In Canada, courts have usually been more conservative in outlook than the legislatures, and could exercise a negative influence.

Having judges decide basically political questions can have a deleterious effect on the judiciary itself. When courts become involved in political controversies, they are rightly subject to political criticism, and lose their image of impartiality and fairness. Even among judges themselves, there will be a substantial amount of lobbying and enmity. The recent bestseller, *The Brethren: Inside the Supreme Court*,[33] is an amazing chronicle of injudicious conduct by American Supreme Court judges torn by differing political views. The end result may be a loss of prestige and independence.

Another argument raised against entrenchment is that it is essentially undemocratic and elitist. Under entrenchment, final responsibility for major social issues is taken from the people, acting through their elected representatives, and given in the final analysis to five members of the Supreme Court. The rationale is that legislatures cannot be trusted to make proper decisions about fundamental rights, and that the people must be protected from themselves. The response given by opponents of entrenchment is that there is no historical or democratic warrant for judges to act as super-legislators or philosopher kings, and that legislative majorities acting under a parliamentary system have not been a threat to the fostering of human rights. Rather, they have been the champions of liberty. As well, the practice of Canadian federal governments of appointing judges primarily on the basis of political allegiance does not foster confidence in the judicial settlement of political issues.

The contention based on democratic concerns may be expanded to suggest that entrenchment results in an erosion of democratic responsibility because the people can no longer assume final responsibility for social changes. It is admitted that democratic majorities will on occasion make mistakes, but they will be able to correct their own mistakes, and learn from the

---

33 Bob Woodward and Scott Armstrong, *The Brethren: Inside the Supreme Court* (New York: Simon and Schuster, 1979)

process. On the other hand, there is no easy way for the courts to correct their mistakes, short of judicial reversal or constitutional amendment. Citizens may also identify constitutionality with wisdom, falsely assuming that what is constitutional is acceptable.

Another criticism of entrenchment is that it unduly fosters litigation, much of which is frivolous as well as expensive. The ordinary remedy to enforce or protect an entrenched right is a lawsuit, and it is debatable whether litigation is the best way to solve human disputes. It may also be the case under entrenchment that privileged people are better able to protect their essential interests than the poor and underprivileged. While the rich or the zealots are challenging the validity of legislation, social reform will be unduly delayed. Certainly, American society has become preoccupied with litigation, which is regarded as a respectable, and in some instances, the only available, instrument of political reform. It is suggested, however, that a legal system works best when it is invoked least, and that increased litigation often is not a desirable social activity.

Another common problem with entrenched bills of rights is that as society changes, some of the specified rights become outdated, others assume undue importance, and new and equally valid claims of rights are ignored. The American 'right of the people to keep and bear arms' has not had a salutary effect on American society, and the right of trial by jury in suits exceeding $20 would block procedural reforms even if the Founding Fathers had been prescient enough to add an inflation factor. There are many rights ignored 50 years ago which would be included in a current bill of rights, and one can safely predict that new rights will be in vogue fifty years from now. These newly competing rights are never given as much credence as the entrenched ones, and social reform is retarded.

In direct contrast to the position that all Canadians should enjoy the same fundamental rights is the contention that entrenchment will be destructive of Canada's federal system. The genius of federalism is to combine the individuality and the variety of the different parts of the country with the strength of the whole. In a country as large and as diverse as Canada, it is important that people in the various regions have a right to differ, and to seek new ideas and solutions, particularly in the sensitive areas found in section 92 of the British North America Act. Federalism serves as a social crucible, in which provinces can experiment and profit from the experience of other provinces. Entrenchment acts as a brake on this process because a final court tends to express a uniform social philosophy, tends to disallow imaginative solutions to social ills, and tends to prefer consistency over provincial diversity. Canada's multicultural nature requires flexibility in its governmental organization but the experience of entrenchment in other federal states indicates that a supreme court reacts more harshly against novel solutions by provincial legislatures.

Another possible argument against entrenchment is that it lulls people into a false belief that their rights are finally secure, and that this attitude is destructive of the vigilance required to maintain a free society. The Canadian Bill of Rights was not a positive factor in protecting human rights, and unsympathetic interpretation of an entrenched bill could produce a similar result. Emphasis on entrenchment could distract attention from utilizing human rights commissions and Ombudsmen to solve individual problems, and from utilizing the political system to solve major social problems.

A final argument against entrenchment is that when protection from oppressive majority action is really required, judicial review will be ineffectual. The two Canadian incidents, which have been frequently cited as justifying an entrenched bill of rights, are the treatment of Japanese-Canadians during the Second World War and the invocation of the War Measures Act during the October crisis of 1970. It is difficult to see how an entrenched bill would have prevented either action. The opinion of the Special Joint Committee of the Senate and the House of Commons on the Constitution, and of the Canadian Bar Association, that a sustained majority opinion will always prevail, has already been quoted. However, the most eloquent rebuttal of the protection argument is found in the writings of Judge Learned Hand: '[T]his much I think I do know – that a society so riven that the spirit of moderation is gone, no Court can save; that a society where that spirit flourishes no Court need save; that in a society which evades its responsibility by thrusting upon the Courts the nurture of that spirit, that spirit in the end will perish.'[34]

ENTRENCHMENT UNDER THE
CANADIAN CHARTER OF RIGHTS AND FREEDOMS

The most salient feature of the Canadian version of entrenchment is that it is a limited version, and does not finally destroy the applicability of the doctrine of parliamentary sovereignty. In most situations, the courts will declare whether a conflict exists between a governmental act and the Charter. Under section 33, however, either Parliament or a provincial legislature may declare in a statute that the statute shall operate notwithstanding sections 2 or 7 to 15 of the Charter. The latter provisions cover Fundamental Freedoms,

34 Learned Hand, *The Spirit of Liberty; Papers and Addresses* (New York: Knopf, 1952), p 181

Legal Rights, and Equality Rights. In these areas, accordingly, Parliament and the legislatures can, by specific declaration, avoid a legal challenge to their legislation, or reverse the result of a judicial determination of conflict. This legislative declaratory power does not extend to democratic rights, mobility rights, language rights or educational rights.

The declaratory power has safeguards against abuse attached to it. A declaration ceases to have effect after five years, although it may be re-enacted. From the context of section 33(1), it may be that the declaration must be contained in the same statute that it is designed to protect, and it is also arguable that the Charter provision, which is overridden, must be specified as well.

The declaratory power negates many of the objections raised against entrenchment because in those cases where a fundamental disagreement over a policy issue exists between the legislative and judicial branches of government, the legislature can eventually prevail. It is suggested, however, that political reality will ensure that a declaration will be made in exceptional cases only, and the experience with provincial human rights legislation in some provinces where a similar technique exists bears this out.

A second important feature of the Canadian Charter is section 1, providing: '1. *The Canadian Charter of Rights and Freedoms* guarantees the rights and freedoms set out in it subject only to such reasonable limits prescribed by law as can be demonstrably justified in a free and democratic society.' As indicated earlier, no right can be interpreted as an absolute. The rights of one conflict with the rights of another, and rights themselves may conflict with each other. Some constitutional documents set out rights in an absolute fashion, such as the American Bill of Rights, but the American courts have accepted many limitations on those rights. Modern international documents confront the legal problem more directly by suggesting when limitations are in order. Article 29(2) of the Universal Declaration of Human Rights provides: 'In the exercise of his rights and freedoms, everyone shall be subject only to such limitations as are determined by law solely for the purpose of securing due recognition and respect for the rights and freedoms of others and of meeting the just requirements of morality, public order and the general welfare in a democratic society.' The International Covenant on Civil and Political Rights utilizes a similar approach: Articles 12, 14, 18, 19, 21 and 22 justify restrictions imposed by law which are necessary in a democratic society to protect national security, public safety, public order, public health or morals, or the rights and freedoms of others.

Section 1 of the Canadian Charter, accordingly, is philosophically sound, and states what would be implied by the courts in any event. Nevertheless,

the wording will lead to interesting challenges concerning its meaning. It will be necessary for the courts to determine:
(a) what are the circumstances or conditions under which a limit on a right or freedom could be described as 'reasonable'?
(b) what is the meaning of the phrase 'prescribed by law'? Does it include regulations, orders-in-council and the common law as well as statutes?
(c) when is a limit 'justified'? What additional requirement is placed on the requirement of reasonableness?
(d) how can such limits be demonstrably justified?
(e) why was the phrase 'can be demonstrably justified' used, rather than 'is demonstrably justified'? What is the legal significance of the difference?
(f) does 'a free and democratic society' refer to Canada alone, or does it include other free and democratic societies? What would happen to a long-standing Canadian law or practice which is not followed outside Canada? Are Canadian traditions sufficient?
(g) what is the burden of proof on an aggrieved person?

The Charter does not make any reference to emergency powers, and these must also stand the test of section 1.

The issue of the burden of proof is especially difficult under the Charter. Many supporters of the Charter argue that if an aggrieved person can show a restriction on a Charter provision, then the onus shifts to the state to show that the limit is reasonable and demonstrably justifiable in a free and democratic society. Section 52 of the Constitution Act, 1982, calls the constitution 'the supreme law of Canada,' and states that any law inconsistent with its provisions is of no force or effect. This section can also be cited in support of the proposition that an accused need go no further than to show an inconsistency between a law and the Charter.

Unfortunately, this popularly held view is not clearly stated, and a contrary argument has been advanced by some federal officials and prosecutors. This position is that a limit of a Charter freedom is not a violation of the Charter. It only becomes a violation when it is unreasonable and not demonstrably justifiable in a free and democratic society, and it is for the accused to establish those conditions.

Proponents of this restrictive view refer to section 24(1) to buttress their argument. Section 24(1) is the enforcement provision, stating that anyone whose rights and freedoms 'as guaranteed by this Charter' have been infringed or denied may apply to a court for an appropriate and just remedy. The contention is that there is no denial of a right or freedom 'as guaranteed by the Charter' unless the conditions stipulated in section 1 have been exceeded.

Adoption of the restrictive approach would have the unfortunate effect of negating much of the benefit of the Charter, and I hope the courts will not accept it. It is difficult for an aggrieved person to do more than to advance, by way of argument, that a law is inconsistent with the Charter. To require him to further show that the law is unreasonable, or that it is demonstrably unjustified in a democratic society could involve such a research or financial burden as to be impossible to meet. It may be that the courts will deal with the qualifications in section 1 only by way of argument, but there surely will be cases when the courts will require empirical evidence to justify a law, and it is suggested that that burden should be on the state.

Section 24(1) is susceptible to restrictive interpretation from another aspect. Application for a remedy may be made by anyone whose rights or freedoms *have been* infringed or denied. Because of the past tense, the argument is being raised that no remedy is available unless the violations of the complainant's rights have already taken place. This interpretation would rule out applications for injunctive or declaratory relief when violations are threatened or pending, and would be a serious defect. The same reasoning has been advanced to suggest that section 24 reverses the very liberal Canadian rules on standing enunciated by the Supreme Court of Canada in the cases of *Thorson*,[35] *McNeil*,[36] and *Borowski*.[37]

An unfortunate choice of words in section 24(2) leads to another problem of proof which is more difficult to avoid. Section 24(2) provides that where evidence has been obtained contrary to the Charter, the evidence shall be excluded 'if it is established' that its admission would bring the administration of justice into disrepute. The negative effect of the admissibility of illegally obtained evidence must be 'established' by someone, and it is unlikely that the prosecution would be interested in doing so. The obvious argument is that the onus is on the accused. The subsection also implies that violation of the Charter alone does not render evidence inadmissible; a deleterious effect on the administration of justice is also required. This view also leads to the contention that the admissibility of evidence may be conditional on the nature of the charge. Arguably, reception of such evidence is more necessary in a serious charge, whereas the public would not care about a minor prosecution. By this rather perverse reasoning, an accused's rights would be less in the hearing of a serious charge than of a minor charge. It is to be hoped that the courts will avoid the consequences of this rather convoluted reasoning by

---

35 (1974) 43 DLR (3d) 1, (1975) 1 SCR 138, 1 NR 225
36 (1978) 2 SCR 662, 84 DLR (3d) 1, 19 NR 570
37 (1982) 1 WWR 97, 130 DLR (3d) 588, 39 NR 331

dealing with section 24(2) applications as a matter of legal argument, not evidence, and by placing any burden involved in the operation of the subsection on the party who ought fairly to bear it.

CONCLUSION

Problems abound in the interpretation of our newly adopted Charter of Rights and Freedoms. The wording of the operative sections, namely 1, 24 and 52, are susceptible to expansive or restrictive interpretations. The entrenchment debate will continue for some time on a judicial level, for judicial perspectives on the merits of entrenchment will influence the effect given to the Charter. Political perspectives on entrenchment also continue to be important, for they will determine the utilization of the override power found in section 33.

Collective versus Individual Rights: The Canadian Tradition and the Charter of Rights and Freedoms

M. James Penton*

Today one hears more and more appeals for collective rights, and one of the major criticisms of the Canadian Charter of Rights and Freedoms is that, to a large extent, it entrenches individual rights but ignores collective rights. For example, French-speaking Quebeckers, whether federalists or separatists, frequently call for legislation to protect *their culture* against that of English-speaking Canadians. Indians and Inuit insist that they be treated as special communities with special rights. Yet when one looks at the matter of collective rights, stressed as part of the Canadian tradition in contrast with the American, it may be argued that from an historical standpoint collective rights have often become collective wrongs for those groups not in the mainstream of Canadian politics. Let us look at certain examples.

Many Canadians, particularly those who are wedded to the 'separate' or religious schools' tradition which exists in most, but not all, provinces, hold that the recognition of collective minority educational rights is much superior to the American system wherein, under Article I of the Bill of Rights, no government at any level can give public financial support to a religious or denominational school. Yet, while it would be naïve to state that there are no serious problems from the standpoint of human rights in the United States tradition, it is equally wrong to ignore the fact that the Canadian tradition has also had its grave and serious flaws.

Quebec, for example, long boasted of its educational tolerance in having three public educational systems: a French Catholic, an English Catholic and and English Protestant. But sometimes this very system, which was created to protect the collective rights of the groups just named, has been used as a

---

* M. James Penton is a Professor of History and Religious Studies at the University of Lethbridge.

means of attacking minority educational rights. Note what happened to the Jehovah's Witnesses in that province. In the 1950s, some of their children were denied the right to attend schools in the French-speaking Catholic system even though they could not speak a word of English and no other schools were available to them. In other instances, Witness children were also denied entry into the English-Protestant system because, allegedly, they were not Protestants. Thus, because they had fallen afoul of the Duplessis regime and many others throughout the province of Quebec, they were, for a time, held not to have any right to education because they were no part of one of the communities who had established educational systems. Although eventually the courts forced local school boards to accept Witness children,[1] for a long time many went without education. And even when the schools were opened to them, often French-Canadian Jehovah's Witness children were forced to attend English-Protestant schools because they were Protestants.

During the first quarter of this century, the Mennonites thought that they had special rights to their own school system in Manitoba and Saskatchewan. Such 'rights' did them little good, however, and those provinces – not regarding the Mennonites as politically significant – chose to force their children into the public schools. As a result, thousands of Mennonites chose to leave Canada and move to Mexico.[2]

More to the point, however, is the fact that in recent years Catholics in both Saskatchewan and Alberta have been forced to send their children to Catholic schools, whether they wanted to or not. Curiously, the right of the parent to determine what sort of an education his children should have has been overridden by the courts in favour of the rights of the Catholic community. For a time, the only way a Catholic could send his children to public schools in Saskatchewan and Alberta was to deny his faith![3]

Language rights are, of course, both individual and community rights, and some Canadians, both English and French, have argued that the rights of the community should come before the rights of the individual in this matter. Thus, historically, in those parts of Canada where English-speaking majorities have dominated the political apparatus, they have denied French-speaking Canadians what amounted or should have amounted to an historic right to education and other public facilities in their own language. Nothing

---

1 *Perron v Syndics d'Ecoles de Rouyn*, [1955] Que. QB 841, [1956] 1 DLR (2d) 414. *Chabot v Les Commissaires d'Ecoles de Lamorandiere*, [1957] Que. QB 707; 12 DLR (2d) 796
2 For a brief account of these events, see Frank H. Epp, *Mennonites in Canada* (Toronto: Macmillan of Canada, 1974), pp 333–62.
3 *Bitner v Regina Public School Board No. 4* (1965), 55 DLR (2d) 646 (Sask. CA)

demonstrated that so clearly as the Manitoba school question, but that is only one example. On the other hand, now, just at the time that many English-speaking provinces are becoming at least somewhat more enlightened towards French language rights, Quebec is moving in the opposite direction.

In the past, Quebec often boasted of its liberalism towards its English-speaking minority. In many ways, however, its boasts were rather hollow: Quebec's benevolence was based more on historic and economic necessity than any real commitment to linguistic tolerance. Now, with Bill 101, the present Quebec government is making war on the English-speaking community in the province to such an extent that already a large percentage of that community has migrated to Ontario and Western Canada. When English-language educational opportunities are limited for English-speaking Quebeckers whose parents or older brothers and sisters did not attend English language schools in the province in the past, and when it is even illegal to post a business sign in the English language, it is no wonder that this is what is happening. Yet this is all taking place for one reason and one reason alone: in Quebec, the government, and evidently most of the French-speaking people of that province, think that they have a perfect right to *destroy*, or at least 'ghettoize,' another culture in order to protect their own.

If the choice of the language of education had been left to parents rather than provincial governments in situations where there were significant francophone or anglophone minorities, there can be little doubt that the minorities in question would be linguistically healthier than they are today. As it is, the provinces treat their societies as communities which, from an educational and linguistic standpoint, are to be homogenized, with only New Brunswick acting as a real exception. Thus, English Canada has forcibly assimilated a large proportion of its French population, and Quebec is well on the way to eliminating or at least placing ethnic strictures on its English population. In the long run, this may well mean that for the two major linguistic communities, community rights are only provincial rights – the rights of 'two solitudes' which eventually may become two nations, two countries.

Let us examine some other instances of collective rights in Canadian history. In the nineteenth century, as early as 1808, the Province of Upper Canada recognized the principle of conscientious objection in relation to military service. In an act of that year, the legislature of the province declared:

... That the persons called Quakers, Menonists, and Tunkers, who, from certain scruples of conscience, decline bearing arms, shall not be compelled to serve in said militia, but every person professing that he is one of the people called Quakers, Menonists, or Tunkers, and producing a certificate of his being a Quaker, Menonist, or Tunker, signed by the clerk of the meeting of such society, or by any three or more of the people called Quakers, Menonists, or Tunkers, shall be excused and exempted from serving in the said militia: Provided, nevertheless, that every such person or persons that shall or may be of the people called Quakers, Menonists, or Tunkers, from the age of sixteen to sixty, shall, on or before the first day of December in each and every year, give in his name and place of residence to the treasurer of the district, where he or they shall reside, and pay to such treasurer, to and for the public uses of such district, in time of peace, the sum of twenty shillings, and in time of actual invasion or insurrection, or when any part of the militia of that district shall be called out on actual service, the sum of five pounds ...[4]

Late in the same century, the Canadian federal government exempted three religious communities – the Mennonites who migrated to Manitoba, the Hutterites and the Doukhobors – from military service.[5] In general, the federal government has been relatively faithful to its commitment to those groups. Yet because conscientious objection was regarded as a *community* right rather than an individual right, note what happened during the First World War. Rather curiously, certain denominations which had strong peace church traditions – the Church of Christ, the Disciples of Christ, the International Bible Students, the Pentecostal Assemblies and the Plymouth Brethren – were not recognized under the Military Service Act of 1917,[6] and as a consequence, one young Pentecostal was treated with such brutality that he died. Several International Bible Students were tortured in Canada, sent to England and treated with equal severity there.[7]

What this meant was that Quakers, Mennonites, Hutterites, Doukhobors, Adventists and Christadelphians all had *collective* rights to exemption from military service. But no one else did. Thus, other peace churches were not recognized and sincere conscientious objectors from the major churches or from no religious background were not recognized as having any right to

---

4 The Statutes of the Province of Upper Canada [1792–1831] [Kingston: 1831], p 135. 48 George III Cap. I (1808) as quoted in John S. Moir, *Church and State in Canada, 1627–1967* (Toronto: McClelland and Stewart, 1967), p 153
5 The groups were exempted from military service by orders-in-council which were published in 1873, 1898 and 1899 respectively.
6 Letter from J. Lorne McDougall, clerk of the Central Appeal Judge, to Captain O.S. Tyndale, secretary to the Military Service Subcommittee, Department of the Militia and Defence, Ottawa, 20 May 1918. This letter may be found in MD HQ 1064-30-67.
7 M. James Penton, *Jehovah's Witnesses in Canada* (Toronto: Macmillan of Canada, 1976) pp 56–62

conscientious scruples about military service. 'Theirs was not to reason why; theirs was but to do and die' – or go to jail, be brutalized or be tortured while Quakers, Mennonites and others stayed home peacefully on the farm or wherever else they were.

In the Second World War, the federal government did treat conscientious objectors more equitably. At that time, however, it took the extreme step of outlawing a whole religious community – Jehovah's Witnesses – by the simple expedient of issuing an order-in-council under the War Measures Act. Interestingly, similar actions taken somewhat later by the Australian government were declared unconstitutional. That country has a provision in its constitution which was taken virtually without change from Article I of the American Bill of Rights. Consequently, it guarantees *all* citizens freedom from interference by the government in matters involving religion. But since there was no such provision in the Canadian constitution, the federal government, acting largely at the behest of Roderique Cardinal Villeneuve, the archbishop of Quebec, simply outlawed the Witnesses.[8] Here, under Canadian law, was an example of a collective *wrong*, simply because there was no constitutional guarantee of the individual human right to freedom of religion under Canadian law.

Similar violations of what are generally considered basic human rights relate to various religious and racial groups. In British Columbia after the First World War, Doukhobors and Mennonites were disfranchised; they were prohibited from voting in provincial elections. Later, in an act of what amounted to pure vindictiveness, the federal Conservative government of R.B. Bennett prohibited both the Doukhobors and their descendants from voting in federal elections. The Dominion Franchise Act of 1934 specifically disfranchised 'in the province of British Columbia, every Doukhobor person and every descendant of any such person, whether born in that province or elsewhere, who is by law of that province disqualified from voting at an election of a member of the Legislative Assembly of that Province.' Yet such legal religious bigotry was not limited to Canada's Pacific province. Alberta, too, passed special legislation directed against specific religious communities. Following the Second World War, it passed the Communal Property Act. According to section 92 of the British North America Act, all matters involving property and civil rights (not civil liberties) fall within provincial jurisdiction. Thus, though the Communal Property Act was directed against Doukhobors and Hutterites *alone* by prohibiting them from establishing new agricultural colonies less than forty miles from any other colony and limiting

8 *Ibid*, pp 276–80

such new colonies to a maximum size of 6,400 acres, the courts denied that their religious freedom was affected.[9]

In the area of legislation covering the solemnization of marriage, the various provinces have granted collective *rights* to certain religious communities and denied them to others. Beginning in 1792, the government of Upper Canada granted the right to solemnize marriages to the clergy of the Church of England and to them alone. Only gradually was such authority given to the clergy of other religions during the pre-Confederation period,[10] and discrimination did not end in this area after 1867. Up until after the Second World War, Jehovah's Witnesses were unable to have their marriages solemnized by members of their own faith in any province. Today, while all English-speaking provinces now recognize their ministers as competent to perform legal marriage ceremonies, Quebec does not yet do so. In addition, the Church of Scientology has been denied the authority to have its ministers solemnize marriages in Ontario and, now, in Alberta. That latter province formerly recognized the Scientologists but now refuses to do so and will give no reasons for its action.

What, then, does the Canadian Charter of Rights and Freedoms have to say about the matter of collective versus individual rights? Is it a document in the tradition of the American Bill of Rights and the French Declaration of the Rights of Man and the Citizen? Yes, largely; for it stresses the rights of the individual, yet it does recognize certain collectivist principles of both Canadian and American origin.

Had the Charter as proposed originally by Prime Minister Trudeau and the federal government been entrenched in the constitution, Canadians would have had a declaration of rights committed more to the tradition of individual rights than the present one. But even had the Trudeau proposal been enacted without change, it too included some concessions to the idea of community rights. Specifically, the statement on 'Equality Rights,' which appears as section 15 of the Charter, was part of the prime minister's original proposal, and it definitely recognizes the collective rights of 'disadvantaged' groups. Section 15 says:

(1) Every individual is equal before and under the law and has the right to the equal protection and equal benefit of the law without discrimination and, in particular, without discrimination based on race, national or ethnic origin, colour, religion,

---

9 *Walter et al.* v *Attorney General for Alberta*; *Fletcher* v *Attorney General for Alberta*, [1969] SCR 383; 66 WWR 513
10 See John S. Moir, *Church and State in Canada* (Toronto: McClelland and Stewart, 1967), pp 140–9.

sex, age or mental or physical disability. (2) Subsection (1) does not preclude any law, program or activity that has as its object the amelioration of conditions of disadvantaged individuals or groups including those that are disadvantaged because of race, national or ethnic origin, colour, religion, sex, age or mental or physical disability.

What section 15(2) no doubt means, of course, is that the Charter now provides for what Americans have come to refer to as 'affirmative action.' Thus, in the future, governments, both federal and provincial, may feel it important to discriminate *against* one group of Canadians in order to take affirmative action – to discriminate against certain persons on behalf of another group of Canadians.

But the present Charter contains at least one other provision which recognizes community rights, in this case *provincial* rights, above individual rights. As is well known to practically all Canadians, the original Trudeau charter proposal had to be modified somewhat as a result of pressure exerted on the federal government by the official opposition, most of the provinces and, ultimately, the Supreme Court of Canada. Consequently, section 6 now allows provincial governments to restrict the mobility rights of Canadians from other provinces in a way that would not have been done under the original Trudeau proposal. Subsection (4) of that section states: 'Subsections (2) and (3) do not preclude any law, program or activity that has as its object the amelioration in a province of conditions of individuals in that province who are socially or economically disadvantaged if the rate of employment in that province is below the rate of employment in Canada.'

No doubt more important than either of the two sections just discussed, at least from a political standpoint, are sections 23 and 24 – those portions of the Charter which deal with minority language education rights. Under both the original Trudeau proposal and the present Charter, language educational rights have been treated as collective rather than individual rights. After all, under the British North America Act education lies almost entirely under provincial jurisdiction, and therefore, if section 23 is to say anything meaningful at all, it has to deal with the rights of language minorities – francophones in English-speaking Canada and anglophones in Quebec – rather than the rights of individuals.

Nonetheless, after noting these collectivist aspects to the sections in question, it is still evident that they are primarily directed towards the protection of *individual* or at least *family* rights as against the collective rights of a linguistic majority in any given province. Note the language of section 23:

23. (1) Citizens of Canada (a) whose first language learned and still understood is that of the English or French linguistic minority population of the province in which they reside, or (b) who have received their primary school instruction in Canada in English or French and reside in a province where the language in which they received that instruction is the language of the English or French linguistic minority population of the province, have the right to have their children receive primary and secondary school instruction in that language in that province. (2) Citizens of Canada of whom any child has received or is receiving primary or secondary school instruction in English or French in Canada, have the right to have all their children receive primary and secondary school instruction in the same language. (3) The right of citizens of Canada under subsections (1) and (2) to have their children receive primary and secondary school instruction in the language of the English or French linguistic minority population of a province (a) applies wherever in the province the number of children of citizens who have such a right is sufficient to warrant the provision to them out of public funds of minority language instruction; and (b) includes, where the number of those children so warrants, the right to have them receive that instruction in minority language educational facilities provided out of public funds.

But what does this mean? Basically, it broadens individual and family rights in the area of language education to a greater extent than ever before in Canadian history. True, it does not give Canadians an *absolute* right to have their children educated in either official language anywhere throughout the country, but it does grant French-speaking Canadians living in English-speaking provinces the right to have their children educated in *either* French or English. And, conversely, it grants English-speaking Canadians in Quebec the right to have their children educated in either English or French.

Sections 23 and 24, therefore, strongly buttress individual rights but make necessary and common sense provisions for the fact that the public education of children must be looked on from a practical, collectivist standpoint as well as an individual one. While section 23 stresses the rights of 'citizens of Canada' who speak either French or English at home and section 24 allows them to turn to the courts against violations of those rights described in section 23, section 23(3) (a) and (b) provides for public support for minority language education *only* where the number of minority language children warrants the establishment and support of a school, schools or program. Also, except under the terms of section 23(2), when immigrants from foreign countries settle in Canada, they *must* educate their children in the language of the linguistic majority of the province in which they settle *unless that province itself decrees otherwise.* Thus, language educational rights are circumscribed by such things as the language spoken at home, Canadian citizenship and the size of the local minority language community to which children belong.

Some mention needs to be made here of aboriginal and native treaty rights, the Charter's commitment to multiculturalism and to the existence of denominational, separate or dissentient schools. All of these matters, dealt with in sections 25 to 29, were present in the original Trudeau proposal in one way or another, and whether one likes them or not, their inclusion was probably necessary or wise from an historic standpoint. But they are most interesting provisions, for all of them are collectivist in nature. Thus, Indians and Inuit have certain rights under the British North America Act and section 27 states: 'This charter shall be interpreted in a manner consistent with the preservation and enhancement of the multicultural heritage of Canadians' whatever that means.

Then, finally, there are the now famous 'notwithstanding' clauses of the Charter: sections 32(2) and 33(1)(2)(3) and (4). According thereto, Parliament and the provincial legislatures (acting within their particular sphere of jurisdiction) may, in effect, suspend sections 2 or 7 through 15 of the Charter of Rights. And there can be no doubt that with these provisions much of the Charter's very *raison d'être* may be destroyed by Parliament or the legislatures in the name of a majority or even a plurality of the electorate. Thus, in an ultimate sense, there is nothing to stop Parliament from outlawing unpopular minorities during times of crises anymore than there was during the Second World War. Were Japanese Canadians and Jehovah's Witnesses to become the targets of governmental and popular hostility as they were in 1941 and 1942, they could be proscribed, outlawed or interned just as they were then. In effect, that means that even according to the Charter, the collective rights of the nation or a province may ultimately come before the individual. But, then, even in a country such as the United States, which emphasizes individual rights to the greatest degree, that is ultimately true.

No one can, of course, determine just how the new Canadian Charter of Rights and Freedoms will be interpreted by the courts. Yet the likelihood is that it will have a positive effect in protecting the rights of individuals in a way that they have not been in the past. Legal Rights as described in sections 7 through 14 are now specified very much as they are in the United States Bill of Rights – and much more clearly than they have been in the past. The Fundamental Freedoms discussed in section 2 – freedom of conscience and religion; freedom of thought, belief, opinion and expression, including freedom of the press and other media of communication; freedom of peaceful assembly; and freedom of association – entrenched constitutional rights as they previously were not. Minority Language Education Rights certainly may be protected more forcibly by the courts under sections 23 and 24. But what about the more overtly collectivist sections of the Charter? What will happen with respect to them? Again, it is difficult to say, but they will no doubt be used by governments, majority and minority groups as 'escape clauses' to avoid certain provisions of the Charter and will also become major sources of litigation.

Affirmative action in the United States has already brought at least one major case before the country's Supreme Court, and more will no doubt follow. If history is any guide, the same sort of thing will happen in Canada shortly. Aboriginal rights will no doubt soon come into conflict with the rights of women, both of which are guaranteed by the Charter, but the likelihood is that Indian women will soon gain the same legal rights as Indian men. Section 28 seems to make that clear. Mobility rights will probably be respected generally, and since not many will want to move to more depressed provinces for employment anyway, section 6(4) will most likely *not* become a hotly disputed proviso. As far as separate or denominational schools are concerned, the issues surrounding them have largely, although not wholly, been settled in the courts already.

What about the 'notwithstanding' provisions? Will they be used or not? Outside Quebec that remains to be seen. In spite of the general optimism on the part of many civil libertarians that they will not be, I personally feel that they will. A charter or bill of rights is more likely to be violated by governments in times of war or emergency than at any other time. The history of the United States demonstrates this fact. Yet such charters or bills, nonetheless, *do serve* as some buttress against the most extreme behaviour of public officials. Also, after wars and emergencies, individuals can go to court and obtain some redress of grievances. But the 'notwithstanding' clauses may permit governments and public officials to violate human rights with the greatest impunity during wars and emergencies without any fear that later they may be forced to account for their actions. This, I believe, is a serious defect in the Charter. Nonetheless, the Charter will very probably be a major buttress in defence of civil liberties in Canada. All of us should hail its enactment and entrenchment as a positive step in the history of our nation.

Judicial Statesmanship and the Canadian Charter of Rights and Freedoms

Rainer Knopff and F.L. Morton*

[The power of the courts] is immense, but it is a power springing from opinion. They are all-powerful so long as the people consent to obey the law; they can do nothing when they scorn it. Now of all powers, that of opinion is the hardest to use, for it is impossible to say exactly where its limits come. Often it is as dangerous to lag behind as to outstrip it.

The federal judges therefore must not only be good citizens and men of education and integrity, qualities necessary for all magistrates, but must also be statesmen; they must know how to understand the spirit of the age, to confront those obstacles that can be overcome, and to steer out of the current when the tide threatens to carry them away, and with them the sovereignty of the Union and obedience to its laws.
Alexis de Tocqueville[1]

On 17 April 1982, the Charter of Rights and Freedoms became part of 'the supreme law of Canada.' As the judges attempt to breathe life into this 'parchment barrier,' they will have to come to terms with the compromise between activism and restraint wrought by the politicians. By 'activism,' we mean the judicial readiness to overrule the more overtly political branches of government in the name of controlling constitutional standards; 'judicial restraint' refers to the opposite disposition.[2] On the one hand, entrenchment and the clear direction to strike down laws inconsistent with the constitution

---

* Rainer Knopff an Associate Professor, and F.L. Morton, an Assistant Professor, are both with the Department of Political Science at the University of Calgary.
1 Alexis de Tocqueville, *Democracy in America*, trans George Lawrence, ed J.P. Mayer (Garden City, New York: Doubleday, 1969), pp 150–1
2 Peter H. Russell, *Leading Constitutional Decisions*, 3rd ed (Ottawa: Carleton University Press, 1982), p 14

were intended to overcome ambiguities in the existing Bill of Rights that provided a convenient 'cover' for extreme restraint. On the other hand, the proponents of judicial restraint managed to secure a provision for the legislative override of key sections of the Charter – in effect, the 'legislative review of judicial review,' as Peter Russell has put it.[3] The judges are thus confronted with an admonition to make more energetic use of the new Charter than they did of the Diefenbaker Bill of Rights, *and* a warning not to go too far.

It may be doubted that the middle road thus indicated exists, or if it does, that our judges will find and travel it. Some claim that the override provision will, at best, buttress existing judicial timidity and, at worst, make politically unpopular decisions impossible to sustain; in either case, they charge, the clause makes a mockery of the claim that rights and freedoms are now entrenched. Others insist, to the contrary, that the political disadvantages inherent in resorting to the override make its use unlikely; that Canada's legal profession (and hence the judiciary of the future) is becoming increasingly activist; that even the current Supreme Court has indicated its willingness to be more activist in the enforcement of entrenched constitutional provisions than it has been in its interpretation of the statutory Bill of Rights; and that the override may actually encourage activism among traditionalist judges, who can take comfort from the fact that the legislature remains supreme.[4] We contend that, although either outcome is possible, neither is desirable and further, that in the long term the extreme of activism cannot be sustained. The middle road implicit in the Charter exists and is the course of judicial statesmanship in the enforcement of any bill of rights, whether or not an overt legislative override exists. The override merely makes explicit the inherent limitations of judicial power in a democratic context.

These limitations on judicial power are especially important when constitutional provisions are interpreted not only to veto policy initiatives but also to require positive action on the part of governments. The 'language' and 'equality' provisions of the Charter are particularly apt to raise this problem. If the judicial interpretation of the equal protection clause of the American Fourteenth Amendment illustrates the danger of extreme activism in the enforcement of such rights, the interpretation of the corresponding clause of the 1960 Canadian Bill of Rights shows that the extremes of restraint are equally counterproductive. In light of this history, we evaluate the potential

---

3 Peter H. Russell, 'The Effect of a Charter of Rights on the Policy-Making Role of Canadian Courts,' *Canadian Public Administration* 25 (1982): 32
4 The arguments are summarized by Russell in *ibid*, pp 15-21.

of the equality provision of the new Charter for promoting the middle road of judicial statesmanship.

I

The necessity of judicial statesmanship in the enforcement of a charter of rights is a function of the liberal democratic order such a charter is intended to secure. Procedurally, liberal democratic government rests on the consent of the governed which, in practice, means the processes of representative democracy. Substantively, liberalism defines the purpose of government as the protection of rights. These principles are allied in the sense that majority rule prevents minority tyranny, but they conflict whenever majority opinion denies the freedom or equality of minorities. The enduring problem of liberal democracy is maintaining a just balance between its procedural and substantive requirements, or between rights and consent.[5] Judicial review of a charter of rights is one of a number of institutional responses to this problem.

The American founders of judicial review were acutely aware of the tension between the liberalism and the democracy of liberal democracy. They proposed a complex institutional solution, which was designed to balance responsiveness to the 'cool and deliberate sense of the community' with sufficient governmental independence to defend 'the people against their own temporary errors and delusions.'[6] The vesting of politically significant power in appointed judges with life tenure was the most extreme example of the attempt to secure a political role for sober reflection independent of immediate public whim. Others included the indirect selection and lengthy fixed terms of senators and the president, and the principle of representation itself.

II

If all forms of the political distance created by the founders were intended to give weight to the 'rights' side of the rights/consent dilemma, the judiciary

5 See generally Harry V. Jaffa, *Crisis of the House Divided* (Seattle: University of Washington Press, 1973); and Martin Diamond, *The Founding of the Democratic Republic* (Itasca, Ill.: F.E. Peacock Publishers, 1981). Cf Abraham Lincoln's 'Peoria Speech' (re the Nebraska Act), October 1854, in Roy P. Basler, ed, *The Collected Works of Abraham Lincoln* (New Brunswick, NJ: Rutgers University Press, 1953), II, pp 247–83; and his 'Springfield Speech' (re the *Dred Scott* decision), June 1857, in *ibid*, pp 389–410. See also Rainer Knopff, 'Pierre Trudeau and the Problem of Liberal Democratic Statesmanship,' *Dalhousie Review* 60 (1980–81), pp 712–26.

6 *The Federalist Papers; Alexander Hamilton, James Madison, John Jay* (New York: New American Library, 1961), p 384. See generally *Federalist* nos 10 and 51.

exercising judicial review was particularly well equipped to do so, not only because of its greater independence, but also by virtue of its training.[7] Indeed, were it not for the fact that the judiciary is the 'least dangerous,' as well as the most independent branch,[8] one might be tempted to suggest that these characteristics point more to a tyranny of rights over consent than to a proper balance between the two. In fact, the unarmed character of the Court underscores the impossibility of such judicial tyranny because, in the most decisive sense, judgments must generate consent to be effective.

In order to generate the required consent, courts must remember that, in a democratic age, the capacity of appointed judges to stand against the public depends upon a general perception that they are not speaking merely in their own name – i.e. imposing on the nation their particular policy preferences – but in the name of long-range principles enshrined in the constitution. Furthermore, the perception that judges speak in the name of the constitution is an improvement upon the belief that they speak in their own name only if the constitution is, itself, an object of respect. As James Madison observed, an effective constitution depends on '... that veneration which time bestows on everything, and without which perhaps the wisest and freest governments would not possess the requisite stability.'[9] Such respect is neither self-generating nor self-sustaining. Whether or not a constitution comes to enjoy it depends largely on the court's skill in choosing and handling its battles with the legislature, especially at the beginning. The extremes of either activism or restraint will almost certainly undermine it; activism by inviting non-compliance, and restraint by causing a court to interpret entrenched rights to fit legislation it does not wish to overrule. As the post-*Drybones* interpretation of the 1960 equality clause shows, the latter approach leads to a series of irreconcilable precedents which can hardly enhance the reputation of the judiciary or of the document it is interpreting.[10]

At first glance, the ability of the American Supreme Court to make one controversial decision after another, often with minimal textual support, and frequently overturning established and popular law or practice, tends to obscure the fragility of judicial authority and to depreciate the case for judicial statesmanship. The apparent triumph of American activism, in other

---

7 *Federalist Papers*, supra note 6, no 78; and de Tocqueville, *Democracy in America*, supra note 1, pp 263–70
8 *Federalist Papers*, supra note 6, no 78
9 *Ibid*, no 49
10 This is especially so in the 'Indian Act' cases. See Walter S. Tarnopolsky, *The Canadian Bill of Rights*, rev ed (Toronto: McClelland and Stewart, 1975), pp 148–63 and ch VIII. And see *A.-G. Canada* v *Canard* (1975), 52 DLR (3d) 548 (SCC).

words, implies the irrelevance, if not the cowardice, of restraint. Perhaps nothing so dramatically illustrates the power and independence of the American Court as the *Watergate Tapes Case*, where a single stroke of the judicial pen accomplished what the combined strength of the House and Senate could not. It was not always thus. The first exercise of judicial review involved a similar confrontation of the Court and the president, and the outcome was not nearly so predictable. A comparison of *Marbury* v *Madison*[11] and *U.S.* v *Nixon*[12] reveals the dramatic difference between the authority of a court before and after the convention of judicial review is firmly established. More importantly, the former case illustrates the kind of statesmanship that made the latter possible.

The full story of *Marbury* v *Madison* has been too often and too well told to repeat in detail here. It is sufficient to emphasize the fact that Chief Justice John Marshall claimed the power to judicial review – using it to strike down part of a statute authorizing him to issue the *mandamus* requested by Marbury, to which Marbury was otherwise entitled – in order to avoid threatened non-compliance by the executive, and perhaps even personal impeachment.[13] This successful first exercise of judicial review was the necessary precondition for the convention of 'automatic' compliance with Supreme Court decisions. The dispute could easily have issued in a very different result, establishing the opposite convention of discretionary compliance. John Marshall has long been memorialized for initiating the practice of judicial review in unlikely circumstances. Less emphasized has been the implicit lesson that, in establishing judicial authority, less may sometimes be more.[14]

One may conclude that the test of a judicially enforceable constitution is *not* the absence of a 'notwithstanding' clause, but the establishment of a convention of compliance. To state it differently, where a *non-obstante* clause *does* exist, a convention of legislative restraint in its use must develop. As in the American case, the establishment of such a convention in Canada will depend partly on judicial statesmanship.[15]

11 1 Cranch (US) 137 (1803)
12 418 US 683 (1974). For a more extended comparison of the two cases that makes a similar point, see Archibald Cox, *The Role of the Supreme Court in American Government* (Oxford: Oxford University Press, 1976), pp 3–11.
13 See, for example, Robert G. McCloskey, *The American Supreme Court* (Chicago: University of Chicago Press, 1960), pp 40–2.
14 See *ibid*, ch 2, esp p 47: '[P]aradoxical though it may seem, the Supreme Court often gains rather than loses power by adopting a policy of forbearance.'
15 Some argue that such a convention already exists with respect to identical override provisions in existing Canadian bills of rights, and that this convention will be transferred to section 33 of the Charter. This argument emphasizes that the override provision in the

III

The necessity of judicial statesmanship varies with the circumstances. What made Marbury such a *tour de force* was Marshall's ability to avoid a direct confrontation, which he was likely to lose, without creating the impression that the Court was simply yielding to political pressure. The problem of compliance – and hence the need for statesmanship – was acute because the available legal remedy, the *mandamus*, required positive action from a high political figure. The judicial enforcement of rights and liberties will not always involve this circumstance. Defence of the Legal Rights entrenched in the Charter, for example, typically requires court supervision not of governments and legislatures, but of law enforcement officials and bureaucrats.[16] The protection of the Fundamental Rights, such as freedom of expression, may entail the voiding of legislation, and thus raises the spectre of conflict to a greater extent; still, the legislature is being told what *not* to do rather than what it *must* do. Problems of compliance may exist in both cases, but they are clearly more serious when judges issue an affirmative order to the more political branches.

Recent decades have seen the steady expansion of a realm of human rights and fundamental freedoms 'which can be adequately remedied only by the issuance of a decree providing affirmative ongoing relief.'[17] The problem with such remedies is compounded when they entail the reallocation of pub-

---

1960 Canadian Bill of Rights was invoked only once – during the 'October Crisis' of 1970 to sustain extraordinary police powers – and that identical clauses in the three provincial bills of rights have not been abused.

There is some truth to this, but one must remember that the new Charter, unlike any of its predecessors, applies to both levels of government. Civil liberties issues could, thus, become entangled with federalism quarrels. Many provinces already doubt the impartiality of the 'federal' Supreme Court. If the Court uses the Charter to strike down a locally popular provincial law, its decision is likely to be condemned as an infringement of 'provincial rights' regardless of its substantive merit.

16 See Paul Weiler, *In the Last Resort: A Critical Study of the Supreme Court of Canada* (Toronto: Carswell, Methuen, 1974), p 209; Alexander Bickel, *The Supreme Court and the Idea of Progress* (New York: Harper & Row, 1970), p 32; and Paul Cavalluzzo, 'Judicial Review and the Bill of Rights: Drybones and its Aftermath,' *Osgoode Hall Law Review* 9 (1971): 545. For some startling examples of problems of compliance even in this area, see Donald L. Horowitz, *Courts and Social Policy* (Washington, DC: Brookings Institution, 1977), chs 5 and 6.

17 Judge Frank M. Johnson, 'The Role of the Judiciary with Respect to the Other Branches of Government,' in Walter F. Murphy and C. Herman Pritchett, eds, *Courts, Judges, and Politics: An Introduction to the Judicial Process*, 3rd ed (New York: Random House, 1979), p 69

lic funds, as they often do. The power of the purse is perhaps the most fundamental of all legislative powers and, not surprisingly, its elected trustees are hostile to any attempt to preempt its disbursement by other branches of government. Examples of such rights are economic and social rights such as the right 'to work' or to 'just and favourable conditions of work.' Judicial enforcement of such provisions requires the courts to abandon traditional and well understood legal remedies – such as the writ of *mandamus*, which is properly used to enforce only a specific duty – in favour of 'judicial legislation.' As Joseph Jaconelli points out,

[The] typical social right which requires affirmative action on the part of the State is, of necessity, so ill-defined that it would be extremely difficult to identify what, for example, are 'just and favourable conditions of work.' And even if it were possible to reach agreement on the precise details of the goal in view, its implementation would require such constant supervision as to necessitate an unprecedented change in the nature of the judicial function.[18]

Except for the minority language education guarantees, the Charter does not contain such positive rights requiring affirmative policy, though section 15(2) permits it. It does contain the more traditional anti-discrimination clause, however, and such clauses can be interpreted in a manner that leads to judicial legislation. In the United States, for example, enforcement of the equal protection clause of the Fourteenth Amendment against hostile southern states since the 1954 *School Desegregation Decision* has led to the controversial practice of 'court-ordered busing.'[19] Faced by reluctant policy-makers, some Federal District Court judges have implemented their orders by assuming the administration of local school districts, in effect replacing elected school boards.[20] This experience has substantially altered the character and function of the federal judiciary in American politics. Having acquired the habits and tools for such affirmative judicial policy-making in the area of school desegre-

---

18 Joseph Jaconelli, *Enacting a Bill of Rights: The Legal Problems* (Oxford: Oxford University Press, 1980), p 101
19 See *Brown* v *Board of Education*, 347 US 483 (1954); *Green* v *Kent County School Board*, 391 US 430 (1968); *Swann* v *Charlotte-Mecklenburg County Board of Education*, 402 US 1 (1970); *Keyes* v *School District No. 1, Denver*, 413 US 189 (1973); and *Milliken* v *Bradley*, 418 US 717 (1974).
20 See Jack W. Peltason, *Fifty-Eight Lonely Men* (New York: Harcourt, Brace & World, 1961); Lino A. Graglia, *Disaster by Decree: The Supreme Court Decisions on Race and the Schools* (Ithaca, NY: Cornell University Press, 1976); and Nathan Glazer, *Affirmative Discrimination* (New York: Basic Books, 1975).

gation, the courts have gone on to play a similar role in prison reform,[21] state mental health policies,[22] federal housing programs,[23] and public funding for abortion.[24] This has recently led to perhaps the most serious episode of 'court-curbing' since the court-packing crisis of 1937.[25]

In its famous *Drybones* decision, the Canadian Supreme Court indicated that it might follow the lead of its American counterpart. Speaking for the majority, Justice Ritchie rejected an interpretation 'pursuant to which ... the most glaring discriminatory legislation against a racial group would have to be construed as recognizing the right of each of its individual members "to equality before the law," so long as all the other members are being discrimi-

---

21 *Hamilton* v *Schiro*, 338 F. Supp. 1016 (E.D. La. 1970), further relief ordered *sub. nom. Hamilton* v *Landrieu*, 351 F. Supp. 549 (1972); *Hamilton* v *Love*, 328 F. supp. 1182 (E.D. Ark. 1971), contempt granted, 358 F. Supp. 338 (1973), contempt citation revoked, 361 F. Supp. 1235 (1973)

22 *Wyatt* v *Stickney*, 325 F. Supp. 781 (M.D. Ala., 1971), 334 F. Supp. 1341 (1971), 344 F. Supp. 373 (1972), 344 F. Supp. 387 (1972), affirmed in part *sub. nom. Wyatt* v *Aderholt*, 503 F2d 1305 (5th Cir. 1974). In this case the federal district court judge ordered state mental hospitals to adhere to some eighty-four minimum standards of care and treatment. Compliance with this order raised Alabama's expenditures on mental institutions from $14 million (1971) to $58 million (1973). See Horowitz, *supra* note 16, pp 4–7, and Nathan Glazer, 'Should Judges Administer Social Services,' *The Public Interest* 50 (1978): pp 69–80.

23 *Hills* v *Gautreux*, 455 US 284 (1976). See Irving Welfeld, 'The Courts and Desegregated Housing: The Meaning (if any) of the Gautreux Case,' *The Public Interest* 45 (1976): pp 123–35.

24 *McRae* v *Mathews*, 421 F. Supp. 533 (1976); *Harris* v *McRae*, 65 L.Ed. 2d 784 (1980). This was the 'Hyde Amendment' case. The Hyde Amendment, adopted in 1976, prohibited the expenditures of Medicaid funds for abortion except to save the life of the mother or in cases of rape or incest. Judge Dooley of the Federal District Court in Brooklyn ruled that these restrictions violated the First and Fifth Amendments, and ordered payments to be restored. On appeal to the Supreme Court, 247 congressmen and senators joined in an *amicus curiae* brief, which argued that Judge Dooley's decision 'in the most fundamental way subverts the Constitution of the United States by making meaningless the reservation to Congress of the right to determine when "money shall be drawn from the Treasury."'

25 A recent count indicated 27 bills pending in Congress that are designed to restrict or to remove federal court jurisdiction to hear cases dealing with abortion, school prayer and non-voluntary busing for school integration. (See *Congressional Quarterly Weekly Report* (30 May 1981): 947–51.) In March of 1982, the Senate passed a bill that would virtually eliminate court-ordered busing. Also in March, a Senate committee favourably recommended an anti-abortion bill for the first time. The other prong of the attack on the federal courts is through the appointment process. True to their 1980 Platform, President Reagan and the Republican majority in the Senate have exercised their joint appointment power to elevate 'avowed believers in judicial self-restraint' and decentralization to federal judgeships. (See US *News and World Report* (15 February 1982): pp 33–4.)

nated against in the same way.'²⁶ In a concurring judgment, Justice Hall likened such a purely formal definition of equality to the infamous 'separate but equal' doctrine of *Plessy* v *Ferguson*, and suggested that if the Canadian provision was analogous to the Fourteenth Amendment, it was to the Fourteenth Amendment of *Brown*, not of *Plessy*.

The social situations in *Brown* v *Board of Education* and in the instant case are, of course, very different but the basic philosophic concept is the same. The Canadian Bill of Rights is not fulfilled if it merely equates Indians with Indians in terms of equality before the law, but can have validity and meaning only when ... it is seen to repudiate discrimination in every law of Canada by reason of race, national origin, colour, religion, or sex in respect of the human rights and fundamental freedoms set out in s.1 in whatever way that discrimination may manifest itself not only as between Indian and Indian, but as between all Canadians whether Indian or non-Indian.²⁷

The Court quickly drew back from this definition of equality, however. In the infamous sequel to *Drybones*, the *Lavell* case, Justice Ritchie (again for the majority) insisted that equality before the law 'is to be treated as meaning equality in the administration or application of the law by the law-enforcement authorities and the ordinary courts of the land' – a definition difficult to distinguish from the one he had rejected in *Drybones*.²⁸ Moreover, Ritchie also rejected the Fourteenth Amendment – and thereby Hall's concurrence with his own judgment in *Drybones* – as a guide for the interpretation of the Canadian equality provision.²⁹

It is not unreasonable to suppose that this turnabout was motivated in part by a fear that a *Brown*-like interpretation of the Canadian Bill of Rights would force Canadian judges to follow their American brethren into the political thicket. A focus on equality in the administration of the law does not require the courts to second-guess a political judgment on the reasonableness of the legislative classification itself. To the extent that the *Drybones* approach does require such judgments, it raises the prospect of judicial legislation and thus, of conflict with the more 'political' legislators. Interestingly, even Justice Laskin, who registered a powerful dissent in *Lavell*, was at pains to repudiate the American doctrine of 'reasonable classification,' and to demonstrate that our Bill of Rights left much less room for interpretive discretion. He clearly implied that, since they were bound by tighter wording,

26 *R.* v *Drybones*, [1970] SCR 282 p 297
27 *Ibid*, p 300
28 *A.-G. Canada* v *Lavell*, [1974] SCR 1349 p 1366
29 *Ibid*, p 1365

our judges could not be considered to be usurping the political function when they upheld the Bill of Rights against conflicting legislation.[30]

This reluctance to engage in judicial legislation was present among the justices even in the *Drybones* case. There it took the form of a dissent from the majority's judgment that the Bill of Rights was more than an interpretive guide and could override even clearly conflicting legislation. This interpretation, said Justice Abbott, 'necessarily implies a wide delegation of the legislative authority of Parliament to the courts ... it would require the plainest words to impute to Parliament an intention to extend to the courts such an invitation to engage in judicial legislation.'[31] By the time of *Lavell*, this view had come to prevail.[32] The overriding effect of the Bill having been firmly established, however, the danger of judicial legislation in the area of equality could be reduced only by contracting the definition of equality in order to minimize the prospect of conflicting legislation.

Such extreme deference to legislative policy will now be more difficult. More than any other, the equality section of the new Canadian Charter constitutes a rejection of previous jurisprudence, which even conservative judges will be hard put to ignore. To the 1960 protection of 'equality before the law and the protection of the law' have been added the guarantees of 'equality *under* the law' and 'equal benefit of the law,' additions that were intended to reverse the restrictive judicial interpretations given to the old wording in *Lavell* and *Bliss* respectively.[33]

Against this background, it will be difficult for judges to maintain the purely formal definition of equality propounded in *Lavell*. The guarantee of

30 *Ibid*, pp 1386–7
31 *Supra* note 34 p 299
32 In an intervening case, *Curr* v *The Queen*, [1972] SCR 889, Abbott concurred with Laskin, who explicitly approved the American 'switch in time that saved nine,' which was motivated by 'the realization that [the] Court [had] enter[ed] the bog of legislative policy-making' in its 'substantive due process' jurisprudence (at 902). In this case, Laskin also formulated the theory, which reappears in *Lavell*, that the Canadian Bill of Rights provides less interpretive elbow-room than the American Fourteenth Amendment (*loc cit*). He also made a distinction between 'judicially manageable standards' and the mere substitution of judicial policy preferences for legislative policy preferences (pp 889–90), a distinction that reappeared in his *Morgentaler* opinion (see below p 196).
33 *A.-G. Canada* v *Lavell*, *supra* note 28; *Bliss* v *A.-G. Canada* (1977), 16 NR 254. It was the women's movement that pressed for these charges, and it seems that women's groups intend to make good use of them by bringing to the Court a 'blizzard of litigation' on 'almost every issue of concern ... abortion, divorce, pornography, prostitution, maternity benefits, employment, sexual assault, daycare.' There are even plans to establish 'legal defense funds' to pay for such litigation. David Blaikie, 'Courts Will Determine Quality of Victory,' *Calgary Herald*, 26 March 1982, p B12

'equality *under* the law' will almost certainly turn the enumerated grounds of discrimination into 'suspect' classifications. On the other hand, it is generally acknowledged that not *all* classifications based on these or other criteria should be prohibited. The courts will thus be forced to develop what they have hitherto preferred to avoid, namely, 'some criterion of equality akin to the doctrine of reasonable classification.'[34] The Charter thus forces on the Court a task which was logically implied by its *Drybones* holding but carefully avoided thereafter. As Peter Hogg remarks, 'It is easy to see why Canadian judges find the doctrine [of reasonable classification] unpalatable: it forces the court to leave the safe area of conventional legal materials, and embark on an inquiry into the rationality and acceptability of legislative policy.'[35] This now unavoidable task clearly increases the potential for conflict between courts and legislatures, and thereby provides both a new field for judicial statesmanship, and the opportunity for counter-productive activism.

In itself, however, the finding of an 'unreasonable' legislative classification requires no more than the voiding of the offending statute and, although this raises the possibility of conflict, it is not as dangerous as a judicial order to undertake a positive policy. As we have seen, equality clauses are also capable of generating this most problematic form of judicial review.

Whether this happens in Canada depends largely on the extent to which the equality clause reaches into the private sphere. In theory, equality and liberty are closely related; in practice, equality is in tension with the political and economic liberties because the latter create a private sphere in which 'private discrimination' may flourish. The boundaries of the private sphere are secured by government action, but it thrives by virtue of government inaction (what is not forbidden is permitted). Its defence by the judiciary, then, requires only the annulling of offending legislation. Overcoming private discrimination, on the other hand, requires positive state action, usually limiting the very private sphere constituted by the other liberties. Some degree of such action may be justified by the self-contradiction inherent in the use of liberty to deny the very equality which engenders it.[36] The question is whether such action should be constitutionally required and enforceable by courts.

At one time, the federal government advocated a constitutionally entrenched prohibition of private discrimination, but that proposal has not

---

34 Peter Hogg, *Constitutional Law of Canada* (Agincourt: Carswell, 1977), p 441
35 *Loc cit*
36 For extended discussion of this contradiction, see Jaffa, *Crisis of the House Divided supra* note 5.

found its way into the Charter.[37] Section 52 of the Constitution Act, 1982, gives the courts only the power to strike down 'laws' that are inconsistent with the constitution, including the Charter. Section 15, the equality clause, guarantees equality 'before and under the *law*' and 'the right to the equal protection and equal benefit of the *law*,' and in this respect follows the 1960 wording. It is true that section 15(2), which permits 'affirmative action,' speaks not only of laws but also of 'programs' and 'activities,' and the latter words are capable of an interpretation that would embrace the private sphere. But section 15(2) is permissive. It allows 'benign' discrimination, and positive policy is not required to overcome what is permitted. It is only *prohibited* private discrimination that requires active remedies, which the courts would have to enforce, and section 15(1), the prohibitive section, extends only to *laws*. There is no analogue in the Charter to section 15(2) of the old Bill of Rights, which defined the term 'law' as used in that Act, but there is no reason to believe that it will be interpreted differently. Finally, section 32 limits the application of the Charter 'to the Parliament and government of Canada' and 'the legislature and government of each province.' It would seem, then, that only public discrimination is prohibited by the Charter. In this instance, at least, the wording of the document minimizes one of the dangers inherent in judicial enforcement of entrenched equality provisions.

The problem is not wholly solved by limiting the reach of an equality clause to public discrimination, however. The concept of discrimination, or unconstitutional inequality, is itself open to an expansive interpretation that would lead to the same result as if the clause had extended to private discrimination. More specifically, if the test for unconstitutional public discrimination becomes the presence of a 'discriminatory impact' (usually as measured by statistical imbalance), whether or not the state intended to cause it, then the courts could again find themselves in the position of requiring the positive policy necessary to remedy the imbalance.

The building of penitentiaries, for example, is clearly a form of public action. Given the social fact that there is typically a much higher number of male than female criminals, policy-makers may find it reasonable to maintain fewer prisons for women than for men. In Canada, the disproportion has been such that only one federal penitentiary for women exists. It is difficult to read discriminatory intent into such a policy, yet it is undeniable that a higher proportion of female prisoners will be housed far from family and friends. If this constitutes unconstitutional discrimination, then the constitu-

---

37 Government of Canada, *The Constitution and the People of Canada* (Ottawa: Information Canada, 1969), p 54

tion, through the courts, would require the government either to dismantle the prison system altogether, or to take positive (and rather expensive) steps to remedy the imbalance. In effect, such an interpretation of the equality clause would force the government to respond to and overcome forces in the private or societal sphere – in this case the tendency of fewer women to engage in criminal activity – that are tangential to the mischief at which the legislation is directed.

How likely is it that the discriminatory impact of even neutral policies will become the test of unconstitutional public discrimination? One of the new provisions in section 15 of the Charter is the guarantee of 'equal benefit of the law,' a phrase that opens the door to such an interpretation. Against this, one may point to the Court's awareness of the problems inherent in such an expansive definition of unconstitutional inequality. In his *Morgentaler* opinion, Justice Laskin, one of the more activist judges on the Court, rejected the proposition that differential access to legal abortion based on 'place or area of residence (where remote from hospitals or where there is a dearth of qualified physicians) and economic status,' constituted a violation of the equality clause of the 1960 Bill of Rights. Said Laskin,

This is a reach for equality by judicially unmanageable standards, and is posited on the theory that the Court should either *give directions* for the achievement of relative equality of access to therapeutic abortion committees and approved hospitals to overcome an alleged legislative shortcoming, or should strike down not only subss. (4) and (5) of s.251 (which would leave an unqualified prohibition of abortion) but the whole section as being inseverable.

I do not regard s.1(b) of the Canadian Bill of Rights as charging the courts with supervising the administrative efficiency of legislation or with evaluating the regional or national organization of its administration, *in the absence of any touchstone in the legislation itself* which would indicate a violation of s.1(b) including the specified prohibitions of discrimination by reason of race, national origin, colour, religion or sex.[38]

Weighing on the other side of the scale is the judicial and quasi-judicial interpretation of federal and provincial anti-discrimination *legislation*, which is rapidly moving toward the test of 'discriminatory effect' as measured by statistical imbalance.[39] The chance of this 'human rights' jurisprudence being

38 *Morgentaler* v *The Queen*, [1976] 1 SCR 616 p 635 [emphasis added]
39 See William Black, 'From Intent to Effect: New Standards in Human Rights,' *Canadian Human Rights Report* 1 (1980), c/1.

incorporated into judicial interpretation of the Charter is probably reduced, however, by the mere existence and reach of human rights legislation. In the United States, the Fourteenth Amendment is also limited to prohibiting discrimination by public or state action, but in an historical context of flagrant racial discrimination in which legislative remedies were unavailable and unlikely to be enacted, 'state action' has been interpreted broadly. It covers not only discriminatory *laws*, but also discriminatory administration of neutral laws, and even extends to apparently 'private' discrimination when the latter is sanctioned by state action.[40] In Canada, at the time of entrenchment, all eleven jurisdictions have enacted comprehensive human rights codes which apply not only to private discrimination, but also to the public administration of legislative policy.[41] Thus, in the case of the penitentiary issue outlined above, it was the Canadian Human Rights Commission that recently found that the existing distribution of prisons for men and women violated the code.[42] It is usually in the administration of otherwise neutral laws that 'discriminatory effect' becomes an issue, and to the extent that this is already being handled under human rights legislation, the Court may not be tempted to find *unconstitutional* discrimination 'in the absence of any touchstone in the legislation itself.'

With respect to the equality clause, then, the new wording clearly compels greater judgment on the part of the Court in determining the reasonableness of legislative classifications. Furthermore, the 'equal benefit' provision creates the opportunity to engage in direct judicial legislation. On the other hand, the clear emphasis on public discrimination and the availability of statutory remedies for 'discriminatory impact' provide support for the prevailing atmosphere of judicial restraint.

IV

The wording of the Charter may affect the direction and style of judicial review but is unlikely to determine it. The capacity of judicial ingenuity to circumvent even apparently clear drafting is well known, and the wording of the Charter is certainly not without ambiguity. Ultimately, effective judicial

---

40 See *Shelley* v *Kramer*, 334 US 1 (1948); *Burton* v *Wilmington Parking Authority*, 365 US 715 (1961); and *Moose Lodge* v *Irvis*, 407 US 163 (1972). See Walter Berns, 'Racial Discrimination and the Limits of Judicial Remedy,' in Robert A. Goldwin, ed, *100 Years of Emancipation* (Chicago: University of Chicago, 1963), esp pp 196–210.
41 Walter S. Tarnopolsky, *Discrimination and the Law in Canada* (Don Mills: R. De Boo Ltd, 1982), pp 380–3
42 Canadian Human Rights Commission, *Newsletter-Bulletin*, 5 (January, 1982): p 5

statesmanship will depend on the political theory that comes to inform the jurisprudence of the Court and the perceptions of its public. As Justice Cardozo has said:

> Implicit in every decision where the question is, so to speak, at large is a philosophy of the origin and aim of law, a philosophy which, however veiled, is in truth the final arbiter. It accepts one set of arguments, modifies another, rejects a third, standing ever in reserve as a court of ultimate appeal. Often the philosophy is ill co-ordinated and fragmentary. Its empire is not always suspected even by its subjects. Neither lawyer nor judge, pressing forward along one line or retreating along another, is conscious at all times that it is philosophy which is impelling him to the front or driving him to the rear. Nonetheless the goad is there. If we cannot escape the furies, we shall do well to understand them.[43]

We have suggested that an entrenched charter of rights attests to the liberal component of a liberal democratic regime, but the judicial enforcement of such a charter ignores the regime's democratic component at its peril – in short, judicial statesmanship depends on an appreciation of the rights/consent dilemma of classical liberalism. Counter-productive extremes of either activism or restraint occur whenever this tension is denied and one of the components is exalted above the other. Such denials may come from either the left or the right. Both the property-conscious 'substantive due process' activism of the United States Supreme Court in the early decades of this century, and the more recent egalitarian activism of the Warren Court, exhibit a marked preference for results (rights) over process (consent), a preference typified by Chief Justice Warren's characteristic response to the merely legal argument of a constitutional question: 'Yes, yes, yes, but is it right? Is it good?'[44]

Today, the danger comes chiefly from the left, or from that stream of modern liberalism which arises out of Rousseau's critique of the classical liberalism of Hobbes and Locke.[45] The rights/consent dilemma is a perma-

---

43 Benjamin N. Cardozo, *The Growth of the Law* (New Haven: Yale University Press, 1924), p 25, quoted in Weiler, *supra* note 16, p 236
44 Alexander M. Bickel, *The Morality of Consent* (New Haven: Yale University Press, 1975), p 120
45 In *The Morality of Consent*, *ibid*, Bickel presents a similar analysis of the theoretical presuppositions of the judicial activism of the Warren Court. He too understands the problem as a tension between liberty and equality, and between the substantive and procedural requirements of liberal democracy, and identifies two distinct theoretical approaches to this problem. However, while we identify Locke and Rousseau as the

nent one, requiring unceasing statesmanship, only for classical liberalism, which holds that human nastiness (including inegalitarian prejudice) is as deeply rooted in nature as is political equality and freedom. The disciples of Rousseau, on the other hand, deny that selfishness is natural and can, therefore, envision what would be unthinkable to an exponent of the older liberalism: 'a social state in which men would wish to benefit themselves only in ways that are beneficial or at least not harmful to others, [a state in which] men's perfect integration into the community would be indistinguishable from their perfect freedom to do as they please.'[46] Once this state is reached, the rights/consent dilemma disappears. On the way to this state, moreover, existing prejudice need not be accommodated; it is the result not of nature, but of 'the system' and the important thing is to change this system, by force if necessary. Consent may thus have to be abandoned, though only temporarily. This theory encourages aggressive judicial intervention precisely because of the belief that it need only be temporary.

In fact, this mode of thought is hostile to modern constitutionalism, which requires that the pursuit of goals be tempered by considerations of process, and which is founded on the classical liberal reading of human nature. Liberal constitutionalism is *limited* government, depending on the restraint of office-holders, including the judiciary. If Rousseau's reading of nature is accepted, this constitutionalism may have to be abandoned in favour of a temporary but benign imposition of rights against what is perceived as unenlightened consent. Proponents of the older liberalism would respond that a 'system changing' strategy cannot ignore consent only temporarily because it is nature, not the system, that is at fault; the application of force would, therefore, be permanent. For that very reason, however, they would deny that such a strategy could be sustained by the judiciary, an institution possessed of neither sword nor purse. They would agree with de Tocqueville

---

originators of these two approaches, Bickel places them both in the same camp – what he calls the 'contractarian' tradition. He argues that this Locke-Rousseau tradition supports excessive judicial activism, and contrasts them with Burke, who is said to provide support for a Lincolnian statesmanship. This interpretation misreads both Locke and Burke, and neglects the profound influence of Locke on both the Founders and Lincoln. In fact, it is Locke, not Burke, who provides the most solid appreciation of what Bickel correctly identifies as the 'Lincolnian tension.' Rousseau is indeed the enemy, but not because of his contractarianism *per se*, as Bickel's assimilation of Locke and Rousseau suggests. See Jaffa, *supra* note 6; Leo Strauss, *Natural Right and History* (Chicago: University of Chicago Press, 1953), chs 5 and 6; and George P. Grant, *Lament for a Nation* (Toronto: McClelland and Stewart, 1970), ch 5.

46 Joseph Cropsey, 'Conservatism and Liberalism,' in his *Political Philosophy and the Issues of Politics* (Chicago: University of Chicago Press, 1977), pp 124–5

that judicial insensitivity to public opinion in the name of rights can only destroy the judiciary itself.

The necessity of the judicial statesmanship we have described depends on which of these theories more closely approximates the truth; the prospect of it being practised depends on which one becomes the 'inarticulate major premise' of the legal community.

PART FOUR: THE CANADIAN CHARTER OF RIGHTS AND FREEDOMS

Some Perspectives on the Canadian Charter of Rights and Freedoms

Walter S. Tarnopolsky*

First of all, may I remind you that this is part of a series of meetings that a number of us from Canada have been fortunate enough to have with some American scholars. Since some of what I will be referring to this afternoon will have a meaning only in the context of what went on in these meetings, I will try to make the necessary connections. If I do not, then perhaps it can come out in the question period later.

One of the things that one has to start with, in considering the future effect of the new Charter,[1] is to remember that in the British North America Act,[2] apart from a few group rights, there are no protections for individual rights. Yesterday, one of our American guests, Professor Berns, suggested that the best way to understand Canada was to look at a coin which says, 'Elizabeth by the Grace of God,' as this is the fundamental principle of our constitution. I would suggest that that has about as much relevance to Canada as has the American coin which says, 'In God We Trust.' Essentially, neither the Americans nor we really believe what we say.

The fundamental proposition from which one has to start, is found in the Preamble to the British North America Act, which says that the new country is to be federally united 'with a Constitution similar in Principle to that of the United Kingdom.' And so, until the enactment of the Canadian Bill of Rights[3] and the other provincial bills of rights, it was the three principles coming out of that Preamble that determined our civil liberties, namely,

---

* Walter S. Tarnopolsky is Director of the Human Rights Centre at the University of Ottawa.
1 *Canadian Charter of Rights and Freedoms*, part I of the *Constitution Act*, 1982
2 30 & 31 Vict., c 3
3 SC 1960, c 44; RSC 1970, Appendix III

federalism and two fundamental doctrines of the English Constitution – parliamentary supremacy, and the Rule of Law. I shall not deal with those principles, but I think that one cannot view the Charter without seeing them as part of our constitutional foundations.

In assessing the Charter of Rights and Freedoms agreed to in November 1981, we have to try to see whether there could be a difference from the application of the Canadian Bill of Rights. In order to determine that, I would suggest that there are three main criteria one has to consider. The first is constitutional status, the second is content, and the third, measures of enforcement. I am going to deal with the three in turn.

(1) *Constitutional Status* Those of you who have looked at decisions of the Supreme Court of Canada concerning the Canadian Bill of Rights will know that the Supreme Court never did accept the Bill of Rights as being constitutional. At most, some called it 'quasi-constitutional,' but most of the references were to the fact that it is statutory. The new Charter, by section 52 of the new Constitution Act, 1982, is made the primary law of the country and any law in Canada which is contrary to the constitution (including the Charter), is, to the extent of the inconsistency, of no force or effect. To that extent there is a change. I hope that as a result the courts will realize that they are interpreting the constitution and not a mere statute. I would hope that they might take into consideration such statements as that made by Lord Sankey in 1932, in the famous *Persons* case,[4] when he held that women might be 'persons' for purposes of appointment to the Senate. You will remember that amongst the things he said was that: 'The British North America Act planted in Canada a living tree capable of growth and expansion within its natural limits. The object of the Act was to grant a Constitution to Canada ... Their Lordships do not conceive it to be the duty of this Board – it is certainly not their desire – to cut down the provisions of the Act by narrow and technical construction, but rather to give it a large and liberal interpretation ...'[5] I could go on with other quotations that we have had with respect to the difference between a constitutional instrument and a statutory instrument, and with the hope that I would have that the courts will pay attention to that difference in their interpretation of the Charter, but time does not permit.

The second major characteristic of the existing Bill of Rights, which is changed in the Charter, is that the existing Bill does not apply to the provinces. The situation at present is that, although all ten provinces have anti-

4 *Edwards* v *A.-G. of Canada*, [1930] AC 124
5 *Ibid*, 136

discrimination legislation,[6] only Saskatchewan,[7] Quebec,[8] and Alberta[9] have bills of rights dealing with the fundamental freedoms. Only Quebec and Saskatchewan include legal rights, but the Saskatchewan provision is very narrow. Quebec has the widest provison on this point. All the other provinces do not have anything restraining parliamentary supremacy, which they have gained through the British North America Act, other than the electoral process. To that extent, since by section 32(1) the Charter applies to all of the provinces as well as to the federal government, we now have a major change. I would suggest, other than in the case of the province of Quebec which has the most comprehensive bill of rights, that the Charter constitutes a major addition.

(2) *Content* I have argued in the past that entrenchment is not as important in determining whether a bill of rights will be given overriding power as whether it purports to have that overriding power. Constitutional status, the issue of whether a bill of rights can be easily amended or not, is one thing. One has, however, to look at whether the words do so specifically provide.

I think that the Charter is a major change from the existing Bill of Rights in at least two ways. Supreme Court majorities in Canada have created two main deficiencies in the Canadian Bill of Rights. The first was that they relied upon section 1 of the Canadian Bill of Rights, which says, 'It is hereby recognized and declared that in Canada there *have existed and shall continue to exist* ... the following human rights and fundamental freedoms.' Based upon that clause, majorities on the Supreme Court have said that the Bill of Rights did not add to our rights and freedoms. In fact, all it did was to crystallize what was in existence at that time. I call this the 'frozen concepts' interpretation. I could go on with illustrations of the difficulties rising out of this, but instead I would just like to say that the Charter makes a change in that it speaks in the present tense, and therefore constitutes a basis for interpreting it as of the time when the Charter is being applied. If one takes into consideration what I referred to earlier from Lord Sankey's decision in the *Persons* case, then we are dealing with 'a living tree' which is capable of growth and which should be interpreted in a large and liberal manner.

The second defect which arose out of the Canadian Bill of Rights, and which the Charter should now overcome, is that the Bill of Rights does not

---

6 For citations to these statutes, and a discussion of their application, see W.S. Tarnopolsky, *Discrimination and the Law in Canada* (Don Mills: R. De Boo Ltd, 1982)
7 *Saskatchewan Human Rights Code*, RSS 1978, c S-24.1, part I
8 *Charter of Human Rights and Freedoms*, SQ 1975, c 6
9 *Alberta Bill of Rights*, SA 1971, c 1

explicitly provide that laws and practices, which are inconsistent with it, shall be inoperative, void, and of no effect. It merely declares that the laws of Canada, unless a 'notwithstanding' clause is used, shall be so 'construed and applied' as not to abrogate, abridge, or infringe the human rights and fundamental freedoms proclaimed. Many courts asked themselves: 'Does that mean anything more than the fact that we have to construe a statute, if we possibly can, in accordance with the Bill of Rights; but that if we cannot so construe it, then we have to apply it according to its plain terms?' Well, there is a leading decision known as the *Drybones*[10] case, in which the Supreme Court did say that, based upon section 2, laws which were inconsistent would have to be held inoperative to the extent of inconsistency. Nevertheless, that issue continued to be one that provided an opportunity for a reluctant Court to decline to apply the Bill of Rights.

The Charter constitutes a change from that. I have already mentioned that section 52, subsection 1 of the Constitution Act, 1982, provides that the constitution (including the Charter) is the supreme law of Canada and any law that is inconsistent with the provisions is, to the extent of inconsistency, of no force or effect. To the extent that there was timidity or obfuscation in the existing Bill, that presumably has now been removed under the Charter.

I cannot deal with all of the changes that the Charter proposes from the existing Bill of Rights. Let me, however, refer to only a few. The first thing to note is that the Canadian Bill of Rights is not repealed by the Charter and section 26 preserves rights not otherwise overridden. Therefore, the Canadian Bill of Rights, to the extent that it is not inconsistent with the Charter, continues to operate. That becomes rather important in a number of ways.

One of these is that by section 6 of the Canadian Bill of Rights, when the War Measures Act[11] was proclaimed, any action taken under the War Measures Act is not considered to be an abrogation, abridgement or infringement of the Bill of Rights. The Charter, on the other hand, makes no mention of the War Measures Act, and therefore presumably we have to rely upon section 1 of the Charter to deal with emergency situations. How that will operate with section 6 of the War Measures Act we will, of course, have to wait and see. However, it is necessary to suggest that any federal action under the War Measures Act will now have to be subjected to the Charter and, therefore, even though it may not be considered a contravention of the Canadian Bill of Rights, it might yet be considered in contravention of the Charter unless it is considered a reasonable limitation under

10 *R* v *Drybones*, [1970] SCR 282; (1969), 9 DLR (3d) 473
11 RSC 1970, c W-2

section 1. There is the possibility, under section 33 of the Charter, for an overriding clause – the *non-obstante* clause – to be adopted. So, the Parliament of Canada could enact an amendment to the War Measures Act or any other emergency legislation and provide that 'notwithstanding the Charter' so and so can go on. But, on the other hand, unless that override power is applied explicitly section by section to the Charter, the Charter applies, unless one can find another reasonable limitation under section 1.

Another matter left out of the Charter, which is in the Bill of Rights, is that section 3 of the Bill of Rights requires the Minister of Justice to examine every bill, and every regulation, to see whether they are in conformity with the Bill of Rights, and to report any inconsistency to Parliament. That is not available under the Charter, but presumably with respect to federal legislation, there is no reason why section 3 should not continue to operate.

As far as the Fundamental Freedoms are concerned, although section 2 of the Charter is somewhat more extensive and has a different arrangement than does section 1 of the Canadian Bill of Rights, I do not think that there is any major change. In order to know what these Fundamental Freedoms are going to be, we will have to wait to see what the courts are going to do with the 'limitations' clause in section 1.

What is new in the Charter is the right of every citizen to vote in elections to the House of Commons and to the provincial legislative assemblies. I suppose we would think that not unthinkable in any case. Nevertheless, section 3 of the Charter guarantees that. For most of our history, all kinds of people did not have that right. Whether it was women, until approximately World War I, or people of Asiatic origin, until after World War II, or the native peoples, until 1960, there certainly were times when many people in Canada did not have the right to vote.

Also new in the Charter is section 6, which deals with Mobility Rights, the right of every citizen to enter and remain in Canada, and of every citizen and landed immigrant to move and take up residence and to pursue the gaining of livelihood in any province. That was not in the Canadian Bill of Rights. Some people have argued that, ever since decisions of the Judicial Committee of the Privy Council just at the turn of the century, that right was probably part of our law in any case. However, whatever vagueness was left as a result of those cases is now taken care of by section 6. There is a saving provision in section 6, which is that any province which has an employment rate below the national average can favour its own residents over those of other provinces.

With respect to the Legal Rights, which in the Charter are sections 7 to 14 inclusive, one has some changes. In the first place, there are three legal rights in the Canadian Bill of Rights that do not appear in the Charter. The first of these is that section 2(a) of the Bill of Rights prohibits arbitrary exile. There is no direct equivalent in the Charter, although I think I would argue that under section 6, 'the right of every citizen to enter, remain in and leave Canada' is a prohibition against exile. Nevertheless, that may be open to some question. The second omission, which is a rather interesting one, is that the Charter does not contain a general right to a 'fair hearing' for the determination of one's rights and obligations, as does section 2, subsection (e) of the Bill of Rights. Again, we have in the Charter, section 7, which speaks of the right to life and liberty, and the right not to be deprived thereof, except in accordance with the principles of fundamental justice, which must cover this right.

The biggest gap in the Charter is the fact that we do not have the equivalent of the protection of property and the right not to be deprived thereof except by due process of law, which is in section 1(a) of the Bill of Rights. It is not in the Charter. Therefore, obviously, with respect to the federal sphere, section 1(a) of the Bill of Rights would continue to operate. Nevertheless, there is nothing which is equivalent to that in the Charter with respect to the provinces.

The main addition to the Legal Rights in the Charter is a prohibition against 'unreasonable search or seizure.' Another very important addition is the right, not only of retaining and instructing counsel upon arrest or detention, but the right to be informed of this right. Another right, which may be less important, but a number of people felt very concerned about it, is the right to trial by jury for offences where the maximum penalty is imprisonment for five years or a more severe penalty. Another addition is a prohibition against retroactive punishment. Another is the protection against double jeopardy. I would guess that these and the other Legal Rights in sections 7 through 14 will probably be among the most litigated in future adjudication.

Briefly, I will turn to sections 16 to 23, which deal with language rights. Sections 16 to 19 apply and extend the language rights which now apply to the federal government, under section 133 of the BNA Act, to the federal government and to New Brunswick. Further, section 20 includes various language communication rights, which do not now apply as against the federal government under section 133, although they do through the Official Languages Act. Section 21 of the Charter preserves section 133 of the BNA Act, which protects language rights in Quebec, and section 23 of the Manitoba Act, which protects language rights in Manitoba. Section 22 declares that there is a preservation of other languages, whether the rights with respect to these are pre-existing or hereafter required.

The most important change, of course, is section 23, which provides for Minority Language Education Rights. These are only for citizens of Canada. They do not apply to immigrants. It is a right to English and French language schools in all parts of Canada. There is a protection for Quebec against certain aspects of section 23, in that section 59 of the Charter provides that the first part of section 23, regarding the rights of those who continue to reside in the same province, only operates against the province of Quebec when the legislature so decides. There are parts of section 23 dealing with what are called 'Canada rights,' that is, the right of a Canadian changing province of residence to continue to have English or French language education for his or her children. It is a clause which will probably cause the greatest difficulty in Quebec. It is a clause that I feel would be extremely difficult for the courts to enforce, because the Minority Language Education Rights provision is subject to a test of 'where numbers warrant.' I find it difficult, within the tradition of our courts, to see how they can decide when it is necessary to provide transportation, when to build schools, when to add a room, when to add separate physical facilities. How our courts will handle this, I think, is going to be one of the big questions. Will we move to the American system, where the courts start to administer some of the institutions? Most of us hope that that will not be the case. Nevertheless, that is certainly one of the most difficult clauses.

I think one of the provisions which caused the greatest discussion was section 1, which is the 'limitations' clause. I think that the greatest opposition of public interest groups, at the time that the Joint Committee met during the winter of 1980 and 1981, was to the original version of this section. It provided that the Charter guarantees rights and freedoms subject only to such reasonable limits as are generally accepted in a free and democratic society with a parliamentary system of government. Those of us who opposed it argued that there was going to be no limitation in this provision. How could one possibly argue that a legislature, which reflects the majority, is not enacting legislation which is generally accepted in a system with a parliamentary system of government? I have suggested that the provision here was wide enough 'to drive a tank through.'

I think there is no doubt that such a clause would not accord with our international responsibilities. There has been a great deal of discussion as to whether one should have a limitations clause at all. I think one main argument in its favour is that there are limitations clauses in all of the major international bills of rights, whether you refer to the European Convention of Human Rights or to the International Covenant of Civil and Political Rights,[12] which Canada ratified and which is, therefore, binding upon Canada. The main thing is that these limitations clauses are only such as are 'prescribed by law,' which was not in the original version. They are only such as are proven to be 'necessary' in a free and democratic society. And then the third and most important difference is that under both the European Convention and the International Covenant, there are really three levels of rights with respect to which the limitations clause applies. *In normal times*, the limitations clause applies only to the Fundamental Freedoms and Mobility Rights. *Only in time of emergency officially proclaimed* can restrictions be put on Legal Rights. And *even* in time of emergency officially proclaimed, there are absolutely non-derogable rights. The most obvious of these is the prohibition against torture or cruel and unusual treatment or punishment. These three gradations did not appear in the original provision, and the third still does not appear in the provision we now have.

Section 1 of the Charter now provides that the rights and freedoms are guaranteed, 'subject only to such reasonable limits prescribed by law as can be demonstrably justified in a free and democratic society.' I think the most important question here is not really whether one should have a limitation clause. Nobody argues that the Fundamental Freedoms could ever be interpreted in an absolute fashion. In the United States, the First Amendment provides: 'Congress shall make no law' abridging freedom of speech, press, religion, and assembly. Nevertheless, the American Supreme Court has held that there are legitimate limitations on these fundamental freedoms.

What I think is crucially important is: Where shall the onus lie? Is it merely going to be our courts applying what they think is a demonstrably justified limitation, or is it someone else? I would argue that clearly it cannot be the person who is being condemned. Surely, if an accused has been denied a right to counsel, it is not up to him or her to argue that this is a reasonable limit. The only way that one can read section 1 is that the onus has to lie upon the government, or upon whoever is relying upon the particular restrictive provision.

I will now address the Equality Rights provisions, with respect to which there was probably the most representation before the Joint Committee. These are sections 15, 27 and 28. The more important ones from the point of

---

12 For the text of these documents see Ian Brownlie, *Basic Documents on Human Rights* (Oxford: Clarendon Press, 1971).

view of representations were 15 and 28. Let me just say that section 27 provides that the whole Charter must be interpreted 'in a manner consistent with the preservation and enhancement of the multicultural heritage of Canadians.' At least with respect to the Equality Rights of section 15, one could argue in favour of more equitable participation in our public services and in the spending of funds for cultural purposes.

If you read the opening clause of section 15, you will have to conclude, as I have suggested elsewhere, that it is the camel which is designed by a committee charged with drawing up a horse, because it reads that 'every individual is equal before and under the law and has the right to the equal protection and equal benefit of the law without discrimination and, in particular, without discrimination based on race, national or ethnic origin, colour, religion, sex, age or mental or physical disability.' Although it is a four-humped camel, the fact is it was so drafted in reaction to what the Supreme Court of Canada had done to the 'equality before the law' clause, which is in section 1(b) of the Canadian Bill of Rights. You will recall that in the *Lavell*[13] case concerning Indian women, Mr Justice Ritchie not only made reference to the 'frozen concepts' theory, which I referred to earlier, but also went on to say that there was no infringement in this case of 'equality *before* the law,' in the sense of people coming equally before the courts of the land. Therefore, he held that the provision was not invalid. Because of the 'frozen concepts' interpretation, Mr Justice Ritchie thought it was necessary to consider what 'equality before the law' meant prior to 1960, the year the Canadian Bill of Rights was enacted into law. This view of 'equality before the law' harkens back to 1885 when Dicey defined 'equality before the law' within the Rule of Law context. In reaction to such an approach, the drafters of the Charter added the clause about equality 'under' the law, and this was why the equal protection clause was included. But that was not all.

In the *Bliss*[14] case, which involved unemployment insurance benefits, the woman concerned had enough weeks to qualify for regular benefits, but not enough weeks to qualify for maternity benefits. Because she was pregnant, she could not qualify for regular benefits, since she was obviously not able to work. She was caught. One of the distinctions made was that the discrimination was not between women and men, but between pregnant women and everyone else, which was not prohibited. Another reason given for denying relief was that the case dealt with benefits, not protection. Thus, we now

---

13 *A.-G. for Can.* v *Lavell*; *Isaac* v *Bédard*, [1974] SCR 1349; 38 DLR (3d) 481
14 *Bliss* v *A.-G. for Can.*, [1979] 1 SCR 183; 92 DLR (3d) 417

have the equal benefits provision. It is important to point out that, presumably, the legislators have indicated their very clear intention to require Equality Rights in all possible applications of the law.

Let me refer very briefly to two other things coming out of section 15. One is that I do not expect it to be applied in an absolute fashion. Our courts will eventually have to evolve, if they do not directly adopt and copy, the American approach (which is a three-level scrutiny test).[15] Thus, distinctions made on the basis of race, religion, and national or ethnic origin (particularly the first two), are considered 'inherently suspect.' Unless the restriction is justified on the basis of an 'overriding state purpose, which could not be accomplished in a less prejudicial fashion,' then the distinction fails. One American author suggests that, on the basis of race, if you put aside the issue of segregation and whether segregation was discrimination, the only case of racial discrimination which was upheld was the *Korematsu*[16] case during World War II. This case concerned the internment of the Japanese. On the basis of 'strict scrutiny,' laws are 'inherently suspect' and it is almost impossible to show a solid basis for distinction. Then there is the 'minimal scrutiny' test, which applies to all cases other than these, with two exceptions. In distinctions made on the basis of indigence, the receipt of social welfare benefits, and so on, in which the test is that of 'minimal scrutiny,' the onus is on the one challenging the distinction to show that it was 'not rationally related to a legitimate legislative purpose.'

One of the things that explains the American Equal Rights Amendment, and why Canadian women pushed for section 28 in the Charter (which is the equivalent of the American ERA), was that sex never made it with race and religion into the 'inherently suspect' category in the United States. In recent years, some people have suggested that there is a form of 'intermediate' scrutiny, in which sex and legitimacy have been fitted. In terms of intermediate scrutiny, one has to show an 'important' government objective, which is somewhat little less than an 'overriding' objective, but more than a merely legitimate one. Presumably, sex and legitimacy stand in this intermediate category.

With regard to section 15, we have a number of listed grounds. I would suggest that other than age and physical and mental handicap, with respect to which there are obvious *bona fide* occupational qualifications, all the other named grounds, now including sex because of sections 15 and 28, would move into the inherently suspect category. With respect to sex, those of us in

---

15 See Polyvios G. Polyviou, *The Equal Protection of the Laws* (London: Duckworth, 1980).
16 *Korematsu* v *United States*, 323 US 214 (1944)

the human rights commissions suggest that there are only two *bona fide* occupational qualifications – sperm donors and wet nurses. Other than that, there are no other *bona fide* occupational qualifications concerning sex, except possibly privacy and decency. The categories of race, national or ethnic origin, colour and religion are not only inherently suspect, but almost impossible to prove as being *bona fide* qualifications. With respect to age and physical and mental handicap, we might move into the intermediate category and, obviously, with respect to those classifications not listed, the 'minimal scrutiny' test might be suggested as applying.

Subsection 2 of section 15 gives protection for affirmative action programs. There is a great deal of misunderstanding in Canada about the effect of the *Bakke*[17] case in the United States, because the *Bakke* case was not decided on the basis of the American equal protection clause in the Fourteenth Amendment. It was decided on the strict wording of the Civil Rights Act of 1964. In our case in Canada, other than Quebec and Newfoundland, every province and the federal government, in their anti-discrimination laws, have specific provisions for affirmative action programs. Therefore, subsection 2 may not have been necessary. For excessive caution, it was put in.

Let me conclude on section 15 with another observation. I do not think that section 15 is going to apply to what is called 'private action.' It applies to 'state action' and, therefore, within Canada it will in no way replace the continued enforcement of all our anti-discrimination or human rights codes. It may inspire some of them to expand into the fields of physical and mental disability, to the extent that they are not already included. Otherwise, I do not see it affecting the administration of our human rights codes except with respect to legislative action. With respect to governmental administrative action, both section 15 and the human rights codes will overlap.

(3) *Measures of Enforcement* To non-lawyers, it must sound very strange (although perhaps considering the opinion most people have of lawyers, it is not so strange), to think that we would talk of a right where there is no remedy. But the majority of our Supreme Court in the famous *Hogan*[18] case did do so. Hogan was driving with his girlfriend and was asked to come to the police station to take a breathalyzer test. He arrived at the police station and asked his friend to phone his lawyer. She proceeded to do so. The lawyer arrived at the police station before Hogan took the breathalyzer test, so he asked to speak to the lawyer. The policemen said, 'No, you have no right to speak to your lawyer. In fact, if you do not take the breathalyzer, you will be

---

17 *Regents of the University of California* v *Bakke*, 438 US 265 (1978)
18 *Hogan* v *The Queen*, [1975] 2 SCR 574; 48 DLR (3d) 427

charged for failing and refusing without reasonable excuse to take the breathalyzer.' He was hoping at the stage that Hogan would make the mistake that I am sure just about everybody would make, including most lawyers. Certainly, I probably would have done the same thing which Hogan did and that is to take the breathalyzer. He then argued at trial that he was denied his right to counsel. He argued that one might apply the American 'exclusionary rule' to exclude the evidence. There was a long discussion in the Supreme Court as to whether the exclusionary rule should automatically have followed in that case. Nevertheless, Mr Justice Ritchie said that, just because the right to counsel, which is set out in the Canadian Bill of Rights, was denied, it does not mean that we necessarily have to apply the exclusionary rule. And he said there is nothing he could see to override the common law rule (which was judge-made), i.e., that evidence, even if illegally obtained, is admissible, if relevant and probative. In the light of that kind of a decision, you now have section 24 of the Charter, which provides that 'Anyone whose rights or freedoms, as guaranteed by this Charter, have been infringed or denied may apply to a court of competent jurisdiction to obtain such remedy as the court considers appropriate and just in the circumstances.' Then the section goes on, in subsection 2, to deal explicitly with the exclusionary rule, and it provides that if it is shown that rights or freedoms have been denied, the evidence will be excluded 'if it is established that, having regard to all the circumstances, the admission of it in the proceedings would bring the administration of justice into disrepute.'

There are just two points I want to make concerning subsection 2. The first is that it is not an *absolute* exclusionary rule. There is a clear distinction here between section 24 and the American exclusionary rule. There is a test, i.e., the courts will have to exercise a discretion. The second point is the question: what are the factors to consider? My answer to that is, of course, I do not know. At this stage, nobody knows. I would hope that it is not going to be just what would shock the judges' conscience. Perhaps one might use a kind of 'community standard.' Perhaps we will have tests similar to those set out in a recent decision, known as the *Rothman*[19] case, in which Mr Justice Lamer, in reference to confessions, provided some possible tests for determining whether the use of this evidence would bring the proceedings of justice into disrepute. He said that all the circumstances have to be considered: the manner in which the statement was obtained, the degree to which there was a breach of social values, the seriousness of the charge, the effect the exclusion would have on the result of the proceedings, etc. He

19 *Rothman* v *The Queen*, [1981] 59 CCC (2d) 30; 121 DLR (3d) 578 (SCC)

went on, by the way, to make a statement on which I shall close, which is this: 'It must also be borne in mind that the investigation of crime and the detection of criminals is not a game to be governed by the Marquis of Queensbury Rules.'[20] Obviously, we are going to have some kind of balance as far as section 24 is concerned. The important thing, however, is that there is now a *clear provision*, in subsection 1, providing a remedy if rights are contravened, and a clear provision in subsection 2 to turn to the exclusionary rule if the Court thinks that the circumstances so justify.

APPENDIX

The Canadian Charter of Rights and Freedoms: An Overview
(1) *Constitutional Status*

(a) Whereas the *Canadian Bill of Rights* has been described as being merely 'statutory' (see Ritchie, J. in *Robertson and Rosetanni* v *The Queen*, [1963] SCR 65, 645–5; Martland, J. in *Regina* v *Burnshine*, [1975] 1 SCR 693, 702) or at most 'quasi-constitutional' (Laskin, J. in *Curr* v *The Queen*, [1972] SCR 889, 899), the *Charter* now constitutes part I of the *Constitution Act*, 1982.

(b) Whereas the *Canadian Bill of Rights* did not apply to the provinces, the new *Charter* does.

(2) *Content*

(a) Whereas s 1 of the *Bill* declares that the rights and freedoms 'have existed and shall continue to exist,' which has led to the proposition that it protects only those rights in existence in 1960 (see Ritchie, J. in *Robertson and Rosetanni* v *The Queen*; Martland, J. in *Regina* v *Burnshine*; and Ritchie, J. in *Miller and Cockriell* (1976), 70 DLR 3d 324), the *Charter* proclaims these freedoms in the present tense (see e.g., ss 2 or 7)

(b) Whereas s 2 of the *Bill* provides that laws of Canada shall 'be so construed and applied' as not to be inconsistent with the rights and freedoms recognized in the *Bill*, s 52(1) of the *Constitution Act*, 1982, proclaims that the constitution (including the *Charter*), is the supreme law and that any law which is inconsistent is of no force or effect.

(c) The Bill is not repealed by s 53 of the *Constitution Act*, 1982, and so continues to operate to the extent it is not overriden by the *Charter*.

(d) By s 6 of the *Bill* the *War Measures Act* is exempted from compliance, whereas the *Charter* makes no mention of the *War Measures Act*, which leaves it rather to be dealt with under the 'limitations' clause in s 1 of the *Charter*.

---

20 *Ibid*, 74 (CCC), 622 (DLR)

(e) Whereas s 3 of the *Bill* requires the federal Minister of Justice to scrutinize all proposed laws and statutory instruments, there is no such responsibility under the *Charter*.

(f) Although s 2 of the *Charter* expresses the fundamental freedoms somewhat more elaborately than does s 1 of the *Bill*, there is probably no major substantive change. The outlines of these freedoms will come through the interpretation of the 'limitations' clause in s 1.

(g) Sections 3, 4 and 5 of the *Charter* are new, although ss 4 and 5 are provided for in ss 20 and 50 of the BNA Act.

(h) The 'Mobility Rights' of s 6 of the *Charter* are new provisions.

(i) The *Charter* leaves out three 'legal rights' to be found in the *Bill*: ss 2(a), 2(c) and 1(a): on the other hand, the *Charter* includes such new rights as ss 8(1), 10(b), 11(f), 11(g), 11(h).

(j) Sections 16 to 20 provide that English and French shall be the official languages of Canada and New Brunswick, whereas s 21 preserves the application to Quebec of s 133 of the BNA Act and to Manitoba of s 23 of the *Manitoba Act*. Section 23 is a wholly new provision for 'minority language educational rights.'

(k) Section 1 of the *Charter* provides for reasonable limits. Since Canada has ratified the International Covenant on Civil and Political Rights and since this Covenant and the European Convention on Human Rights also provide for specific limitations clauses, the comparison might be made with these as to limitations that would be 'demonstrably justified in a free and democratic society.'

(l) Section 33 of the *Charter* constitutes the *non-obstante* provision under which legislative bodies in Canada can specify that their laws shall operate 'notwithstanding' the *Charter*. It would appear that such action is not reviewable.

(m) Section 15(1) adds to the 'equality before the law' clause of s 1(b) of the *Bill*, three additional clauses on 'equality *under* the law,' the 'equal *protection* of the law' and 'the equal *benefit* of the law.' Would this now be sufficient to cover every possible application of the law? To what extent might there now be a review similar to the three tests used in the United States, i.e. 'strict scrutiny,' 'intermediate scrutiny' and 'minimum scrutiny'? What is the effect of s 28?

(n) Section 15(2) purports to protect 'affirmative action.'

(o) In view of s 32(1) of the *Charter*, as well as the wording of s 15(1), and the fact that every jurisdiction in Canada has an anti-discrimination statute, it would appear that s 15 is not intended to apply to 'private action.'

(p) In any case, by s 32(2), s 15 does not have effect until three years after the coming into force of the *Charter*.

(q) Section 27 purports to constitutionalize the federal government policy proclaimed in 1971 of 'bilingualism within a multicultural context.'

The Canadian Charter of Rights and Freedoms with Special Emphasis on Quebec-Canada Relations

Donald Smiley*

The debate about the Canadian Charter of Rights and Freedoms has *not* been very satisfactory and I only wish that such discussions as have been occurring at this late date had taken place when the Charter was 'in the gristle' rather than in its stage of final enactment by the Parliament of the United Kingdom. The debate was, in my mind, superficial and unsophisticated from three points of view.

First, even in the higher reaches of academia we have heard almost nothing of the old debates about natural law and natural rights and the contemporary formulations of rights by such scholars as Ronald Dworkin, Robert Nozick and John Rawls. It was R.H.S. Crossman who said that nations in the British parliamentary tradition usually had a very weak tradition of natural law thinking. In general, Canadian political and legal philosophers appear to have lost an unusually favourable opportunity for raising this and other matters of theoretical concern about the nature and justifications of human rights in the context of the discussion over the Charter.

Second, we have not looked very hard at the experience of other nations. It may be that as we come to do so we will rely *too* heavily on the American example and it is my general disposition to think that the circumstances and traditions of the United States are so different from those of Canada that the American experience will be somewhat misleading. The American courts play and have played a somewhat different role in that system of government. There is in the United States a long tradition of civil rights jurisprudence. The Bill of Rights protects a much more limited set of claims than does the Charter. American civil rights thinking and law have been decisively shaped by the traditions of natural law and natural rights but Canada's

* Donald Smiley is Professor of Political Science at York University.

has not. If we were to look elsewhere I should suggest some careful attention be paid to the experience of India under its 1949 Constitution and the complex jurisprudence surrounding the Declaration of Rights in part III of that Constitution. It is both perverse and parochial when effecting fundamental political change not to look at the experience of other jurisdictions. Yet it requires the most exquisitely sensitive political judgment to determine the significance of such experience for one's own nation.

Third, there has been relatively little discussion of the possible consequences of the Charter for the workings of our political institutions and for the Canadian political culture more broadly.[1] What is the likely impact of the Charter on the kinds of persons appointed to our senior appellate courts? How does one move the judges, as the Charter directs, from a positivist to an activist tradition of jurisprudence? What are the possible implications of the Charter for executive agencies charged with the protection of human rights such as federal and provincial human rights commissions and the office of the Commissioner of Official Languages? What are the consequences for the protection of the rights of official-language minorities of the Charter rejecting the bilingual districts device as recommended by the Royal Commission on Bilingualism and Biculturalism in its 1967 Report? Is it likely that the Charter will do something to wean citizens away from their provincialism as Canadians come increasingly to define themselves as possessors of certain rights embodied in the Canadian constitution and protected in the last instance by a national institution, the Supreme Court of Canada?

For myself, the general debate about the constitutional entrenchment of human rights is somewhat sterile, and in particular the controversy about whether or not entrenchment as such is 'democratic.'[2] Rather, in my view, the crucial questions are ones of institutional efficacy. From this perspective, one of the major failures of the Charter experience is not the more extensive constitutional protection of rights *per se* but rather the somewhat indiscriminate entrenchment of a very large number of very diverse claims. Although I do not have the time to give the reasons for those judgments, I believe that the entrenchment in the Charter of democratic and legal rights is a gain and that a persuasive if not conclusive case can be made for the entrenchment of

---

1 I have made a preliminary attempt in this direction in *The Canadian Charter of Rights and Freedoms*, 1981, Discussion Paper Series (Toronto: The Ontario Economic Council, 1981) particularly ch 7, 'The Probable Consequences of the Charter.'
2 This argument has gone on in the United States since the early days of the republic. For an admirably balanced account of the literature and the issues see Leonard W. Levy, *Judgments: Essays on American Constitutional History* (Chicago: Quadrangle Books, 1972), 'Judicial Review, History, and Democracy,' pp 24–63.

the Fundamental Freedoms (belief, expression, religion, association). However, I have less faith in the efficacy of the courts in respect to the rights of official language minorities and of the native peoples and in making social policy decisions in respect to Equality Rights.

The coming into effect of the Charter will be the most radical break ever made in a constitutional and legal tradition hitherto characterized by continuity and incremental change.[3] Even the Confederation settlement of 1864–67 embodied a high degree of continuity – the new Dominion was to be organized under the Crown 'with a Constitution similar in Principle to that of the United Kingdom,' the traditional independence of the judiciary was to remain, the civil law was to continue to prevail in Quebec and the English common law in the other provinces, and even in respect to the federal aspects of the new constitution, the provinces were put in the same constitutional position in respect to the authorities of the Dominion as were these latter authorities in relation to the Imperial government.[4] Changes subsequent to 1867 through judicial review, explicit constitutional amendment and evolving practices have all been piecemeal. Yet the major burden of effecting the decisive rupture made with the Canadian past is imposed on the elements of the governmental system most institutionally attuned to incrementalism – the courts of law. The Charter is honeycombed with general phrases which are unknown to Canadian law or that of any other jurisdiction – 'the principles of fundamental justice,' 'such reasonable limits prescribed by law as can be demonstrably justified in a free and democratic society,' the where-numbers-warrant provision in respect to education in the minority official language, proceedings which 'would bring the administration of justice into disrepute' and the like.

Apart from giving meaning to such phrases, the judiciary is charged with defining and ranking a very large number of claims on the community in respect to which the Parliament and the provincial legislatures were hitherto the final authorities. As the Charter becomes a part of Canadian law, we can

---

3 Prime Minister Trudeau has also been associated with Canada's other break with its past – the creation of what Stefan Dupré has called 'the institutionalized cabinet' and with very new patterns of executive decision-making more generally. The authors of the Constitutional Resolutions of December 1981 seem to have wanted to make clear to Canadians that a decisive break with the constitutional past was being made by adding as Schedule 1 of the Resolution, provisions renaming previous constitutional measures since 1867 – for example, the British North America Act, 1867 is now to be the Constitution Act, 1867.

4 Through reservation and disallowance and the appointment of provincial Lieutenant-Governors by the Governor-in-Council

expect lawyers on behalf of their clients to raise a whole new group of claims in the lower courts – to the utter bewilderment of justices of the peace, magistrates and judges manifestly ill-prepared to decide on such matters. In the nature of judicial review, it will take the Supreme Court of Canada decades or even longer to give authoritative meaning to the Charter. In the meantime, some of the most fundamental aspects of the legal system are in utter disarray and the assertion by the defenders of the Charter that its enactment will make rights more sure and certain cannot be sustained.[5] Competent lawyers have also told me that the Charter is badly drafted and under the conditions it was contrived Canadians would be almost providentially fortunate if this did not prove to be so. For example, it is not completely clear in respect to several rights whether these apply to corporations or only to individuals. Section 28 relating the equality of males and females might plausibly be interpreted so as to override affirmative action programs for women authorized under section 15(2), and so on.

The primary impulse for the enactment of the Charter was *not* the better protection of human rights in Canada – the record of successive Trudeau governments in respect to human rights is, to be charitable, an indifferent one. The Charter, along with the other reforms passed by the Parliament of Canada in December 1982, was in its origins a response to the exigencies of Quebec's place in Confederation. While the history of recent efforts to reform the Canadian constitution is complex, in a proximate sense the beginnings of the process culminating in the Charter were in the Quebec referendum campaign on sovereignty/association in the spring of 1980. During this campaign, Prime Minister Trudeau, as well as his federal Liberal colleagues from Quebec and several of the premiers of the other provinces, promised that if the electorate gave a 'No' verdict, something rather imprecisely designated as 'renewed federalism' would come about. The Quebec voters by a fairly decisive margin of 60/40 rejected the sovereignty/ association alternative. During the summer of 1980, there were intensive negotiations among the ministers of the eleven governments charged with intergovernmental and constitutional affairs. At a September 1980 meeting of first ministers, it was impossible to secure agreement on any significant aspects of constitutional reform. Subsequent to the September meeting, the federal government introduced into Parliament a Resolution providing for

---

[5] Admittedly the Charter removes some of the former ambiguities related to the federal-provincial distribution of power in respect to human rights matters. For details of this see Walter S. Tarnopolsky, *The Canadian Bill of Rights*, 2nd rev ed (Toronto: McClelland and Stewart, 1975), ch II.

the patriation of the constitution, a wholly Canadian amending formula and a charter of rights and freedoms. The support of only two provinces, Ontario and New Brunswick, was secured for this initiative. The constitutional events of the next year were bewildering in their complexity and culminated in November 1981 with the agreement among the federal government and all the provinces but Quebec on a much revised version of the Resolution of the preceding year.

Two distinct but intertwined questions can be asked about the November Resolution in the context of relations between Quebec and the wider Canadian political community. First, was the Resolution a fulfilment of the promise of 'renewed federalism' made to the voters of Quebec in the 1980 referendum campaign? Secondly, was the passage of the Resolution by Parliament in the face of Quebec dissent a breach of Canadian constitutional convention? My answer to the first question is 'No,' to the second 'Yes.'

Debate within Quebec since 1960 makes plain at least to me that 'renewed federalism' during the 1980 referendum could be taken to mean only constitutional changes safeguarding and extending the powers of the political authorities of that province. This kind of demand has been a constant for Quebec provincial politicians since the discussions of explicit constitutional reform began two decades ago.[6] The Charter manifestly restricts the powers of the government and legislature of Quebec, although the extent of such restrictions will be known only through subsequent judicial interpretation. The November Resolution was a betrayal of the Quebec electorate.

My second question involves constitutional convention. The late Sir Ivor Jennings gave three crisp and authoritative tests for defining whether a usage, practice or custom had the status of a convention. 'We have to ask ourselves these questions: First, what are the precedents; secondly, did the actors in the precedents believe they were bound by a rule; and thirdly, is there a reason for the rule?'[7]

The relevant precedents in the matter under discussion would appear to be those past amendments explicitly altering the constitutional distribution of legislative powers between Parliament and the provinces – the amendments of 1930, 1931, 1940, 1951 and 1964. Parliament requested Westminster to amend the constitution in these circumstances only after the consent of all the provinces had been secured, and in the case of the 1930 amendment, the

---

6 See generally Edward McWhinney, *Quebec and the Constitution, 1960–1978* (Toronto: University of Toronto Press, 1979).
7 Sir William Ivor Jennings, *Law and the Constitution*, 5th ed (London: University of London Press, 1959), p 134

consent of only the western provinces directly affected. However, these precedents do not by themselves determine that the November Resolution breached Canadian constitutional convention if we accept as authoritative the majority decision of the Supreme Court of Canada rendered on 28 September 1981 to the effect that requests for amendments altering the federal-provincial distribution of powers required, by convention, not unanimity but a 'substantial measure of provincial consent.'

The next test involves the major political actors giving some indication that adherence to the rule is obligatory. The most relevant precedent here appears to be that surrounding the Victoria Charter of 1971. The Charter contained significant changes in the distribution of powers between Parliament and the provinces and was agreed to by the federal government and the governments of all the provinces except Quebec. After the Quebec premier had given notice of his government's dissent from these changes, there was no serious discussion to the effect that the Charter should be embodied in a Resolution requesting Westminster to amend the Canadian constitution in these terms. In this instance, and I would claim it to have a direct and crucial relevance to the matter under review, the major political actors gave tacit approval to the principle that Quebec's assent was required for amendments altering the federal-provincial distribution of powers.[8]

Jenning's third criterion relates to the reason for the rule. Conventions must have some rationale in the fundamental nature of the political order. In my view, the first-line protection of the rights of the francophone society of Quebec is, and has been since Confederation, the powers of the legislature and government of that province.[9] On this basis, convention dictates that those powers should not be restricted without Quebec's assent.[10] It appears

8 Another possible precedent relates to the dropping of the Fulton-Favreau formula for patriation and constitutional amendment after Quebec's dissent had been registered. However, this measure did not directly affect the federal-provincial distribution of power.

9 In his recent book *The French-Canadian Idea of Confederation, 1864–1900* (Toronto: University of Toronto Press, 1982) Arthur I. Silver gives extensive documentation for his conclusion that the French-Canadian forces behind Confederation were primarily concerned with provincial autonomy. See particularly chs II, III and IV. This is in marked contrast with Peter B. Waite's view in *Life and Times of Confederation, 1864–1867; Politics, Newspapers, and the Union of British North America* (Toronto: University of Toronto Press, 1962) where the argument is advanced that the primary French-Canadian aim was to secure strength in the central government.

10 So far as I can find out, the use of the term 'convention' in the context of federal-provincial relations began only with the legal challenges mounted by three of the provinces to the federal Resolution of October 1980. Significantly, the 1965 White Paper on Constitutional Amendment uses the term 'principles' to designate traditionally accepted procedures of amendment. The concept of convention was first elaborated of course in

to me to be constitutionally irrelevant that the government of Quebec is composed of members of a political party whose *raison d'être* is to remove that province from the Canadian Confederation.

In the short run, the political consequences for Quebec politics of the 'consensus' of 5 November has been to trigger events leading the Parti Québécois to turn its back on *étapisme*. According to the position of the Parti Québécois as adopted in February 1982 after the decisive victory by the 'moderates' in the party, the next provincial election is to be fought on the sovereignty issue. If the party receives a majority of the popular vote, it will take immediate steps towards sovereignty wherein economic association with Canada is not to be a precondition of Quebec independence. The previous Parti Québécois policy adopted in 1974 divorced the sovereignty issue from that of the Parti Québécois' electoral fortunes. On the basis of this distinction, the party won decisive electoral victories in 1976 and 1981 after campaigns in which sovereignty was downplayed and sustained a decisive defeat in the sovereignty/association referendum of 1980. The commitment to sovereignty has been, since the beginnings of the party, the Parti Québécois' major electoral liability. It is plausible to argue that had constitutional reform not been effected in the face of Quebec dissent, the government's conduct would increasingly have been motivated by the objective of retaining power with decreasing emphasis on the cause of Quebec independence.

Not only did the November 'consensus' lead to a recrudescence of Quebec separatism but it also denied the moderate federalist forces in Quebec provincial politics a defensible constitutional position on which to stand. In my opinion, the *Beige Paper* of Claude Ryan's Liberals presented in 1980 was constructive both in spirit and in substance and would have provided a useful starting point for constitutional discussion leading to a genuinely renewed federalism. This general thrust towards reform has been, at least for the time being, foreclosed.

To the extent that the Charter is interpreted by the courts to sustain the position of the English-speaking minority in Quebec, I would expect further tensions in Quebec-Canada relations. Section 23(1)(b), which extends the rights of minority-language education to children whose parents have had their education in Canada in that language, is quite clearly incompatible with existing Quebec law. As a non-Quebecer, I would expect vigorous resistance from the francophone community of Quebec to this and perhaps other provi-

A.V. Dicey's classic *Introduction to the Study of the Law of the Constitution* (London: Macmillan) whose first edition appeared in 1885 and referred to relations within the governmental system of the United Kingdom. The term was later extended to relations between the UK authorities and governments of the Empire/Commonwealth.

sions of the Charter which restrict the powers of the Quebec authorities in respect to culture, language and education.

The Charter and the methods by which it was put into place gives the separatist government of Quebec an opportunity to challenge the legitimacy of the existing constitutional order to which the Parti Québécois gave at least nominal allegiance before. We can reasonably expect that government to use every legal means at its disposal to challenge the validity of the Charter and the primacy of Quebec law over its provisions. The 'notwithstanding' clause of section 33 relating to the Fundamental Freedoms and to Legal and Equality Rights gives the Quebec authorities the opening to negate major elements of the Charter and, in effect, to establish a very different regime of rights in Quebec than the one prevailing elsewhere in Canada.[11] So far as the other provinces are concerned, this *non-obstante* provision is in my view a defensible compromise between the demands of parliamentary sovereignty and of a constitutionally entrenched regime of human rights. However, in the case of Quebec, this provision lays a basis for challenging the legitimacy of the Charter and the Canadian constitutional system more generally.

Many of the supporters of the Charter have acted as if they believe that the constitutional entrenchment of rights was such a desirable thing to accomplish that the means by which this was done were, if not irrelevant, at best of secondary importance. Yet anyone familiar with human rights matters must realize that a fastidious respect for procedure is of the essence and that justice has both procedural and substantive elements.

To conclude, the Canadian Charter of Rights and Freedoms had its origins in the exigencies of Quebec-Canada relations and it is justifiable to evaluate the Charter in terms of its actual and anticipated impact on these relations. From this viewpoint, an adverse judgment must be rendered. The Charter was put in place by a procedure that breaks the constitutional convention which safeguards Quebec's fundamental interests. This procedure has led both to a recrudescence of Quebec nationalism in its more virulent forms and to undermining the constitutional position of the moderate federalists in Quebec. In this process, the separatist government of Quebec has been granted an opportunity it did not have before to challenge the legitimacy of the existing constitutional order and to assert the primacy of Quebec law over the Canadian constitution.

11 After the November conference was held the Parti Québécois government introduced Bill 89 into the Quebec National Assembly using the *non-obstante* provision of the Charter in the more extensive way. Section 28 exacts that the amended Quebec Charter of Human Rights and Freedoms shall operate notwithstanding the provisions of 2 and 7 to 15 of the Constitution Act, 1982.

The Implications of the Canadian Charter of Rights and Freedoms

Barry Strayer*

There are a few points that I would like to cover, which may appear random but are nonetheless well worth noting at this time. The first thing I would like to do is comment on some of the comments that Professor Smiley made. He appears to be saying that we ought not to have a Charter of Rights unless we know all of the implications, every application that might be made of it in the future. I think if we had waited for that, we would never have had a Charter of Rights. I dare say that on that basis there would never have been an American Bill of Rights. What is the Canadian Supreme Court likely to do with the Charter? Can we know, or foresee if they are going to be particularly imaginative in their approach to it? We do not know that, but I dare say that when the American Bill of Rights was ratified in 1791 nobody knew that in the United States either. What would have been the assessment of the judiciary in the United States at that time, and what would the prediction have been as to what they would do with the Bill of Rights? Keep in mind that in 1791, the Harvard Law School had not even been invented yet and thus could not provide the guidance to the Supreme Court which it now does! But today, in Canada, we have a number of excellent law schools and departments of political science to give us ample advice as to what is being done wrong.

I believe Professor Smiley has created something of a man of straw in how the Charter has failed or will fail to meet its objectives, because he defines in his own way what the objectives were for the Charter and then maintains that the Charter does not meet those objectives. He says the Charter had nothing to do with the better protection of human rights, rather it had to do with national unity. But national unity, according to Professor Smiley, could only

---

* Barry Strayer is Assistant Deputy Minister of Justice for the Government of Canada. The views expressed here are the personal views of the speaker and not necessarily those of the Government of Canada. Accompanying references have been supplied by the editor.

be preserved by transfers of power to provinces or at least to the province of Quebec. I think those are rather large assumptions, which are not necessarily borne out by the facts. After some twenty-odd years of being engaged in this process of constitutional reform, I do not think that the history of the Charter is quite that black and white.

In the first place, while I think the better protection of human rights is not the sole justification for the Charter, it certainly was one of the principal motivations for its adoption. Admittedly, different people and different governments will have engaged in the process of adoption with a variety of motivations but that does not mean that the protection of rights was not an important factor. Also it is easy to ask: how can a government, which arguably has abridged human rights in the past in some other context, now validly put forward a constitutional Charter of Rights? I do not see why those two things are necessarily incompatible. As I shall elaborate upon later, I think the effect of the Charter may well be significant in areas in which the government of Canada has been accused of denying rights in the past.

With regard to the circumstances surrounding the development of the Charter, these too were neither simple nor straightforward. Professor Smiley's suggestion is that what the people of Quebec were being promised during the referendum campaign was a 'renewed federalism,' which we are to understand was to involve substantial transfers of jurisdiction to the provincial governments or at least to the government of Quebec. That transfer has not happened. It is not for me as a public servant to comment on the political activities of my masters, but I would have to say that I would be surprised to find out that federal spokesmen in the referendum campaign were promising massive transfers of jurisdiction to the provinces, and I find it hard to believe that very many people listening to them would have understood them to be saying that.

Obviously, there was a lot of ambiguity in the referendum debate. I do not know, and I am not sure that anyone else knows, exactly what the assumptions were of the majority of Quebecers. It was unclear at the end of the day as to what was going to follow after any particular result in the referendum.

We are, in some quarters today, being led to believe that this Charter and the other changes in the constitution are being rammed down the throat of Quebec. That, of course, proceeds on the assumption that the government of Quebec is the only representative of the people of Quebec. I would be quick to admit that the government of Quebec has not agreed to the Charter and has not agreed to the other constitutional amendments. There is now a case in the Quebec Court of Appeals on the question of whether, in terms of constitutional conventions, the consent of Quebec ought to be obtained before these constitutional changes are made. While we do not know what the decisions will be,[1] we know from our experience in the Supreme Court in the fall of 1981 that the Supreme Court of Canada said that conventions, whatever they may be, are not legally binding rules.[2]

We are, in this context, told that the Charter is undermining cultural duality, the cultural duality which in this particular theory is equated with the views of the present government of Quebec as far as the francophone part of the duality is concerned. That is one arguable position. But I think it is also important, particularly for our American visitors, to be aware of the fact that there is another arguable position which I am afraid they have not heard very much about in this forum. That other position implicitly believes that the francophone community has a home everywhere in Canada; that although eighty-five per cent of the francophone community is in the province of Quebec, it also exists outside the province of Quebec in places where they do not send any members to the National Assembly of Quebec. It is a community which has survived in spite of very great adversity and through no credit to the anglophone majority, but it has survived. There is a point of view that the constitutional settlement ought to recognize better the role of that community outside of Quebec as well as that of the English minority in Quebec. This Charter does contribute to that recognition, because it provides minority language rights for francophone minorities outside of Quebec. Thus, we have a particular point of view, one analysis of the Canadian duality, represented in this Charter. We have another view of the Canadian duality represented by the present Government of Quebec, which advocates independence for Quebec as the embodiment of francophone North America. We do not know yet which view of the francophone role in Canadian society the people of Quebec may ultimately take. But I do not think that we can say that this Charter is an abnegation, a suppression of cultural duality.

On the question of why we have a Charter, we should also be aware that its history did not commence in 1980. One can find over the past thirty years at least, various initiatives for a Charter for the purpose of the better protection of human rights, long before the Quebec referendum was ever thought of. The CCF party, the forerunner of the NDP, had this as part of its program,

---

1 *Remboi à la Cours d'appel relatif à une résolution concernant la Constitution du Canada*, subsequently decided 7 April 1982 that the consent of the Government or the National Assembly of Quebec was not required. This decision was then appealed to the Supreme Court of Canada where it was heard in June 1982. In its decision, the Supreme Court held that Quebec did not have a 'veto.' See: *Quebec Veto Reference: In the Matter of a Reference to the Court of Appeal of Quebec concerning the Constitution of Canada* (6 December 1982) Unreported.

2 *Reference Re Amendment of the Constitution of Canada* (1981), 125 DLS (3d) 1

that there should be a constitutional charter of rights.[3] Pierre Trudeau was writing about it in the 1950s.[4] John Diefenbaker was obviously interested in it at the time of the Canadian Bill of Rights but felt that politically it was not feasible in 1960. We had various committees, public bodies and so forth expressing interest in it in the 1970s. Two parliamentary committees had recommended a constitutional bill of rights.[5] The Canadian Bar Association recommended a bill of rights in its report on the constitution,[6] the *Beige Paper* did as well,[7] as did the Pépin-Robarts Report.[8] So there was a building momentum for one and I think that it is fair to say that a good part of that momentum was related to the intrinsic value of a charter of rights for the protection of rights and freedoms. This predated the referendum of Quebec by many years. We also know that in the last year or two the substance of the Charter has been a matter of great public debate in this country, and that according to the public opinion polls, there has been a growing support for the concept.

It is true that there are other purposes which clearly are being served by the Charter, apart from the intrinsic protection of the rights which are listed in it. There was clearly an intention – there I agree with Professor Smiley completely – to strengthen national unity. This Charter is seen by some people as an instrument of national integration strengthening the things which Canadians might recognize that we have in common, in the face of so many things that we fervently insist we do not have in common. One has to keep building a country like this over and over again. There are very strong

3 See CCF National Office, *Report of the First National Convention held at Regina, Sask., July 1933* (mimeographed). Section 9; and David Lewis and Frank Scott, *Make This Your Canada; A Review of C.C.F. History and Policy* (Toronto: Central Canada Publishing Co., 1943), p 184. ('With a new constitution, guaranteeing full protection to minorities and embodying the democratic civil liberties, ... [Canada] can march forward to an era of national unity and progress such as she has never known.' *Ibid*).
4 P.E. Trudeau, *Federalism and the French Canadians* (Toronto: Macmillan of Canada, 1968), pp 52–60
5 Canada, Parliament, Special Joint Committee of the Senate and of the House of Commons on the Constitution of Canada, *Final Report* (Ottawa: Queen's Printer, 1972), pp 18–25; Canada, Parliament, Special Joint Committee of the Senate and of the House of Commons on the Constitution of Canada, *Minutes of Proceedings and Evidence*, issue no 20, 3rd Session, 30th Parliament, 1977–78 (Ottawa: Queen's Printer, 1978)
6 Canadian Bar Association, Committee on the Constitution, *Towards a New Canada* (Toronto: Canadian Bar Foundation, 1978), ch 4
7 Constitutional Committee of the Quebec Liberal Party, *A New Canadian Federation* (Montreal: Quebec Liberal Party, 1980), pp 31–4
8 Canada. Task Force on Canadian Unity, *A Future Together: Observations and Recommendations* (Ottawa: Department of Supply and Services, 1979)

forces of particularism all around this country, and the Charter is one force moving in the other direction. I do not think this is an intrinsically dangerous thing: far from it. There are, of course, also provisions in the Charter for language rights which have a particular justification in protecting the survival and mobility of the two official language groups from coast to coast.

It may be helpful, in looking at section 33, to reflect back a little bit on the nature of the debate in Canada over the incorporation of the Charter in the constitution. Americans may be a bit mystified by this 'notwithstanding clause,' in section 33, but I am sure that they are fully familiar with the debate which has been going on in the United States over the question of the entrenchment of rights versus majority rule.[9] There has been a whole cottage industry developed on this subject in the United States. People agonize and beat their breasts about it in writing but the general conclusion usually seems to be, after two or three hundred pages of analysis, that judicial review is probably here to stay and that there is something to be said for having rights in the Constitution. The debate in the United States became increasingly vocal as a result of what were seen as the eccentricities of the Warren Court and the public dispute over judicial activism, which gained such momentum at that time.[10]

In Canada, we have had a somewhat similar debate and, of course, the American debate has spilled over the 49th parallel to some extent. The debate in Canada has been articulated more in terms of parliamentary supremacy, and the opposition to having a Charter of Rights has been largely expressed in terms of the antagonism between entrenched rights and parliamentary supremacy.[11]

Parliamentary supremacy is usually justified here as being the best method of representing majority opinion. I think we have had a lot more faith in Parliament, in parliamentary institutions in Canada, than the Americans have had. I think the problem with the United States is that it had an

9 See Henry Steele Commager, *Majority Rule and Minority Rights* (New York: Oxford University Press, 1943).
10 See Alexander M. Bickel, *The Supreme Court and the Idea of Progress* (New York: Harper and Row, 1970); Archibald Cox, *The Warren Court: Constitutional Decision as an Instrument of Reform* (Cambridge, Mass.: Harvard University Press, 1968); John Hart Ely, *Democracy and Distrust: A Theory of Judicial Review* (Cambridge, Mass.: Harvard University Press, 1980); and Jesse H. Choper, *Judicial Review and the National Political Process: A Functional Reconsideration of the Role of the Supreme Court* (Chicago: University of Chicago Press, 1980).
11 See Ontario, Royal Commission Inquiry into Civil Rights, *Report Number Two* (Toronto: Queen's Printer, 1969); and Douglas A. Schmeiser, 'The Case against Entrenchment of a Canadian Bill of Rights,' *Dalhousie Law Journal* 1 (1973–74): pp 15–50.

unhappy childhood. In the eighteenth century, Americans came to be somewhat alienated from parliamentary institutions, particularly the Parliament in London. We, happily or unhappily, inherited the parliamentary system but became more or less 'self owned and operated' under it. The concept of responsible government, which we inherited before Confederation, had not been developed before American independence. We have thus had a more favourable view of Parliament and of government and we have not had this antagonism towards government to the same degree as the Americans have had. Therefore, it struck many of our citizens as unwise, unnecessary, and perhaps downright dangerous to detract from the concept of parliamentary supremacy with an entrenched Charter.

I fully agree with Professor Smiley that there has been a lot of hyperbole on the side of the advocates of the Charter. I think false hopes have probably been raised and extravagant statements have been made as to what the Charter can do. On the other hand, the opponents of the Charter have also engaged, from time to time, in hyperbole, and we have heard a good deal about 'government by judges' and the 'destruction of parliamentary supremacy and the parliamentary system as we have known it,' etc. One does find echoes of this conflict in the actual text of the Charter as it was finally settled.

Professor Tarnopolsky talked about section 1, the one that says, that clearly contemplates, that there can be limitations on rights, as long as they are prescribed by law, and as long as they can be demonstrated as being reasonable and justified. That clearly signals to the courts that legislatures or Parliament can impose limits on these rights, but they are going to have to answer to a court if anybody challenges those limitations.

The question of emergency powers looms large in many people's minds. There has been some confusion, I think, as to what the effect of the Charter is going to be on the War Measures Act. I do want to spend just a moment on that because some mention here was made of the discussion of this problem in the parliamentary committee. I was in the parliamentary committee when this was discussed and I think there was confusion there as to what the *issue* was. I think the situation is, with respect to the War Measures Act, that it can stay on the books. It does not have any effect from day to day, it only has effect when it is proclaimed. It can be proclaimed by the cabinet but they must then justify its use to Parliament within so many days. However, once proclaimed, then what? Again, the Act does not have any immediate effect on anybody until some regulations are made under it. It is at that point, once the regulations are made, that they might be challenged in courts under the Charter, and if they are, then it would be necessary for the government to come along and demonstrate to the courts why these regulations are justified. If the Charter had been in operation in 1970, I would imagine that some people would have invoked the Charter to challenge, in certain respects, the regulations that were made at that time.

The mere existence of the Charter is not going to wipe out the War Measures Act, but it may well have some bearing on how the War Measures Act, or any similar Act that is put in place, is used. At the point where the Act is actually used, the government is probably going to have to come forward and give some demonstration as to why this use is reasonable and justified in these particular circumstances. So as far as I can see, this is going to make a difference.

Because of its uniqueness and implications, it is important to address specifically section 33, commonly known as the 'notwithstanding clause.' It is the one which was added in the dying hours of the November Constitutional Conference. It was not in the original proposal put forward to Parliament in the fall of 1980, but it became a basis for a compromise in November of 1981 and I think that in spite of some understandable concerns about it in various parts of the country, it has not seriously undermined the value of the Charter. By making it possible to have a Charter, applicable in all jurisdictions, it has by that means achieved an important goal. The section basically states that Parliament or a legislature may override certain sections of the Charter, as long as it does so expressly, and as long as it renews its override every five years. By way of example, let us say that Parliament wants to provide for the retirement of civil servants at the age of forty. It might have some difficulties justifying that in relation to section 15, which says that people should be treated equally, notwithstanding their age. If the government had some doubts about being able to justify such a law under section 1, it could put in a clause under section 33 saying that notwithstanding section 15 of the Charter, this compulsory retirement provision is to apply.

Perhaps that sounds rather horrendous and, in theory, it leaves it open to Parliament to make mincemeat of the Charter. However, I do want to emphasize three or four positive aspects of the overriding clause. In the first place, the override provision does not apply to all sections of the Charter. It does not apply to the Democratic Rights. Parliament or a legislature cannot use this override power to nullify guarantees in sections 3, 4 and 5 with respect to the right to vote, the requirement that legislatures sit no more than five years and that they sit annually. So the integrity of the legislative process is preserved, and Parliament or a legislature cannot use its override power to perpetuate its own life or to rig the electoral system so that the opposition could never gain power.

I would have been happier, personally, if the override had not been made applicable to section 2, which guarantees the Fundamental Freedoms, such as freedom of assembly and freedom of speech and so forth. The override clause does not apply to language rights. I think it is important to note that the override clause is almost certainly going to be difficult to use. That is perhaps its greatest value. Parliament or legislatures will be very reluctant, it seems to me, to use the clause. Any government that comes into its House with a bill in which there is a notwithstanding clause is immediately going to attract to itself a lot of very pointed attacks. (I say that with a slight hesitation because Quebec has such a clause in its Charter and I think it has been used six or seven times.) Also note that under section 33, the override has to be renewed. There is a 'sunset clause' so that if you override the Charter in a particular respect, and the override is not renewed in five years, it becomes inoperative.

I think that the claims regarding the importance of the override clause have been exaggerated, in that it will not be of very much help to bureaucrats. It allows Parliament or legislatures specifically to override clauses in the Charter, but it does not allow bureaucrats to do so. It therefore means that in the administration of the laws, public officials, whether they are federal officials, provincial officials, municipal officials, police officers, or whoever, are going to have to obey the provisions of the Charter unless Parliament or the legislatures have specifically authorized them not to do so. It is the history of violations of human rights that they are quite often inadvertent, or at least unauthorized, certainly unauthorized by higher authority. Therefore, if police officers, for example, are refusing to allow people counsel, it is almost certain that no Parliament of Canada is going to authorize police officers to hold people and charge them without giving them the right to consult counsel. So if police officers engage in this sort of practice, they are going to be subject to the Charter and subject to the enforcement provisions in section 24 and elsewhere. The override clause is not going to be of any help to the officialdom which administers the law from day to day.

In fact, the override clause could have a very positive effect on both the legislative and judicial processes. As for the former, the existence of section 33 may bring about a narrower interpretation of the scope of limitations permissible under section 1. It may be said that certain indirect limitations of rights cannot be upheld under section 1 since it would have been open to the legislative body expressly to override such rights under section 33, if that were really necessary. This approach would at least force legislators to consider specifically if they really wanted to restrict certain otherwise guaranteed rights.

As for the judicial process, the existence of section 33 may encourage courts to take a more active approach, striking down laws or practices that appear to conflict with the Charter, knowing that if those laws or practices seem of sufficient importance to democratically-elected legislatures they can always overcome the judicial decision by the use of the overriding clause, section 33, to abridge the rights affected. The Court will simply be forcing the legislature to consider the consequences of its action specifically, and make a conscious decision whether the denial of rights is justified as a trade-off for some public good. It will be forced to review that decision every five years. The courts thus do not need to feel that they are frustrating the democratic process, but are forcing it to work more consciously.

Panel: Questions and Answers*

DONALD SMILEY If I have misunderstood it is my fault, but what I did not say, Professor Strayer, was that the Government of Canada or the Quebec members of the Government of Canada were not one group of authentic voices for the Quebec community. What you are really saying is that because there is a separatist government in Quebec, and you think the reasons that they gave for not agreeing to the Charter are insubstantial, these reasons are illegitimate. I cannot accept that! The broader political context is in terms of national unity. As I understand my American constitutional history, the creation of the federal Bill of Rights was the result of a campaign to ensure that the Constitution was ratified by the people of the states. What they wanted was protection against the national government. Your second line I find even less convincing. It is, 'Well, we do not live in a perfect world and you, Smiley, have been living in the elevated, atmosphere of Political Science Departments too long.' I do not think that is a fair comment.

In the summer of 1965, I worked with one of the most distinguished constitutional lawyers in Canada, Frank Scott, trying to work out the modalities of securing language rights. We came up with the notion of bilingual districts. Out of that enterprise, we also drafted a constitutional amendment for the protection of minority official language rights. It was an essential fact of this proposal that there would be new bilingual districts after each census. People within those districts would have *prima facie* access to all public services in both official languages. An important decision was made in 1981, that minority language rights would be better protected by the 'where numbers warranted' clause in relation to schools, and in relation to the significant demand for them. That seems to me to be important.

---

* This panel discussion, which took place on March 12, 1982 at the University of Western Ontario, relates to the previous three papers.

One could go on to remedies. As Professor Tarnopolsky pointed out, that will require the expenditure of public money in order to make some of these rights effective. How within the context of the British parliamentary tradition does one get public money appropriated in securing the rights of the physically handicapped, or official language minorities and other groups?

I think we are quite entitled to ask each other these specific questions. The Charter was drafted under the worst possible kind of conditions. The parliamentary committee made changes, as did the first ministers, ten of whom agreed to a short document not expressed in legal language. As I understand it, there were new things coming in over the Telex minute by minute right up until the time that the Charter was enacted by Parliament. I do not think it is improper to say that the Charter is not very good, not something of which to be very proud. This Charter is probably going to cause us great distress in the future.

BARRY STRAYER On the second question first, my 'counsel of perfection comment,' I would just like to make two points. First, there has been more thought put into the Charter than might be recognized. Now that is not to say that we are absolutely sure what some court someday is going to do. But we have, in fact, addressed every question we could think of and we have had an awful lot of them tossed at us over the course of the development of the Charter. We have had to address them, and we have not had the time or resources to go over all these things with everyone who might have concerns about them. Many of the problems referred to have been addressed much more fully than might be assumed. But at the end of the day, nobody can be quite sure how a court is going to interpret a section and these interpretations will assuredly change over time.

On the question of the political legitimacy of the whole package, I do not think anybody involved in the process was happy with the way it turned out since the government of Quebec did not agree. I do not pretend to argue that the government of Quebec is not one legitimate interlocutor for the people of Quebec. But it is not the *only* one. When after very long and difficult efforts, no agreement is reached, when it is possible on one side for the government of Canada, which also represents the people of Quebec, to form an opinion as to what they think is acceptable to those people, when there seems to be no prospect of getting agreement with the government of Quebec on anything reasonable, and that view is shared by nine other provinces, I do not think it is so unreasonable for ten governments to go ahead. I am just asking that the other side of the issue be addressed. I am not asking Professor Smiley to agree with the conclusion that was reached. Many will disagree with it, but I think the other point of view had to be put as fairly as possible. That is what I was trying to do, because nobody else had done it for the benefit of our American colleagues.

QUESTION I have a question primarily for Professor Tarnopolsky in relation to what he said about section 15 of the Charter. For the first time, that section made some sense to me after he explained that American court interpretations of equality treat different kinds of equality rights in different ways. He talked about 'minimal scrutiny' and 'strict scrutiny' as applied to different kinds of rights. Strict scrutiny would apply to race, religion and ethnic origin but for other factors such as mental and physical disability, there might be minimal scrutiny. If that in fact is the case, were the groups that represented people with mental and physical disabilities told that they might fall into a different category in terms of how they would be treated by the courts? If informed people are aware that those rights are to be interpreted in different ways for different people, why could we not have had that written into the Charter so that people would know for sure that there were different categories of equality rights for different kinds of people?

WALTER TARNOPOLSKY No one had brought that to their attention at the time. Remember, I am just guessing now what might be the way the Court could go and I am basing it upon a similar problem faced by the American courts. I am suggesting, however, that if you think about the categories such a result will be inevitable. The fact is that age is, at some point, a *bona fide* occupational qualification, whether it be at the bottom end or at the top end. Unless one believes that a physical handicap unrelated to the job performance is so irrelevant that you do not have to even consider it a *bona fide* occupational qualification, there are *bona fide* occupational qualifications, which run headlong into some cases of physical and mental disability. It is just what we have had to face in the enforcement of anti-discrimination legislation. It is inevitable. So, the only way out of that, I have suggested, is through these three categories of scrutiny. I do not know how else it could be handled. It is also clear that section 15 prohibits distinctions on other grounds without reasonable cause.

One of the things that one wonders is, could all this have been put in? I do not think so. I think that even now section 15 is too wordy. I have explained it in the light of the reactions to what the Supreme Court did with a simple clause like 'equality before the law.' We would not want to make section 15 even more complicated. This is, of course, my problem with Professor Smiley. He says he is not a lawyer, but he expects perfection in terms without waiting for a court to define them. In the end, the courts are going to interpret rights. You can take anything, whether it is in the constitutional field, in bills of rights, or in ordinary statutes and the end result will depend upon who does the interpreting. There is no way that one can absolutely ensure that a legal drafter is going to have his or her intention applied in the courts. It is just impossible. I am not sure that the people who have agreed upon section 15 necessarily had in mind what I am suggesting. I am merely suggesting what I think the courts will have to deal with in regard to that clause.

QUESTION I applaud Professor Smiley's concerns and his role as critic of the Charter of Rights, and I think he is very correct in pointing out that maybe the Charter of Rights has been overblown. In light of his remarks, how would he respond to the Parti Québécois, which went into the referendum citing immense problems with the concepts of Canadian federalism? They cited examples where the British North America Act was not meeting the needs of Quebec. This has been a recurring theme in Quebec politics. In light of his criticisms of the Charter, what justification would the Parti Québécois have in saying that Trudeau and the provincial premiers did not bargain in good faith? The federal Liberals and the other provincial premiers, by not meeting the needs of Quebec, and by making no effort whatsoever to modify a system that has already spawned a very strong separatist movement, have enabled the Parti Québécois to espouse the goal of independence. I would like to know what Professor Smiley's alternative is and how can he reconcile those two political extremes?

DONALD SMILEY I think it would have been perfectly legitimate for the Government of Canada, in the last session of negotiations, to go for the patriation and amendment of the constitution with whatever degree of provincial consent was forthcoming. I rather liked the Victoria formula which gave Quebec the permanent veto over the most important amendments. How one is to deal with this government is not clear. Professor Tarnopolsky says that people like me interpret what laws say too literally. I think that we have to say that sometimes one has to interpret what politicians say with a certain degree of flexibility as well. I have never, like some Canadians, idealized the Parti Québécois. I thought that it was a political party like others whose primary motives were to be in power and to stay in power. Perhaps the Parti Québécois could have been waited out. Also, I would have thought that it is terribly important to those of us who want Canada to stay together that there be an important federalist alternative in Quebec politics. I think we have made life very difficult for federalists in Quebec. I think that there is a disposition in Trudeau's mind that one must have a confrontation to resolve the constitutional question once and for all. I do not believe that one can operate on those premises without more conflict than I as a peaceful man am willing to tolerate.

QUESTION Considering that we cannot see too far into the future, I am wondering about the possibility of amending the constitution if occasions to do so should arise. When we look at the American experience with the long battle over the ERA and with the new battles over the human life amendments, I was wondering if you foresee any problems in this whole area for our own experience?

WALTER TARNOPOLSKY I think if one looks at the American experience, it is quite clear that there have been no real amendments to the original ten amendments (which is the Bill of Rights) except to add to them. The American historical experience would not indicate that it is very likely that provisions in a bill of rights are going to be amended. With all the criticism one hears about the Charter, compared to the International Covenant of Civil and Political Rights, compared to the European Convention on Human Rights, compared to all the bills of rights that the Commonwealth countries had given to them by English lawyers (who drafted more bills of rights than anyone else in the world), you do not see great variation. Obviously, we have a little more, like language rights. Compare the Charter to the Quebec Charter and you will see the variations again. One by one they are not that great. I do not see, as far as the Charter is concerned, any major departures. As far as the Constitutional Conference is concerned, I think everyone attending was guessing that amendment is not likely in the near future. The economic issues seem to be of greater concern.

There is one conference that, according to the Canada Act, must be held within one year of the coming into force of the Charter. That one could be very important as it deals with the native peoples. On the other hand, there is another provision in section 49, which says that within fifteen years there has to be another Constitutional Conference. So we are quite sure we will have one no longer than 15 years after the first one with the native peoples. The general feeling that most of us had is that probably the first case of crisis might come when the Supreme Court of Canada invalidates part of Bill 101, which contravenes the 'Canada clause' (section 23), which allows Canadians from other provinces who go to Quebec to have their children educated in English. When that comes, then we will see what the reaction will be. I have no doubt that it would help a great deal in overcoming a crisis, if Ontario were to move by then, to apply language protections at least against the legislature and courts. Whether that is going to happen, we do not know.

QUESTION I have a two-part question. Professor Tarnopolsky refers to the interrelationship of section 28 with section 15 and the discrimination on the basis of sex. My feeling is that there might be an interpretation by the courts because of section 28 that might serve to limit the rights on the basis of race, or colour, or ethnic origin. In other words, why do they see the need to include section 28 to distinguish sex from all others? Secondly, what effect does section 33 have upon the rights enumerated in section 28? Section 33 specifically refers to the fact that you can override with respect to section 15 but section 28 says that, notwithstanding anything in this Charter.

WALTER TARNOPOLSKY I think clearly that section 28 cannot be overridden by section 33. If you go to the 1947 Privy Council Appeals case, in reference to the provision in section 101 of the British North America Act, which provides for an alternative court of appeal upon which the Parliament of Canada established the Supreme Court, the Judicial Committee said notwithstanding anything in this Act means essentially that. The power is there. I think that those words clearly mean that under section 28 you cannot make a distinction between men and women. Is that going to downplay the others? Who knows? I would have thought that if you look at American history, sex did not make it into the 'inherently suspect' category. Some people reached an 'intermediate scrutiny' category, thus one can see why it was put in. There were two other things that were factors in this decision. One was the existence of section 12(1)(b) of the Indian Act dealing with discrimination against Indian women. There was a certain fear on the part of women that if you looked at section 27, which says that 'this Charter shall be interpreted in a manner consistent with the preservation and enhancement of the multicultural heritage of Canadians,' there were certain women who felt that some cultural heritage in Canada includes a lower standing for women and they pointed to 12(1)(b) amongst others. They were afraid that section 27 might then be used to lower the position of sex under section 15 and so section 28 is intended to follow immediately after to raise that back up. There is no doubt now that section 28 cannot be overridden by section 33. One of the questions that arose, and I think is going to create the greatest difficulty under this, is whether because of section 28 you cannot have an affirmative action program under subsection 2 of section 15 in favour of women. That, frankly, is the biggest anomoly or the biggest possible conflict. I have argued that that is not so, but that the right to which section 28 refers to in reference to section 15 is set out in subsection 1. Subsection 2 is merely an interpretation of the equality clauses, and therefore the reference cannot be made to the affirmative action programs. That is a possible area of conflict. I think the only way to resolve it is to view section 15(1) as the granting of the right and section 15(2) as a partial interpretation of what the right includes.

QUESTION Professor Strayer contended that the notwithstanding clause would be very difficult to use, yet only two days ago the Department of National Defence allowed that they would like to be exempted on several grounds: the right to counsel, the right to discriminate against women, or the right to discriminate against people who in conscience hold political views. In light of such developments, do you think departments will demand specific exemptions from time to time?

BARRY STRAYER It does not surprise me that the Department of National Defence would like to be excluded. It probably sees special problems for the armed forces. However, I would not hold my breath waiting for the legislation that would exclude them from the Charter. I think that we are probably a long way from that happening. It is true that all departments are supposed to be looking at their legislation and seeing how it relates to the Charter, and I think there will be some anxieties. Undoubtedly, people will see problems. A lot of that has already gone on, and those problems have been discussed. I think we are quite a long distance from that clause being used federally and I would be surprised if it is used very readily. I think you only need imagine the debate in the House of Commons if such an exception clause were proposed. It would attract a penetrating scrutiny and I cannot imagine ministers being very enthused about taking such an amendment like that to Parliament except in the clearest case of necessity.

ROY MCMURTRY I would just like to congratulate the panelists on a very excellent and entertaining presentation. I think these discussions are enormously important to the future of a country, particularly in relation to the new constitution, and the Charter of Rights. At the same time, despite the imperfections, despite the uncertainty, I would like to think that we, as Canadians, would recognize that this is a very significant chapter in the nation's history that is being concluded. We have reached a stage of our development which has demonstrated that despite our regional, cultural and other diversities, there is a political will to make this country work. I think the new constitution, despite its imperfections, does represent very much that political will. I hope you will all get behind it and make it work.

APPENDICES

APPENDIX A

Authors and Contributors

William Beaney
Professor of Law
University of Denver

Paul Bender
Professor of Law
University of Pennsylvania

Walter Berns
Resident Scholar
American Enterprise Institute
Washington, DC

R.G.L. Fairweather
Chief Commissioner
Canadian Human Rights Commission

David H. Flaherty
Professor of History and Law
The University of Western Ontario

Rainer Knopff
Department of Political Science
University of Calgary

W.R. Lederman
Professor of Law
Queen's University

William R. McKercher
Department of Political Science
The University of Western Ontario

The Hon R. Roy McMurtry
Attorney General
Ministry of the Attorney General
Queen's Park

Paul L. Murphy
Professor of History
University of Minnesota

F.L. Morton
Department of Political Science
University of Calgary

Aryeh Neier
Vice Chairman
Helsinki Watch and Americas Watch
  Committees
New York

S.J.R. Noel
Department of Political Science
The University of Western Ontario

M. James Penton
Professor of History
University of Lethbridge

The Hon Gordon Robertson
President
The Institute for Research
  on Public Policy
Ottawa

Douglas A. Schmeiser
Professor of Law
University of Saskatchewan

Donald V. Smiley
Professor of Political Science
York University

Barry Strayer
Assistant Deputy Minister of Justice
Government of Canada

Walter S. Tarnopolsky
Director
The Human Rights Centre
University of Ottawa

André Tremblay
Professeur Titulaire
Faculté du droit
Université de Montréal

Alan F. Westin
Professor of Public Law
  and Government
Columbia University

APPENDIX B

The Canadian Charter of Rights and Freedoms

PART I SCHEDULE B CONSTITUTION ACT, 1982

CANADIAN CHARTER OF RIGHTS AND FREEDOMS

Whereas Canada is founded upon principles that recognize the supremacy of God and the rule of law:

Guarantee of Rights and Freedoms

Rights and freedoms in Canada

1. The *Canadian Charter of Rights and Freedoms* guarantees the rights and freedoms set out in it subject only to such reasonable limits prescribed by law as can be demonstrably justified in a free and democratic society.

Fundamental Freedoms

Fundamental freedoms

2. Everyone has the following fundamental freedoms:
   (*a*) freedom of conscience and religion;
   (*b*) freedom of thought, belief, opinion and expression, including freedom of the press and other media of communication;
   (*c*) freedom of peaceful assembly; and
   (*d*) freedom of association.

Democratic Rights

Democratic rights of citizens

3. Every citizen of Canada has the right to vote in an election of members of the House of Commons or of a legislative assembly and to be qualified for membership therein.

Maximum duration of legislative bodies

4. (1) No House of Commons and no legislative assembly shall continue for longer than five years from the date fixed for the return of the writs at a general election of its members.

Continuation in special circumstances

(2) In time of real or apprehended war, invasion or insurrection, a House of Commons may be continued by Parliament and a legislative assembly may be continued by the legislature beyond five years if such continuation is not opposed by the votes of more than one-third of the members of the House of Commons or the legislative assembly, as the case may be.

Annual sitting of legislative bodies

5. There shall be a sitting of Parliament and of each legislature at least once every twelve months.

Mobility Rights

Mobility of citizens

6. (1) Every citizen of Canada has the right to enter, remain in and leave Canada.

Rights to move and gain livelihood

(2) Every citizen of Canada and every person who has the status of a permanent resident of Canada has the right
 (*a*) to move to and take up residence in any province; and
 (*b*) to pursue the gaining of a livelihood in any province.

Limitation

(3) The rights specified in subsection (2) are subject to
 (*a*) any laws or practices of general application in force in a province other than those that discriminate among persons primarily on the basis of province of present or previous residence; and
 (*b*) any laws providing for reasonable residency requirements as a qualification for the receipt of publicly provided social services.

Affirmative action programs

(4) Subsections (2) and (3) do not preclude any law, program or activity that has as its object the amelioration in a province of conditions of individuals in that province who are socially or economically disadvantaged if the rate of employment in that province is below the rate of employment in Canada.

Legal Rights

Life, liberty and security of person

7. Everyone has the right to life, liberty and security of the person and the right not to be deprived thereof except in accordance with the principles of fundamental justice.

Search or seizure

8. Everyone has the right to be secure against unreasonable search or seizure.

Detention or imprisonment

9. Everyone has the right not to be arbitrarily detained or imprisoned.

Arrest or detention

10. Everyone has the right on arrest or detention
 (*a*) to be informed promptly of the reasons therefor;

(*b*) to retain and instruct counsel without delay and to be informed of that right; and
(*c*) to have the validity of the detention determined by way of *habeas corpus* and to be released if the detention is not lawful.

Proceedings in criminal and penal matters

11. Any person charged with an offence has the right
(*a*) to be informed without unreasonable delay of the specific offence;
(*b*) to be tried within a reasonable time;
(*c*) not to be compelled to be a witness in proceedings against that person in respect of the offence;
(*d*) to be presumed innocent until proven guilty according to law in a fair and public hearing by an independent and impartial tribunal;
(*e*) not to be denied reasonable bail without just cause;
(*f*) except in the case of an offence under military law tried before a military tribunal, to the benefit of trial by jury where the maximum punishment for the offence is imprisonment for five years or a more severe punishment;
(*g*) not to be found guilty on account of any act or omission unless, at the time of the act or omission, it constituted an offence under Canadian or international law or was criminal according to the general principles of law recognized by the community of nations;
(*h*) if finally acquitted of the offence, not to be tried for it again and, if finally found guilty and punished for the offence, not to be tried or punished for it again; and
(*i*) if found guilty of the offence and if the punishment for the offence has been varied between the time of commission and the time of sentencing, to the benefit of the lesser punishment.

Treatment or punishment

12. Everyone has the right not to be subjected to any cruel and unusual treatment or punishment.

Self-crimination

13. A witness who testifies in any proceedings has the right not to have any incriminating evidence so given used to incriminate that witness in any other proceedings, except in a prosecution for perjury or for the giving of contradictory evidence.

Interpreter

14. A party or witness in any proceedings who does not understand or speak the language in which the proceedings are conducted or who is deaf has the right to the assistance of an interpreter.

Equality Rights

Equality before and under law and equal protection and benefit of law

15. (1) Every individual is equal before and under the law and has the right to the equal protection and equal benefit of the law without discrimination and, in particular, without discrimination based on race, national or ethnic origin, colour, religion, sex, age or mental or physical disability.

Affirmative action programs

(2) Subsection (1) does not preclude any law, program or activity that has as its object the amelioration of conditions of disadvantaged individuals or groups including those that are disadvantaged because of race, national or ethnic origin, colour, religion, sex, age or mental or physical disability.

Official Languages of Canada

Official languages of Canada

16. (1) English and French are the official languages of Canada and have equality of status and equal rights and privileges as to their use in all institutions of the Parliament and government of Canada.

Official languages of New Brunswick

(2) English and French are the official languages of New Brunswick and have equality of status and equal rights and privileges as to their use in all institutions of the legislature and government of New Brunswick.

Advancement of status and use

(3) Nothing in this Charter limits the authority of Parliament or a legislature to advance the equality of status or use of English and French.

Proceedings of Parliament

17. (1) Everyone has the right to use English or French in any debates and other proceedings of Parliament.

Proceedings of New Brunswick legislature

(2) Everyone has the right to use English or French in any debates and other proceedings of the legislature of New Brunswick.

Parliamentary statutes and records

18. (1) The statutes, records and journals of Parliament shall be printed and published in English and French and both language versions are equally authoritative.

New Brunswick statutes and records

(2) The statutes, records and journals of the legislature of New Brunswick shall be printed and published in English and French and both language versions are equally authoritative.

Proceedings in courts established by Parliament

19. (1) Either English or French may be used by any person in, or in any pleading in or process issuing from, any court established by Parliament.

Proceedings in New Brunswick courts

(2) Either English or French may be used by any person in, or in any pleading in or process issuing from, any court of New Brunswick.

Communications by public with federal institutions

20. (1) Any member of the public in Canada has the right to communicate with, and to receive available services from, any head or central office of an institution of the Parliament or government of Canada in English or French, and has the same right with respect to any other office of any such institution where
 (*a*) there is a significant demand for communications with and services from that office in such language; or

 (*b*) due to the nature of the office, it is reasonable that communications with and services from that office be available in both English and French.

Communications by public with New Brunswick institutions

(2) Any member of the public in New Brunswick has the right to communicate with, and to receive available services from, any office of an institution of the legislature or government of New Brunswick in English or French.

Continuation of existing constitutional provisions

21. Nothing in sections 16 to 20 abrogates or derogates from any right, privilege or obligation with respect to the English and French languages, or either of them, that exists or is continued by virtue of any other provision of the Constitution of Canada.

Rights and privileges preserved

22. Nothing in sections 16 to 20 abrogates or derogates from any legal or customary right or privilege acquired or enjoyed either before or after the coming into force of this Charter with respect to any language that is not English or French.

Minority Language Educational Rights

Language of instruction

23. (1) Citizens of Canada
  (*a*) whose first language learned and still understood is that of the English or French linguistic minority population of the province in which they reside, or
  (*b*) who have received their primary school instruction in Canada in English or French and reside in a province where the language in which they received that instruction is the language of the English or French linguistic minority population of the province,
have the right to have their children receive primary and secondary school instruction in that language in that province.

Continuity of language instruction

(2) Citizens of Canada of whom any child has received or is receiving primary or secondary school instruction in English or French in Canada, have the right to have all their children receive primary and secondary school instruction in the same language.

Application where numbers warrant

(3) The right of citizens of Canada under subsections (1) and (2) to have their children receive primary and secondary school instruction in the language of the English or French linguistic minority population of a province
  (*a*) applies wherever in the province the number of children of citizens who have such a right is sufficient to warrant the provision to them out of public funds of minority language instruction; and
  (*b*) includes, where the number of those children so warrants, the right to have them receive that instruction in minority language educational facilities provided out of public funds.

Enforcement

Enforcement of guaranteed rights and freedoms

24. (1) Anyone whose rights or freedoms, as guaranteed by this Charter, have been infringed or denied may apply to a court of competent jurisdiction to obtain such remedy as the court considers appropriate and just in the circumstances.

Exclusion of evidence bringing administration of justice into disrepute

(2) Where, in proceedings under subsection (1), a court concludes that evidence was obtained in a manner that infringed or denied any rights or freedoms guaranteed by this Charter, the evidence shall be excluded if it is established that, having regard to all the circumstances, the admission of it in the proceedings would bring the administration of justice into disrepute.

General

Aboriginal rights and freedoms not affected by Charter

25. The guarantee in this Charter of certain rights and freedoms shall not be construed so as to abrogate or derogate from any aboriginal, treaty or other rights or freedoms that pertain to the aboriginal peoples of Canada including
   (a) any rights or freedoms that have been recognized by the Royal Proclamation of October 7, 1763; and
   (b) any rights or freedoms that may be acquired by the aboriginal peoples of Canada by way of land claims settlement.

Other rights and freedoms not affected by Charter

26. The guarantee in this Charter of certain rights and freedoms shall not be construed as denying the existence of any other rights or freedoms that exist in Canada.

Multicultural heritage

27. This Charter shall be interpreted in a manner consistent with the preservation and enhancement of the multicultural heritage of Canadians.

Rights guaranteed equally to both sexes

28. Notwithstanding anything in this Charter, the rights and freedoms referred to in it are guaranteed equally to male and female persons.

Rights respecting certain schools preserved

29. Nothing in this Charter abrogates or derogates from any rights or privileges guaranteed by or under the Constitution of Canada in respect of denominational, separate or dissentient schools.

Application to territories and territorial authorities

30. A reference in this Charter to a province or to the legislative assembly or legislature of a province shall be deemed to include a reference to the Yukon Territory and the Northwest Territories, or to the appropriate legislative authority thereof, as the case may be.

Legislative powers not extended

31. Nothing in this Charter extends the legislative powers of any body or authority.

Application of Charter

Application of Charter

32. (1) This Charter applies
(*a*) to the Parliament and government of Canada in respect of all matters within the authority of Parliament including all matters relating to the Yukon Territory and Northwest Territories; and
(*b*) to the legislature and government of each province in respect of all matters within the authority of the legislature of each province.

Exception

(2) Notwithstanding subsection (1), section 15 shall not have effect until three years after this section comes into force.

Exception where express declaration

33. (1) Parliament or the legislature of a province may expressly declare in an Act of Parliament or of the legislature, as the case may be, that the Act or a provision thereof shall operate notwithstanding a provision included in section 2 or sections 7 to 15 of this Charter.

Operation of exception

(2) An Act or a provision of an Act in respect of which a declaration made under this section is in effect shall have such operation as it would have but for the provision of this Charter referred to in the declaration.

Five year limitation

(3) A declaration made under subsection (1) shall cease to have effect five years after it comes into force or on such earlier date as may be specified in the declaration.

Re-enactment

(4) Parliament or a legislature of a province may re-enact a declaration made under subsection (1).

Five year limitation

(5) Subsection (3) applies in respect of a re-enactment made under subsection (4).

Citation

Citation

34. This Part may be cited as the *Canadian Charter of Rights and Freedoms*.

APPENDIX C

The United States Bill of Rights

Amendment I
(Ratification of the first ten amendments was completed December 15, 1791.)
Congress shall make no law respecting an establishment of religion, or prohibiting the free exercise thereof; or abridging the freedom of speech, or of the press; or the right of the people peaceably to assemble, and to petition the Government for a redress of grievances.

Amendment II
A well regulated Militia, being necessary to the security of a free State, the right of the people to keep and bear Arms, shall not be infringed.

Amendment III
No Soldier shall, in time of peace be quartered in any house, without the consent of the Owner, nor in time of war, but in a manner to be prescribed by law.

Amendment IV
The right of the people to be secure in their persons, houses, papers, and effects, against unreasonable searches and seizures, shall not be violated, and no Warrants shall issue, but upon probable cause, supported by Oath or affirmation, and particularly describing the place to be searched, and the persons or things to be seized.

Amendment V
No person shall be held to answer for a capital, or otherwise infamous crime, unless on a presentment or indictment of a Grand Jury, except in cases arising in the land or naval forces, or in the Militia, when in actual service in time of War or public danger; nor shall any person be subject for the same offence to be twice put in jeopardy of life or limb; nor shall be compelled in any criminal case to be a witness against himself,

nor be deprived of life, liberty, or property, without due process of law; nor shall private property be taken for public use, without just compensation.

Amendment VI
In all criminal prosecutions, the accused shall enjoy the right to a speedy and public trial, by an impartial jury of the State and district wherein the crime shall have been committed, which district shall have been previously ascertained by law, and to be informed of the nature and cause of the accusation; to be confronted with the witness against him; to have compulsory process for obtaining witnesses in his favor, and to have the Assistance of Counsel for his defence.

Amendment VII
In Suits at common law, where the value in controversy shall exceed twenty dollars, the right of trial by jury shall be preserved, and no fact tried by a jury, shall be otherwise reexamined in any Court of the United States, than according to the rules of the common law.

Amendment VIII
Excessive bail shall not be required, nor excessive fines imposed, nor cruel and unusual punishments inflicted.

Amendment IX
The enumeration in the Constitution, of certain rights, shall not be construed to deny or disparage others retained by the people.

Amendment X
The powers not delegated to the United States by the Constitution, nor prohibited by it to the States, are reserved to the States respectively, or to the people.

THE CIVIL WAR AMENDMENTS

Amendment XIII (1865)
Section 1. Neither slavery nor involuntary servitude, except as a punishment for crime whereof the party shall have been duly convicted, shall exist within the United States, or any place subject to their jurisdiction.
  Section 2. Congress shall have the power to enforce this article by appropriate legislation.

Amendment XIV (1868)
Section 1. All persons born or naturalized in the United States, and subject to the jurisdiction thereof, are citizens of the United States and of the State wherein they

reside. No State shall make or enforce any law which shall abridge the privileges or immunities of citizens of the United States; nor shall any State deprive any person of life, liberty, or property, without due process of law; nor deny to any person within its jurisdiction the equal protection of the laws.

Section 2. Representatives shall be apportioned among the several States according to their respective numbers, counting the whole number of persons in each State, excluding Indians not taxed. But when the right to vote at any election for the choice of electors for President and Vice President of the United States, Representatives in Congress, the Executive and Judicial officers of a State, or the members of the Legislature thereof, is denied to any of the male inhabitants of such State, being twenty-one years of age, and citizens of the United States, or in any way abridged, except for participation in rebellion, or other crime, the basis of representation therein shall be reduced in the proportion which the number of such male citizens shall bear to the whole number of male citizens twenty-one years of age in such State.

Section 3. No person shall be a Senator or Representative in Congress, or elector of President and Vice President, or hold any office, civil or military, under the United States, or under any State, who, having previously taken an oath, as a member of Congress, or as an officer of the United States, or as a member of any State legislature, or as an executive or judicial officer of any State, to support the Constitution of the United States, shall have engaged in insurrection or rebellion against the same, or given aid or comfort to the enemies thereof. But Congress may by a vote of two-thirds of each House, remove such disability.

Section 4. The validity of the public debt of the United States, authorized by law, including debts incurred for payment of pensions and bounties for services in suppressing insurrection or rebellion, shall not be questioned. But neither the United States nor any State shall assume or pay any debt or obligation incurred in aid of insurrection or rebellion against the United States, or any claim for the loss or emancipation of any slave; but all such debts, obligations, and claims shall be held illegal and void.

Section 5. The Congress shall have power to enforce, by appropriate legislation, the provisions of this article.

Amendment XV (1870)

Section 1. The right of citizens of the United States to vote shall not be denied or abridged by the United States or by any State on account of race, color, or previous condition of servitude.

Section 2. The Congress shall have power to enforce this article by appropriate legislation.

APPENDIX D

Select Bibliography

BOOKS

Abraham, H.J. (1982) *Freedom and the Court: Civil Rights and Liberties in the United States* 4th ed (Oxford: Oxford University Press)
Anderson, Sir N. (1978) *Liberty, Law & Justice* (London: Stevens & Sons)
Barker, L.J. and T.W. Barker, jr (1965) *Freedom Courts, Politics: Studies in Civil Liberties* (Englewood Cliffs, NJ: Prentice-Hall)
Basler, Roy P., ed (1953) *The Collected Works of Abraham Lincoln* (New Brunswick, NJ: Rutgers University Press)
Beaney, William M., jr (1972) *The Right to Counsel in American Courts* (Westport, Conn.: Greenwood Press)
Beaney, William M., jr and Alpheus T. Mason (1968) *The Supreme Court in a Free Society* (New York: Norton)
Berger, Morroe (1967) *Equality by Statute: The Revolution in Civil Rights* (New York: Doubleday)
Berger, Raoul (1977) *Government by Judiciary: the Transformation of the Fourteenth Amendment* (Cambridge, Mass.: Harvard University Press)
Berger, Thomas R. (1981) *Fragile Freedoms: Human Rights and Dissent in Canada* (Toronto: Clarke, Irwin & Co, Ltd)
Berns, Walter (1969) *Freedom, Virtue, and the First Amendment* (New York: Greenwood Press)
– (1976) *The First Amendment and the Future of American Democracy* (Basic Books)
Bickel, Alexander M. (1962) *The Least Dangerous Branch: The Supreme Court at the Bar of Politics* (New York: Irvington)
– (1970) *The Supreme Court and the Idea of Progress* (New York: Harper & Row)
– (1975) *The Morality of Consent* (New Haven: Yale University Press)

Black, Charles L. (1960) *The People and the Court; Judicial Review in a Democracy* (New York: Macmillan)
- (1969) *Structure and Relationship in Constitutional Law* (Baton Rouge: Louisiana State University Press)

Black, Hugo L. (1963) *One Man's Stand for Freedom: Mr. Justice Black and the Bill of Rights; a Collection of Supreme Court Opinions* (New York: Knopf)
- (1968) *A Constitutional Faith* (New York: Knopf)

Bolton, P. Michael (1975) *Civil Rights in Canada* (Toronto: International Self-Counsel Press)

Brant, Irving (1965) *The Bill of Rights; Its Origin and Meaning* (Indianapolis: Bobbs-Merrill)

Brownlie, Ian (1971) *Basic Documents on Human Rights* (Oxford: Clarendon Press)

Cahn, Edmond N. (1963) *The Great Rights* (New York: The Macmillan Co)

Canadian Bar Association. Committee on the Constitution (1978) *Towards a New Canada* (Toronto: Canadian Bar Foundation)

Cardozo, Benjamin N. (1924) *The Growth of the Law* (New Haven: Yale University Press)

Cheffins, R.I. and R.N. Tucker (1976) *The Constitutional Process in Canada* 2nd ed (Toronto: McGraw-Hill Ryerson Ltd)

Choper, Jesse H. (1980) *Judicial Review and the National Political Process: A Functional Reconsideration of the Role of the Supreme Court* (Chicago: University of Chicago Press)

Commager, Henry Steele (1958) *Majority Rule and Minority Rights* (Gloucester, Mass.: Peter Smith)

Constitutional Committee of the Quebec Liberal Party (1980) *A New Canadian Federation* (Montreal: Quebec Liberal Party)

Cortner, Richard G. (1975) *The Supreme Court and Civil Liberties Policy* (Palo Alto: Mayfield Publishing Co)
- (1981) *The Supreme Court and the Second Bill of Rights: the Fourteenth Amendment and the Nationalization of Civil Liberties* (Madison: University of Wisconsin Press)

Corwin, Edward S. (1955) *'Higher Law' Background of American Constitutional Law* (Ithaca, NY: Cornell University Press)
- (1964) *American Constitutional History: Essays*. Edited by Alpheus T. Mason and G. Garvey (New York: Harper & Row)

Cox, Archibald (1968) *The Warren Court: Constitutional Decision as an Instrument of Reform* (Cambridge, Mass.: Harvard University Press)
- (1976) *The Role of the Supreme Court in American Government* (Oxford: Oxford University Press)

Cox, Barry (1975) *Civil Liberties in Britain* (Harmondsworth: Penguin)
Cranston, Maurice W. (1973) *What are Human Rights?* (New York: Taplinger Publishing Co, Inc)
Cropsey, Joseph (1977) *Political Philosophy and the Issues of Politics* (Chicago: University of Chicago Press)
Cushman, Robert F. (1971) *Leading Constitutional Decisions* 14th ed (Englewood Cliffs, NJ: Prentice-Hall)
– (1979) *Cases in Civil Liberties* 3rd ed (Englewood Cliffs, NJ: Prentice-Hall)
Dean, H.E. (1966) *Judicial Review and Democracy* (New York: Random House)
Denning, Sir A. (1949) *Freedom under the Law* (London: Stevens & Sons, Ltd)
Diamond, Martin (1981) *The Founding of the Democratic Republic* (Itasca, Ill.: F.E. Peacock Publishers)
Dicey, A.V. (1885) *Introduction to the Study of the Law of the Constitution* (London: Macmillan)
Dorsen, N., P. Bender and B. Neuborne (1976) *Emerson, Haber and Dorsen's Political and Civil Rights in the United States* vol 1 4th ed (Boston: Little, Brown & Co)
Dorsen, N. and P. Bender, B. Neuborne and S. Law (1979) *Emerson, Haber and Dorsen's Political and Civil Rights in the United States* vol 2 4th ed (Boston: Little, Brown & Co)
Dumbauld, Edward (1957) *The Bill of Rights and What It Means Today* (Norman, Okla.: University of Oklahoma Press)
Dworkin, Ronald M. (1977) *Taking Rights Seriously* (Cambridge, Mass.: Harvard University Press)
– ed (1977) *The Philosophy of Law* (New York: Oxford University Press)
Ely, John Hart (1980) *Democracy and Distrust: A Theory of Judicial Review* (Cambridge, Mass.: Harvard University Press)
Epp, Frank H. (1974) *Mennonites in Canada* (Toronto: Macmillan of Canada)
The Federalist Papers; Alexander Hamilton, James Madison, John Jay Introduction by Clinton Rossiter (1961) (New York: New American Library)
Franck, Thomas M. (1968) *Comparative Constitutional Process; Cases and Materials; Fundamental Rights in Commonwealth Nations* (New York: F.A. Praeger)
Freund, Paul A. (1972) *The Supreme Court of the United States: Its Business, Purposes, & Performance* (Gloucester, Mass.: Peter Smith)
– (1977) *Constitutional Law: Cases and Other Problems* 4th ed (Boston: Little, Brown)
Gabin, Sanford B. (1980) *Judicial Review & the Reasonable Doubt Test* (Port Washington, NY: Kennikat Press)
Glazer, Nathan (1975) *Affirmative Discrimination* (New York: Basic Books)
Goldman, Alan H. (1979) *Justice and Reverse Discrimination* (Princeton: Princeton University Press)

Goldwin, Robert A. (1963) *100 Years of Emancipation* (Chicago: University of Chicago)
Gotlieb, Alan, ed (1970) *Human Rights: Federalism and Minorities* (Toronto: Canadian Institute of International Affairs)
Graglia, Lino A. (1976) *Disaster by Decree: The Supreme Court Decisions on Race and the Schools* (Ithaca, NY: Cornell University Press)
Grant, George P. (1970) *Lament for a Nation* (Toronto: McClelland and Stewart)
Griffith, J.A.G. (1977) *The Politics of the Judiciary* (Manchester: Manchester University Press)
Gunther, G. (1980) *Cases & Materials on Constitutional Law* 10th ed (Mineola, NY: Foundation Press)
Haines, C.G. (1959) *The American Doctrine of Judicial Supremacy* (New York: Russell & Russell, Inc)
Hand, Learned (1952) *The Spirit of Liberty; Papers and Addresses* (New York: Knopf)
Hart, H.L.A. (1963) *Law, Liberty and Morality* (Stanford, Calif.: Stanford University Press)
Hartz, Louis (1964) *The Founding of New Societies: Studies in the History of the United States, Latin America, South Africa, Canada and Australia* (New York: Harcourt, Brace and World)
Hogg, Peter W. (1977) *Constitutional Law of Canada* (Agincourt: Carswell)
Horowitz, Donald L. (1977) *Courts and Social Policy* (Washington, DC: Brookings Institution)
Jackson, Robert H. (1941) *The Struggle for Judicial Supremacy* (New Yok: A.A. Knopf)
Jaconelli, Joseph (1980) *Enacting a Bill of Rights: The Legal Problems* (Oxford: Oxford University Press)
Jaffa, Harry V. (1965) *Equality and Liberty: Theory and Practise in American Politics* (New York: Oxford University Press)
– (1973) *Crisis of the House Divided* (Seattle: University of Washington Press)
Jefferson, Thomas *The Papers of Thomas Jefferson*. Edited by Julian P. Boyd (1955) vol 12: 7 August 1787 to 31 March 1788 (Princeton, NJ: Princeton University Press)
Johnson, Donald (1963) *The Challenge to American Freedoms: World War I and the Rise of the American Civil Liberties Union* (Lexington, Ky.: University of Kentucky Press)
Joyce, James A. (1978) *The New Politics of Human Rights* (New York: St Martin's Press)
Kamisar, Y., W.R. LaFave and J.H. Israel (1980) *Modern Criminal Procedure: Cases, Comments & Questions* 5th ed (St Paul: West Publishing Co)
Kelly, A.H. and W.A. Harbison (1970) *The American Constitution* 4th ed (New York: Norton)

Konvitz, Milton R. and Clinton Rossiter, eds (1958) *Aspects of Liberty; Essays Presented to Robert E. Cushman* (Ithaca, NY: Cornell University Press)

Krichmar, Albert (1972) *The Women's Rights Movement in the United States, 1848–1970: A Bibliography and Sourcebook* (Metuchen, NJ: Scarecrow Press)

Kurland, P.B., ed (1975) *The Supreme Court and the Judicial Function* (Chicago: The University of Chicago Press)

Laskin, Bora (1966) *Canadian Constitutional Law: Cases, Text & Notes on Distribution of Legislative Power* (Toronto: Carswell)

Lawrence, David (1936) *Nine Honest Men* (New York and London: D. Appleton-Century Co)

Lederman, W.R. (1964) *The Courts and the Canadian Constitution* Carleton Library no 16 (Toronto: McClelland and Stewart)

Lederman, W.R. and J.D. Whyte (1975) *Canadian Constitutional Law Cases, Notes and Materials* (Toronto: Butterworths)

Lederman, W.R. (1981) *Continuing Canadian Constitutional Dilemmas: Essays on the Constitutional History, Public Law & Federal System of Canada* (Toronto: Butterworths)

Levy, Leonard W., ed (1967) *Judicial Review and the Supreme Court: Selected Essays* (New York: Harper & Row)

– (1972) *Judgments: Essays on American Constitutional History* (Chicago: Quadrangle Books)

Lewis, David and Frank R. Scott (1943) *Make This Your Canada; a Review of C.C.F. History and Policy* (Toronto: Central Canada Publishing Co)

Linden, Allen M. (1976) *The Canadian Judiciary* (Toronto: Osgoode Hall Law School, York University)

Macdonald, R. and J. Humphrey (1979) *The Practise of Freedom: Canadian Essays on Human Rights and Fundamental Freedoms* (Toronto: Butterworths)

Maine, Sir Henry J.S. (1870) *Ancient Law: Its Connection with the Early History of Society and Its Relation to Modern Ideas* 4th ed (London: J. Murray)

Mason, Alpheus T., W.M. Beaney and G. Stephenson (1983) *American Constitutional Law* 7th ed (Englewood Cliffs, NJ: Prentice-Hall)

Mason, Alpheus T. (1956) *Harlan Fiske Stone: Pillar of the Law* (New York: Viking Press)

McCloskey, Robert G. (1960) *The American Supreme Court* (Chicago: University of Chicago Press)

McLaughlin, Andrew C. (1972) *The Foundations of American Constitutionalism* (Gloucester, Mass.: Peter Smith)

McWhinney, Edward (1969) *Judicial Review* (Toronto: University of Toronto Press)

– (1979) *Quebec and the Constitution, 1960–1978* (Toronto: University of Toronto Press)

- (1982) *Canada and the Constitution 1979–1982: Patriation and the Charter of Rights* (Toronto: University of Toronto Press)
MeikleJohn, Alexander (1965) *Political Freedom: The Constitutional Powers of the People* (New York: Oxford University Press)
Meyers, Marvin, ed (1981) *The Mind of the Founder: Sources of the Political Thought of James Madison* rev ed (Hanover, NH: University Press of New England)
Moir, John S. (1967) *Church and State in Canada, 1627–1927* (Toronto: McClelland and Stewart)
Monet, Jacques (1969) *The Last Cannon Shot: A Study of French-Canadian Nationalism, 1837–1850* (Toronto: University of Toronto Press)
Moore, Winston S., ed (1980) *The Role of the Judiciary in America* (The American Enterprise Institute)
Murphy, Paul L. (1968) *Liberty and Justice: a Historical Record of American Constitutional Development* 2nd ed (New York: A.A. Knopf)
- (1972a) *The Constitution in Crisis Times, 1918–1969* New American Nation Series, vol 2. Edited by H.S. Commager and R.B. Morris (New York: Harper and Row)
- (1972b) *The Meaning of Freedom of Speech: First Amendment Freedoms from Wilson to F.D.R.* (Westport: Greenwood)
- (1979) *World War I and the Origin of Civil Liberties in the United States* (New York: Norton)
Murphy, Walter F. (1962) *Congress and the Court; A Case Study in the American Political Process* (Chicago: University of Chicago Press)
Murphy, Walter F. and C. Herman Pritchett, eds (1979) *Courts, Judges, and Politics: An Introduction to the Judicial Process* 3rd ed (New York: Random House)
Neier, Aryeh (1979) *Defending My Enemy: American Nazis in Skokie, Illinois, & the Risks of Freedom* (New York: Dutton)
Newberg, P.R., ed (1980) *The Politics of Human Rights* (New York: New York University Press)
Nowak, J.E., R.D. Rotunda and J.N. Young (1978) *Handbook on Constitutional Law* (St Paul: West Publishing Co)
Peltason, Jack W. (1961) *Fifty-Eight Lonely Men* (New York: Harcourt, Brace & World)
Pennock, J.R. and J.W. Chapman (1977) *Due Process* (New York: New York University Press)
Penniman, Howard R., ed (1981) *Canada at the Polls, 1979 and 1980: A Study of the General Elections* (Washington, DC: American Enterprise Institute for Public Policy Research)

Penton, M. James (1976) *Jehovah's Witnesses in Canada* (Toronto: Macmillan of Canada)

Perry, Richard L. and John C. Cooper, eds (1959) *Sources of Our Liberties* (New York: McGraw-Hill)

Polyviou, Polyvios G. (1980) *The Equal Protection of the Laws* (London: Duckworth)

Presthus, Robert (1973) *Elite Accommodation in Canadian Politics* (Toronto: Macmillan of Canada)

Raphael, D.D., ed (1967) *Political Theory and the Rights of Man* (London: Macmillan)

Russell, Peter H. (1982) *Leading Constitutional Decisions* 3rd ed (Ottawa: Carleton University Press)

Rutland, Robert A. (1955) *The Birth of the Bill of Rights, 1776–1791* (Chapel Hill: Published for the Institute of Early American History and Culture by the University of North Carolina Press)

Schmeiser, Douglas A. (1981) *Cases and Comments on Criminal Law* 4th ed (Toronto: Butterworths)

Schwartz, Bernard (1977) *The Great Rights of Mankind: A History of the American Bill of Rights* (New York: Oxford University Press)

Schwartz, Bernard, ed (1970) *The Fourteenth Amendment Centennial Volume* (New York: New York University Press)

Scott, Frank R. (1959a) *The Canadian Constitution and Human Rights* (Toronto: Canadian Broadcasting Corporation)

– (1959b) *Civil Liberties & Canadian Federalism* (Toronto: University of Toronto Press)

– (1977) *Essays on the Constitution: Aspects of Canadian Law and Politics* (Toronto: University of Toronto Press)

Sellery, George C. (1907) *Lincoln's Suspension of Habeas Corpus as Viewed by Congress* Bulletin of the University of Wisconsin, no 149. History series, vol 1, no 3 (Madison, Wis.: University of Wisconsin)

Shapiro, Martin (1966) *Freedom of Speech: The Supreme Court & Judicial Review* (Englewood Cliffs, NJ: Prentice-Hall, Inc)

Silver, Arthur I. (1982) *The French-Canadian Idea of Confederation, 1864–1900* (Toronto: University of Toronto Press)

Smiley, Donald (1981) *The Canadian Charter of Rights and Freedoms, 1981* Ontario Economic Council Discussion Paper Series (Toronto: Ontario Economic Council)

Stacey, Frank (1973) *A New Bill of Rights for Britain* (Newton Abbot [Eng.]: David and Charles)

Steamer, Robert J. (1971) *The Supreme Court in Crisis: A History of Conflict* (Amherst, Mass.: The University of Massachusetts Press)
Storing, Herbert J. (1982) *The Complete Anti-Federalist* 7 vols (Chicago: University of Chicago Press)
Strauss, Leo (1953) *Natural Right and History* (Chicago: University of Chicago Press)
Strayer, B.L. (1968) *Judicial Review of Legislation in Canada* (Toronto: University of Toronto Press)
The Supreme Court and Individual Rights (1980) (Washington, DC: Congressional Quarterly Inc)
Svnahara, Ann G. (1981) *The Politics of Racism: The Uprooting of Japanese Canadians during the Second World War* (Toronto: James Lorimer & Co)
Tarnopolsky, Walter S. (1975) *The Canadian Bill of Rights* 2nd rev ed (Toronto: McClelland and Stewart)
– (1982) *Discrimination and the Law in Canada* (Don Mills: R. De Boo Ltd)
Tocqueville, Alexis de (1961) *Democracy in America* 2 vols (New York: Schocken Books)
Tribe, L.H. (1978) *American Constitutional Law* (Mineola, NY: Foundation Press)
Trudeau, Pierre Elliot (1968) *Federalism and the French Canadians* (Toronto: Macmillan of Canada)
Vanderbilt, Arthur T. (1955) *The Challenge of Law Reform* (Princeton, NJ: Princeton University Press)
Waite, Peter B. (1962) *Life and Times of Confederation, 1864–1867; Politics, Newspapers, and the Union of British North America* (Toronto: University of Toronto Press)
– (1963) *The Confederation Debates in the Province of Canada / 1865* (Toronto: McClelland and Stewart Ltd)
Weiler, Paul (1974) *In the Last Resort: A Critical Study of the Supreme Court of Canada* (Toronto: Carswell, Methuen)
Westin, Alan F. (1964) *Freedom Now: The Civil Rights Struggle in America* (New York: Basic Books)
– (1967) *Privacy and Freedom* (New York: Atheneum)
Wilkinson, J.H. (1979) *From Brown to Bakke: The Supreme Court & School Integration: 1954–1978* (New York: Oxford University Press)
Whyte, J.D. and W.R. Lederman (1977) *Canadian Constitutional Law: Cases, Notes and Materials* 2nd ed (Toronto: Butterworths)
Woodward, Bob and Scott Armstrong (1979) *The Brethren: Inside the Supreme Court* (New York: Simon and Schuster)
Zander, Michael (1975) *A Bill of Rights?* (London: Barry Rose)

PERIODICALS

Abel, Albert S. (1959) 'The Bill of Rights in the United States: What Has it Accomplished?' *Canadian Bar Review* 37: 147–88
Beaudoin, Gerald A. (1975) 'La Cour Suprême et la protection des droits fondamentaux.' *Canadian Bar Review* 53: 675–714
Berns, Walter (Fall 1972) 'Free Speech and Free Government.' *The Political Science Review* 2: 217–41
Black, William (1981) 'From Intent to Effect: New Standards in Human Rights.' *Canadian Human Rights Reporter* 1: c/1
Bowker, W.F. (1959) 'Basic Rights and Freedoms: What are They?' *Canadian Bar Review* 37: 43–65
Cavalluzzo, Paul (1971) 'Judicial review and the Bill of Rights: Drybones and its aftermath.' *Osgoode Hall Law Review* 9: 545
Clokie, H. McD. (1947) 'Emergency Powers and Civil Liberties.' *Canadian Journal of Economics and Political Science* 13: 384–94
Corwin, Edward S. (1952) 'Bowing Out "Clear and Present Danger".' *Notre Dame Lawyer* 27: 325–59
Dahl, R.A. (1957) 'Decision-Making in a Democracy: The Supreme Court as a National Policy Maker.' *Journal of Public Law* 6: 279–95
Dworkin, Ronald (1981a) 'What is Equality? Part 1: Equality of Welfare.' *Philosophy and Public Affairs* 10: 185–246
– (1981b) 'What is Equality? Part 2: Equality of Resources.' *Philosophy and Public Affairs* 10: 283–345
Ely, J.H. and P.L. Murphy (1980) 'Democracy and Distrust – A Theory of Judicial Review.' *Minnesota Law Review* 65: 158–66
Flint, D. and M.J. Penton (1977) 'Hutterites – Study in Prejudice.' *Canadian Historical Review* 58: 76–7
Frankfurter, Felix (1965) 'Memorandum on "Incorporation" of the Bill of Rights into the Due Process Clause of the Fourteenth Amendment.' *Harvard Law Review* 78: 746–83
Glazer, Nathan (1978) 'Should Judges Administer Social Services.' *The Public Interest* 50: 69–80
Harlan, John M. (1964) 'The Bill of Rights and the Constitution.' *American Bar Association Journal* 50: 918–20
Hunter, Ian A. (1977) 'Civil Actions for Discrimination.' *Canadian Bar Review* 55: 106–30
Knopff, Rainer (1980–81) 'Pierre Trudeau and the Problem of Liberal Democratic Statesmanship.' *Dalhousie Review* 60: 712–26

Laskin, Bora (1959) 'An Inquiry into the Diefenbaker Bill of Rights.' *Canadian Bar Review* 37: 77–134
- (1975) 'The Role and Functions of Final Appellate Courts: The Supreme Court of Canada.' *Canadian Bar Review* 53: 469–81
Lederman, W.R. (1959) 'The Nature and Problems of a Bill of Rights.' *Canadian Bar Review* 37: 4–15
- (June 1975) 'Comparing the Constitutions of Canada and the United States.' *American Bar Association Journal* 61: 710–14
- (1981) 'Canada's Current Constitutional Crisis.' *Parliamentarian* 62: 192–8
Mann, F.A. (October 1978) 'Britain's Bill of Rights.' *Law Quarterly Review* 94: 512–33
Marx, Herbert (1970) 'The Emergency Power and Civil Liberties in Canada.' *McGill Law Journal* 16: 39–91
McKay, Robert B. (November 1959) 'The Preference for Freedom.' *New York University Law Review* 34: 1182–227
McWhinney, Edward (1959) 'The Supreme Court and the Bill of Rights – The Lessons of Comparative Jurisprudence.' *Canadian Bar Review* 37: 16–42
Murphy, Paul L. (November 1981) 'Near v Minnesota in the Context of Historical Developments.' *Minnesota Law Review* 66: 95–160
Neier, Aryeh (1979a) 'Above the Law.' *Nation* 228: 355–6
- (1979b) 'Anti-Abortion a Violation.' *Nation* 228: 34
- (1979c) 'No Waived Right.' *Nation* 228: 650
- (1980) 'Victim Censorship – Expurgating the First Amendment.' *Nation* 230: 737
Pigeon, Louis-Philippe (1959) 'The Bill of Rights and the British North America Act.' *Canadian Bar Review* 37: 66–76
Roche, John P. (1952) 'Executive Power and Domestic Emergency: The Quest for Prerogative.' *Western Political Quarterly* 5: 592–618
Russell, Peter H. (1969) 'A Democratic Approach to Civil Liberties.' *University of Toronto Law Journal* 19: 109–31
- (1975) 'The Political Role of the Supreme Court of Canada in its First Century.' *Canadian Bar Review* 53: 576–96
- (1982) 'The Effect of a Charter of Rights on the Policy-Making Role of Canadian Courts.' *Canadian Public Administration* 25: 1–33
Schmeiser, Douglas A. (1973–74) 'The Case Against Entrenchment of a Canadian Bill of Rights.' *Dalhousie Law Journal* 1: 15–50
Scott, F.R. (1949) 'Dominion Jurisdiction over Human Rights and Fundamental Freedoms.' *Canadian Bar Review* 27: 497–536
Scott, Stephen A. (1976) 'The Supreme Court and Civil Liberties.' *Alberta Law Review* 14: 97–134

Schlafly, Phyllis (August 1979a) 'The Effect of E.R.A.s in State Constitutions.' *The Phyllis Schlafly Report* 13
- (August 1979b) 'E.R.A. and Homosexual Marriages.' *The Phyllis Schlafly Report* 13

Smiley, Donald V. (1969) 'The Case Against the Canadian Charter of Human Rights.' *Canadian Journal of Political Science* 2: 277–91
- (1978) 'Canadian Federation and Challenge of Quebec Independence.' *Publius – The Journal of Federalism* 8: 199–224

Stampp, Kenneth M. (June 1978) 'The Concept of a Perpetual Union.' *Journal of American History* 65: 5–33

Tarnopolsky, Walter S. (1968) 'The Iron Hand in the Velvet Glove: Administration and Enforcement of Human Rights Legislation in Canada.' *Canadian Bar Review* 46: 565–90
- (1975) 'The Supreme Court and the Canadian Bill of Rights.' *Canadian Bar Review* 53: 649–74
- (1976) 'The Supreme Court and Civil Liberties.' *Alberta Law Review* 14: 58–96
- (1979) 'A Bill of Rights and Future Constitutional Change.' *Canadian Bar Review* 57: 626–39

Thayer, J.B. (October 1893) 'The Origin and Scope of the American Doctrine of Constitutional Law.' *Harvard Law Review* 7: 129–56

Van Alstyne, William W. (January 1969) 'A Critical Guide to *Marbury* v *Madison*.' *Duke Law Journal* 1–47

Welfeld, Irving (1976) 'The Courts and Desegregated Housing: The Meaning (if any) of the Gautreux Case.' *The Public Interest* 45: 123–35

Westin, Alan F. (March 1979) 'Privacy in the Banking Relationship – The Federal Government as a Source of Privacy Problems and a Possible Part of the Solution.' *Business Lawyer* 34: 1129–36

GOVERNMENT PUBLICATIONS

Canada (1968) Department of Justice, *A Canadian Charter of Human Rights* (Ottawa: Queen's Printer)
- (1972) Special Joint Committee of the Senate and of the House of Commons on the Constitution of Canada, *Final Report* (Ottawa: Queen's Printer)
- (1978a) Department of Justice, *Constitutional Reform: Canadian Charter of Rights and Freedoms* (Ottawa: Canadian Unity Information Office)
- (1978b) Special Joint Committee of the Senate and of the House of Commons on the Constitution of Canada, *Minutes of Proceedings and Evidence* Issue no 20 3rd Session, 30th Parliament, 1977–78 (Ottawa: Queen's Printer)
- (1979a) Task Force on Canadian Unity, *A Future Together: Observation and Recommendations* (Ottawa: Supply and Services) 1979

- (1979b) Task Force on Canadian Unity, *A Time to Speak* (Ottawa: Supply and Services)
- Constitution Act, 1982, *Canadian Charter of Rights and Freedoms*

Federal-Provincial Conference of First Ministers on the Constitution, Ottawa (8–13 September 1980) 'Documents' (Ottawa: Canadian Intergovernmental Conference Secretariat)

Government of Canada (1982) *The Charter of Rights and Freedoms: A Guide for Canadians* (Ottawa: Supply and Services)

Meeting of the Continuing Committee of Ministers on the Constitution, Montreal (8–11 July 1980) 'Documents' (Ottawa: Canadian Intergovernmental Conference Secretariat)

Ontario (1969) Royal Commission Inquiry into Civil Rights, *Report Number Two* (Toronto: Queen's Printer)

United States Congress (1976) Senate Committee on the Judiciary Subcommittee on Constitutional Rights, *Citizens Guide to Individual Rights Under the Constitution of the United States of America* 5th ed (94th Congress, 2nd Sess)

United States President (1957) *Public Papers of the Presidents of the United States* (Washington, DC: Office of the *Federal Register*, National Archives and Records Service (1953–) Dwight D. Eisenhower)